Processes in individual differences

One of the most fascinating topics in psychology is how and why people come to develop different personalities and abilities – the psychology of individual differences. Questions such as 'why do different children in the same family seem to have such different natures and abilities?', 'what influences the way in which we interpret other people's personalities?', 'how can personality affect the way in which we process information?' and 'is personality shaped by society, our biological make-up or both?' are fundamental to the subject. Unlike many books on the structure and measurement of individual differences, this collection seeks to shed light on underlying processes.

There is now some agreement about the basic structure of human abilities and personality, which makes it possible to provide at least partial answers to the above questions. *Processes in Individual Differences* reviews and explores what is known about the social, biological, genetic and cognitive processes that underlie various aspects of intelligence, personality and mood. It contains contributions from international experts in their fields, and provides non-technical but state-of-the-art descriptions of the processes that underpin various aspects of personality, moods and ability, together with some new empirical results.

Processes in Individual Differences will give the advanced student, the researcher and the professional test-user a good understanding of why precisely people are so very different.

The collection honours the work of Paul Kline, D.Sc., who recently retired from the only chair of psychometrics in the country.

Colin Cooper is Lecturer in Psychology at Queen's University, Belfast.

Ved Varma is a retired Psychotherapist and Educational Psychologist. His previous publications include *The Management of Children with Emotional and Behavioural Difficulties* (1990) and *Stress in Psychotherapists* (1996).

Processes in individual differences

Edited by Colin Cooper and Ved Varma

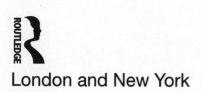

London and New York

First published 1997
by Routledge
11 New Fetter Lane, London EC4P 4EE

Simultaneously published in the USA and Canada
by Routledge
29 West 35th Street, New York, NY 10001

Typeset in Palatino by Routledge
Printed and bound in Great Britain by T. J. International,
Padstow, Cornwall

British Library Cataloguing in Publication Data
A catalogue record for this book is available from the British Library

Library of Congress Cataloguing in Publication Data
Processes in individual differences/
edited by Colin Cooper and Ved Varma.
    p. cm.
    Includes bibliographical references and index.
    1. Individual differences. I. Cooper, Colin, 1954–
    II. Varma, Ved P.
    BF697.P7 1997
    155.2′2–dc21   96–52970
                                                                              CIP

ISBN 0–415–14119–2

Contents

Illustrations

TABLES

List of contributors

Paul T. Barrett Psychometrics Unit, Ashworth Hospital, Liverpool, U.K.

Colin Cooper School of Psychology, Queen's University, Belfast, U.K.

Hans J. Eysenck Institute of Psychiatry, de Crespigny Park, Denmark Hill, London SE5, U.K.

Michael W. Eysenck Department of Psychology, University of London, Royal Holloway and Bedford New College, Egham, Surrey, U.K.

Sarah E. Hampson Department of Psychology, University of Surrey, Guildford, Surrey, U.K.

Arthur R. Jensen Education Department, University of California at Berkeley, California, U.S.A.

Paul Kline Department of Psychology, University of Exeter, Exeter, Devon, U.K.

Paul Lichtenstein Division of Genetic Epidemiology, The Karolinska Institute, Stockholm, Sweden.

Gerry Mulhern School of Psychology, Queen's University, Belfast, U.K.

Nancy L. Pedersen Division of Genetic Epidemiology, The Karolinska Institute, Stockholm, Sweden.

Jim Stevenson Department of Psychology, University of Southampton, Southampton, Hampshire, U.K.

Preface

Research into individual differences stands at a crossroads. There is now some agreement that in order to predict behaviour it is necessary to consider both characteristics of the situation and internal characteristics of the organism – or 'individual differences' – since these two variables may be assumed to interact in complex ways to determine behaviour. There is also some agreement between individual-difference theorists about the number and nature of at least some of these internal characteristics, and their relation to each other, the domains of intelligence/ability and personality having been particularly closely studied.

The challenge is now to understand the mechanisms by which these individual differences operate, and to grasp precisely how they interact with situational variables to predict behaviour. The chapters that follow summarise much of what is currently known about the cognitive, social, physiological and genetic processes that underpin the main areas of individual differences. There are of course gaps – partly in order to keep the book to a reasonable length, and partly because too little is known about some aspects of individual differences to allow sensible process models to be constructed and tested. The psychology of motivation is one such area, with the psychology of mood being only slightly better understood. The primary aim of this work is to examine what is known about theory-driven and empirically verifiable process models in individual differences, and to suggest ways forward.

Colin Cooper
Ved Varma

Introduction

This book was planned as a tribute to Paul Kline, who has recently retired from academic life. Rather than producing some form of eulogy, the editors felt that it would be more appropriate to produce a 'state of the art' synopsis of a topic that is close to Paul's heart: the experimental study of processes that underpin individual differences of various kinds. The purpose of this Introduction is to allow some of his ex-graduate students to reflect on his contribution in a rather more personal way.

At the undergraduate level, Paul Kline was an *exciting* teacher. His lectures imparted knowledge and wisdom with a light dressing of outrageous humour and comment which enthused (and occasionally shocked) his audience. With hindsight his aim was to show that no matter how bizarre a theory may sound, if it was logically consistent, well-validated and addressed an important issue it deserved serious scrutiny. In smaller groups he talked with (rather than *to* or *at*) students, and gave an open, honest, unassuming, supremely challenging and above all enthusiastic view of individual differences.

Paul supervised our PhDs in the 1970s and early 1980s, which was a time when the field of personality was at a low ebb because of situationist arguments. Nevertheless he was convinced that Cattell's and Eysenck's work showed evidence that the personality trait was a useful means of viewing personality, and that Cattell's personality sphere should permit the major source-traits to be identified. Few would now disagree with the former view, at least. He also appreciated the *weaknesses* of these methods better than most, particularly their reliance on self-report data. Hence his continued interest in objective tests of personality, those aspects of psychoanalytic theory that seemed to have some empirical basis and developments in psychometrics (such as G-analysis) which might permit the responses from projective tests to be categorised and analysed reliably.

As a research supervisor he was always available, enthusiastic and supportive, and genuinely interested in the opinions of his graduate students. Rather than slotting research students into a predetermined research programme, he encouraged us to develop our own interests – even though this must have meant far more work for him. As a result of this he ended up supervising theses in areas ranging from Lacanian theories of psychoanalysis through to the factor structure of various popular personality questionnaires; from feminist philosophy to psychometric theory. His incisive mind allowed him quickly to identify false premises, errors of logic and other such pitfalls, yet one always left his office feeling that the original ideas had worth.

In psychometrics he was not a 'details man', an ardent programmer or expert on numerical analysis. Indeed he was notorious for his ability to destroy microcomputers; one popular theory held that it was due to the static electricity generated when he scratched his beard as part of the creative process! Despite this electrical handicap he understood and expounded the principles from a conceptual point of view, and in the days before research methods training he taught us a whole host of other extracurricular academic skills, ranging from writing references to reviewing papers, drafting research proposals, and avoiding having ideas exploited by others. He also stressed the need to publish, so long as the basic experimental design was sound: he made us appreciate that an experiment that is not written up might as well never have been performed.

His approach to the subject has always been tempered by pragmatism. He argued that many fashionable theories were both woefully unimaginative and insufficiently supported by firm experimental data, but held that rigorous experimentation, often based on multivariate techniques, may be able to draw some truths from even the morass of Freudian theory. He has a healthy disrespect for 'psychometric moles' (Cattell's term) who focus on the minutiae of statistical or computational detail rather than on the substantive nature of psychological problems. As every experienced researcher knows, if the theory is sound, the effect-size respectable and data collection good, then the *detail* of data analysis matters rather little. He also maintained that it is *replication*, not one-off sophisticated analyses, that determines the truly substantive nature (or otherwise) of a research result. Several of us feel that this is a lesson that needs to be learnt by those acolytes of structural equation modelling who seem mesmerised by their ability to create largely non-replicable models of such complexity that their path diagrams assume the nature of a plate of spaghetti, and who merrily abandon a model's psychological plausibility in order to improve its fit.

Paul was particularly doubtful of some theoretical and empirical work in social psychology, based on scales where the same item is paraphrased ten times thus ensuring high reliability (it could hardly be otherwise) but which are hopelessly narrow in scope, or where some major theoretical assumption is simply not borne out by the data. For example, the evidence suggests that some tests beloved of social psychologists measure situation-specific responses rather than traits. In his 1988 book *Psychology Exposed or The Emperor's New Clothes* he suggests that many branches of psychology ignore what non-psychologists would regard as the important areas of human functioning but concentrate instead on trivia or closed, hermeneutic systems that can have no relevance to anything of importance. Reviews of this book revealed depths of emotion that could have only one interpretation for anyone with Freudian leanings.

Paul Kline is probably best known for his twenty or so books, almost all of which are single-authored. These range in content from two editions of his standard text on empirical studies of psychoanalytic theory *Fact and Fantasy in Freudian Theory* to works with a substantial psychometric component, such as *Psychometrics and Psychology*, *The Handbook of Psychological Testing* and *An Easy Guide to Factor Analysis*. They were written in an extraordinary fashion. He would be seen walking round his room or up and down the corridor looking preoccupied, clasping his hands behind his back and staring at the floor or ceiling. Then he would dive back into his office and quickly write (quite literally) a chapter or two, in tortured longhand. There were no corrections or drafts; the paragraphs just leapt out onto the pages, fully formed.

Paul is a rather shy, non-authoritarian man, so some quirk of reaction-formation doubtless caused him to lead a research project into the authoritarian personality for the Ministry of Defence. He was really rather glad when he saw a comment on the final report saying that it contained 'nothing of military value'. However it succeeded in its main aim of producing several quite useful psychological papers.

His retirement has ended the Individual Differences tradition at Exeter, where Raymond Cattell and Richard Lynn preceded him. And though most psychologists will know him through his clear, incisive and occasionally formidable books and journal articles, one of us can remember quite distinctly an occasion when he handed back an undergraduate psychometric project explaining gently that it might be quite appropriate to use the word 'questionnairre' in Devon – but not really anywhere else. We wish him well.

Paul Barrett *Psychometrics Unit,*
Ashworth Hospital, Liverpool

Colin Cooper *School of Psychology,*
Queen's University, Belfast

Sarah Hampson *Department of Psychology,*
University of Surrey

Jon May *Department of Psychology,*
University of Sheffield

Corinne Squire *Department of Human Relations,*
University of East London

Chapter 1

Process models in individual differences research

Paul T. Barrett

Personality and ability factors are marvellous shorthand summaries of behavioural regularities: it is so much more parsimonious to speak of high 'verbal ability' than to have to enumerate an individual's skill at spelling, comprehension, use of language, understanding of metaphor and a whole host of other behaviours. However, knowing an individual's profile of ability and personality characteristics (and being able to predict their subsequent behaviour from these traits) does not imply any sort of understanding of the concepts being measured by standard, psychometric tests – many of which are developed atheoretically, through the use of factor analysis. To understand these characteristics, it is necessary to introduce theory-based models that consider how more fundamental processes (be they psychological, biological, social, cognitive, developmental, genetic or whatever) give rise to the behavioural consistencies that we term 'traits'.

Whilst the contributions that follow discuss in some detail what is known about particular process models in certain areas of individual differences research, the purpose of this chapter is to take a more meta-theoretical approach. Following an appraisal of trait theory, it examines precisely why the study of process models is vitally important for all aspects of individual differences. It also suggests that some varieties of process model (such as those based on biological, physiological or biochemical processes) lead more naturally to causal explanations than do others (such as social models). Finally, it provides a brief description of some useful approaches to the biological processes underlying intelligence and personality – several of which are little-known, even to specialists – and suggests how traditional psychometric techniques may need to be revised in the light of process models.

WHAT IS A 'PROCESS MODEL'?

This is an explanatory model of particular behavioural outcomes (perhaps summarised in terms of a trait or state). It hypothesises that a series of specified mechanisms function in certain ways, so *causing* the observed behaviours. This kind of dynamic model can be contrasted with a structural model that seeks to describe the possible components of behaviour, without attempting to state how these components might so produce the behaviour in question. For example, when trying to predict a behavioural outcome we might express the precursors to this behaviour in terms of a series of actions or interlinking processes that can be seen to be the basis or the *how* of the outcome. A structural approach, however, might propose that certain hypothesised components are responsible for producing the behaviour. It might well weight scores or measures of these components to permit an optimal quantitative prediction to be made. However, there is no explanation of *why* or *how* these components produce the outcome.

WHAT ARE INDIVIDUAL DIFFERENCES?

Ostensibly, these are any observed difference between individuals on *any* variable chosen by the observer. Such variables may be latent (e.g., abstract concepts such as 'learning potential' or 'social class') or manifest (such as 'amount of disposable income' or 'scores on Raven's Matrices'). However, if we modify the 'observed difference' component of this definition to include the word *reliable*, we begin to make a distinction between behavioural variability that is attributable to *random* influences and that which is *systematic* or non-random in origin. Further, if we also propose that behavioural variability can be explained with greater accuracy by taking into account individuals' levels of certain hypothesised *intrapsychic* variables – then we have defined the essential nature of individual differences research. The word *intrapsychic* denotes those attributes that an individual may be said to possess that will interact with *environmental* variables so producing measurable behavioural variance amongst individuals. Examples of *intrapsychic* variables are those defining temperament, cognitive ability, motivation and mood. Environmental variables are those that are said to exhibit some influence upon an individual's behaviour but which exist independently of an individual's personal attributes.

For example, if we are interested in determining timed performance on a recognition memory task using emotive word categories, we could obtain a sample of individuals and proceed to generate several sample statistics based solely upon the chronometric indices so generated. One simple model could consider the average recognition time for the group, with the variability around that mean being accorded the status of error. Alternatively we could also consider the level of trait anxiety for each individual and perhaps general cognitive ability. Regression procedures could then be used to explain mean recall time as a function of ability, trait anxiety, and perhaps the interaction between these two variables. It is likely that we would now have greater insight into any *individual's* performance. Although the mean recall would be the same, it would be possible to partition the variance in observed scores such that more of the 'error' is explainable by our two *individual difference* variables. This is essentially the argument put forward by Underwood (1975) in a paper espousing the value of individual difference variables in understanding cognition.

Consider performance on ability tests as an example of the individual differences approach to the study of behaviour. Jensen (1964) reported a study looking at the performance of university students on Raven's Advanced Progressive Matrices. Whereas it is assumed that performance on problem-solving tasks is solely a function of the cognitive abilities of an individual, Jensen explored the hypothesis that speed of problem solving may also be related to the *personality* of the individual. His hypothesis was deduced from Eysenck's theory of the personality variable introversion/extraversion. This predicted that the performance of extraverts (measured as speed of problem solving) would be inferior to that of introverts over a long duration of testing, due to a gradual build-up of reactive inhibition in extraverts. Jensen administered the test to each subject individually, without time limit. However, the total time taken by the individual to complete the test was recorded secretly by the tester. Although the personality variables of extraversion (E) and neuroticism (N) did not correlate significantly with the scores on the test, the correlation between E and the completion duration was -.46 ($p<0.01$). This result indicates that if the test had been administered under timed conditions, the more extraverted individuals might probably have scored higher than the more introverted individuals. Thus the experiment shows that it can be erroneous to assume that performance on ability tests is solely a function of the ability of an individual, given particular test administration conditions that interact with particular features of an individual's personality. Eysenck and Eysenck (1985) and Eysenck (1994) detail further evidence of this particular phenomenon. In other words, 'ability tests' are producing differences between individuals that are not attributable to a single causal variable – ability. Further examples of such approaches in the area of memory and cognition are to be found in Cohen (1994), as well as in Michael Eysenck's chapter in this volume.

WHAT ARE THE AREAS OF STUDY ENCOMPASSED WITHIN INDIVIDUAL DIFFERENCES RESEARCH?

To answer this, I refer to a quotation from Eysenck (1970) who provided a definition of personality as:

> A more or less stable and enduring organisation of a person's character, temperament, intellect and physique, which determines his unique adjustment to the environment. *Character* denotes a person's more or less stable and enduring system of conative behaviour ('will'); *temperament*, his more or less stable and enduring system of affective behaviour ('emotion'); *intellect*, his more or less stable and enduring system of cognitive behaviour ('intelligence'); *physique*, his more or less stable and enduring system of bodily configuration and neuroendocrine endowment.
>
> (Eysenck, 1970, p. 2)

Note here that Eysenck is using the term 'personality' as a composite variable that is viewed as the product of four conceptual entities. I would modify the above definition slightly by dropping the term 'character' and making explicit that 'will' involves the concept of motivation. This has important repercussions as will be seen below. However, it is significant to note that Eysenck is careful not to treat the concepts of motivation/will, emotion, intelligence and biological composition as discrete entities. Although it is easier to examine each of these areas in isolation from each other, the evidence and explanatory process theory that is beginning to emerge from research laboratories suggests that this separation is becoming tenuous, as shown in Jensen's (1964) study discussed above. Experimental studies of individual differences thus require great attention to be paid to experimental design where either the interactions deduced from theory are 'built into' a design, or where experimental manipulation 'controls' the deduced interactions.

Although multivariate data analysis and computing technology have now reached levels of sophistication that enable large-scale data analyses to be undertaken with relative ease, this has brought with it the problems of 'data-dredging' and mindless empiricism. It is now too easy to generate studies that seem no more than an attempt to measure everything and hope that some sense can be made of whatever results can be made to pour forth from the computer. Whereas the pioneers of multivariate psychology (e.g., Cattell, Eysenck and Kline) preached judicious and theory-laden use of the new techniques and advances, many practitioners and researchers nowadays seem to view the techniques as an alternative to careful theory-driven scientific investigation. The author himself almost became wrongly convinced about the capability of the computer to produce, not just prodigious amounts of analysis but, results that were meaningful. Experience taught otherwise!

A second implication of the definition given above is that the four concepts of motivation/will, temperament, intellect and physique are viewed as systems, and systems are defined by structure *and* process. This is very much reflected in the kind of theory proposed by Eysenck and others who are looking for causal models of behaviour. Whereas Cattellian theory initially was very much concerned with *inductive* generation of psychometric structure, Eysenckian theory has been primarily involved with *deducing* the processes that might permit coherent structure to be found within the psychometric domain. Following Eysenck (1994), I think it is essential that the area of individual differences research should move forward from the purely structural models of psychometrics and correlational/covariance analysis of questionnaire data matrices into the direct investigation of causal models of the processes by which such structure manifests itself at the psychometric level. However, as will be noted below, current evidence indicates that this is not going to be a straightforward task.

Finally, before departing this section, it is important to note that the statements made so far are sufficiently generalised to permit the study of individual differences in both the normal and clinical domains. The kinds of process models that may be generated do not rely upon discrete boundaries being constructed between behaviourally normal and abnormal individuals. Rather, such models propose that abnormality is defined by extreme positions on continua, irrespective of whether the continua are largely defined biologically, psychometrically, or socially.

PROCESS IDENTIFICATION AND LEVEL OF EXPLANATION

Before any model (structural or process) can be generated, it is a prerequisite that a phenomenon is detected. That is, in order to attempt to generate an explanatory model, it is incumbent upon a researcher to demonstrate empirically that a phenomenon (e.g., a personality trait) exists to be explained. This seemingly trivial statement, first proposed by Woodward (1989) in the philosophy of science literature, and applied to the psychological domain by Haig (in preparation), has enormous repercussions within the empirical science of psychology. A phenomenon must be both differentiable from other phenomena (uniquely identifiable), and replicable. The phenomena can be either manifest or latent. Once any phenomenon is established as an empirical 'fact', by noting its replicability and reliability of identification, it is then appropriate to generate some explanatory process model that attempts to infer causal inference from the conditions and processes that produce the phenomenon. It does so by assuming the phenomenon to be the dependent variable, and positing several (measurable) lower-level independent variables together with some theoretical model that suggests how these may jointly influence the dependent variable.

When generating causal theories in individual differences, the researcher can choose explanatory processes that reside at four levels of explanation: the social, the cognitive, the psychodynamic and the biological. (I have mentioned the psychodynamic level here as it does attempt to generate process theory, albeit on the basis of little or no empirical foundation.) A process model at the social level will couch explanatory theory in terms of person-to-person interaction and the rules for behaviour that are defined in/by society. As Sarah Hampson indicates in her chapter, the social process model may be defined entirely in a *constructionist* framework (where individual attributes play no part in the model) or in a *constructivist* framework (which posits an interaction between an individual's attributes and the environment within which they operate from moment to moment). The cognitive approach to explaining individual differences can be viewed in global cognition-based theories such as Bandura's (1986) social-cognition theory or Seligman's (Seligman *et al.*, 1979) learned helplessness/optimism attribution-style theory. Alternatively, elementary cognitive tasks (ECTs), such as reaction time, inspection time, analogy item problem solving and memory span, are used to aid in the determination of the processes involved and their processing durations. The term ECT is defined by Carroll (1993) as:

> any one of a possibly large number of tasks in which a person undertakes, or is assigned, a performance for which there is a specifiable class of 'successful' or 'correct' outcomes or end states which are to be attained through a relatively small number of mental processes or operations, and whose successful outcomes depend on the instructions given to, or the sets or plans adopted by, the person.
>
> (Carroll, 1993 p. 11)

Generally, the investigator will use the results from ECTs to infer differences in cognitive abilities. This kind of empirical investigation has been called the 'cognitive correlates' approach by Sternberg (1990). This can be contrasted with the 'cognitive components' methodology, based largely upon the work of Sternberg (1977). Here tasks are broken down into discrete processing components, which are then systematically manipulated in order to observe the timed responses. Finally, at the biological level of explanation, theory generation is specified at the level of biological structures and processes. Generally, biological models of individual differences are proposed as the foundation of the social and cognitive levels of explanatory theory. For example, Eysenck (1988) views intelligence within three facets of understanding – the biological, psychometric (cognitive) and the social/practical domain. It is the biological processes that are considered the precursors of the behaviours which are described within the psychometric domain of investigation. As Eysenck (1988) has indicated, the psychometric domain or level is also influenced by social and environmental processes. That there is a synergy between all three levels of explanation is not in doubt. Rather, it is the overall *directionality* of causal explanation that is contentious (see Hampson, 1992; H.J. Eysenck, 1992; Neisser and Fivush, 1994; Gergen and Gergen, 1988). More explicitly, we might ask whether the interaction between biology, cognition and social processes is equally multidirectional, or whether an individual's biological make-up can determine to a large extent the level and style of both cognitive and social performance.

THE STATIC DESCRIPTION OF INDIVIDUAL DIFFERENCES – PSYCHOMETRICS

It is fair to say that the basis for much of the psychometric description of individual differences in personality has been built upon the concept of the trait, first espoused by Allport (1937) and Stagner (1937). However, the definition of a trait differed markedly between these two individuals, with Allport speaking of traits as initiating and guiding behaviour, with some traits identified as motives and others as stylistic descriptions. Stagner claimed that traits were just convenient descriptions of behaviour, and not explanatory concepts or motivators. Further, he saw no reason to believe that traits were consistent from one situation to the next. Within the domain of intelligence, Spearman (1927) had attempted to identify 'g' – a pervasive unidimensional concept of cognitive ability, identified by him using factor analysis. Thurstone (1938) disagreed with Spearman by proposing a series of factors of intelligence, however, as Eysenck and Eysenck (1985) note, a measure of agreement was finally reached between Spearman and Thurstone in that not only was a general factor shown to be empirically identifiable, but also that several other factors of cognitive abilities were also seen to be identifiable (even though correlated to some extent between one another). Finally, it was Eysenck (1947), Vernon (1950) and Cattell (1957, 1971) who first created the benchmark psychometric solutions for personality and ability variables. With regard to present-day psychometric structure, frankly very little has changed from these seminal efforts. Carroll (1993) has provided a remarkable report of psychometric analyses of more than 460 datasets of ability test items: the results remain very similar to Cattell's original factor structures.

The five-factor model of Tupes and Christal (1961) and McCrae and

Costa (1985) is really no more than a truncated, orthogonalised second-order factor solution that Cattell first demonstrated in 1957 (see also John, 1990). As far back as the early 1980s, both Paul Kline and myself had mused over the proposition that the whole field of psychometrics was stagnating in a methodological cul-de-sac, offering no new insights or substantive psychological knowledge. Eysenck seems to be concurring with this in a recent chapter, stating:

> Altogether, it seems that we are still plagued by the separation of Cronbach's 'Two disciplines of scientific psychology', that is, the psychometric and the experimental. Until and unless we manage to unite these into one seamless garment, new attempts to understand better the nature of personality and intelligence and their interaction will be severely compromised.
>
> (Eysenck, 1994, p. 26)

The problem with psychometric models is that they are essentially sterile, descriptive structures. They are undoubtedly the crucial precursors to the development of substantive process theory but, by themselves, can only offer summary description of covariance between observations. As indicated above, they assist in the identification of psychological phenomena, but not in the attribution of causality. This requires the specification of process, and it is to this class of models that I now turn.

CAUSAL/PROCESS MODELS OF INDIVIDUAL DIFFERENCES

Attribution theory

With regard to models put forward at the social level of explanation, social-cognitive (Bandura, 1986) and attribution theory (Försterling, 1986; Rotter, 1966; Abramson et al., 1978) seem to be the most comprehensive of these approaches. Cognitive theories of personality are based upon the proposition that there are components of cognition that determine how an individual evaluates, interprets and organises information that is considered relevant. Little can be said about these theories other than they seem to exist in isolation from the large body of evidence accrued at the biological and psychometric levels of investigation. Further, there is actually surprisingly little explanatory power within these theories, as many are confined mainly to either clinical situations or specific social processes. For example, Seligman's work in this area has been based upon a reformulation of learned helplessness that was originally based on animal studies (Seligman, 1975). As Sweeney et al., (1986) noted, research based upon human research participants offers little support for this model. Thus it was again redefined as an attributional-style model by Abramson *et al.*, (1978) and has since had some success in explaining certain behaviours. However, the kinds of processes bought forward to provide the explanatory theory are large-scale, and gross in conception. Seligman's theory states that

> attributing lack of control to internal factors leads to lowered self-esteem, whereas attributing lack of control to external factors does not. Furthermore, attributing lack of control to stable factors should lead to helplessness deficits extended across time, and attributing lack of control to global factors should lead to wide generalisation of help-lessness deficits across situations . . .
>
> (Seligman *et al.*, 1979, p. 242)

Although social-cognitive individual differences theory does have some explanatory power, there seems to be a complete avoidance of the more fundamental attributes of individuals. It is true that the cognitive explanations are couched in process form, but these seem to involve yet more assumptions about hypothesised processing components of cognition that themselves need empirical examination. Thus such models are really not very parsimonious. Furthermore, because they rely on concepts that simply fail to emerge from cross-situational analyses of behaviour – 'non-traits' such as 'internal locus of control' about which Kline (1993) makes several pithy comments – it is difficult to see how these models can possibly work. 'Experiments' in this area merely involve correlating scores on various questionnaires, and inferring causal models from certain patterns of correlations. However, since all the data generally come from the same domain (self-report, or rating) it is always possible that the correlations emerge because some other variable (social desirability, for example) will affect some people's scores on both measures. This may give the false impression that two constructs are causally related. I am unsure whether proceeding with theory generation at this level, in apparent ignorance of the more fundamental individual differences theory being currently proposed at the biological level, will prove optimal in the long term.

Hampson's social constructivist model of personality (1992, 1995)

Another, less comprehensive and perhaps more focused, approach is that put forward by Sarah Hampson (see her chapter in this book). Hampson's social constructivist model of personality is based upon the premise that personality is a dynamic function both of an *observer* and an *actor* (self-observer). An individual observer is assumed to interpret another individual actor's behaviour, and respond accordingly. The actor is also assumed to adopt the role of self-observer, and make corresponding adjustments to behaviour that are then in turn interpreted by the observer, and so on. The constructivist approach acknowledges that biological mechanisms and behavioural traits will form part of this interactive process in that they affect the *intra-individual* component of the *inter-individual* interaction. However, the concept of personality is seen ultimately as a constructive process, that is formed directly as a function of the interaction between two or more individuals. It is especially important to distinguish the key philosophical distinction that lies behind the theory generated within social constructionism and that formed within a social constructivist position. This distinction revolves around the proposition that personality is not a reality, to be observed similarly by independent observers, but rather is a social creation that is being continually defined by actors and observers. Hampson's model acknowledges the concept of an independent reality, but also proposes that social interaction is an additional defining feature of both the language and concept of personality.

M.W. Eysenck's processing efficiency theory of anxiety (1992)

This is an approach to theory generation that tries to explicate the cognitive processes involved in anxiety-related behaviours. Essentially, it is an attempt to explain cognitive performance as a function of state anxiety. The latter concept is concerned with levels of anxiety that are transient and situation-dependent, as contrasted with trait anxiety which is considered a relatively enduring and stable attribute for an individual. However, as Eysenck and Calvo (1992) indicate, measurements of these two concepts generally correlate at around 0.70, hence there is a close relationship between the two. At the heart of the theory is the proposition that high-anxiety individuals differ from those with low anxiety, based upon the amount of information processing and attentional resources available for any task that involves elements of stress. He has coined the clinical term 'hypervigilance' to describe the excessive level of processing resources that are committed to detecting and processing threat-related stimuli or events within a high-anxiety individual. Because of this tendency to maintain a heightened level of threat-detection, behavioural performance in the highly anxious individual is negatively affected. Eysenck and his co-workers have now carried out many experiments to demonstrate that the fundamental proposition of the theory is supported by empirical results. In addition, as is apparent from his chapter in this book, he has gone further than most in attempting to demonstrate that the concept of anxiety is perhaps best defined in terms of cognitive processes that rely less upon the notion of biologically mediated response mechanisms and more upon learned cognitive processes. Although this theory is solely concerned with explaining individual differences in anxiety, it is nevertheless interesting to contemplate the extrapolation of this process-oriented approach to other areas of individual differences research.

H.J. Eysenck's biological model of personality (1957, 1967)

This biologically based model proposes that introversion/extraversion is a function of the levels of activity (*arousal*) within a cortico-reticular loop, involving processing within the reticular formation through the Ascending Reticular Activating System and the cerebral cortex. Introverts are hypothesised to have greater levels of activity within this loop, hence are characterised as having greater cortical arousal than extraverts. Neuroticism is thought to be a consequence of the level of activity within the visceral brain (consisting of the hippocampus, amygdala, cingulum, septum and hypothalamus). Individuals who show a greater level of neurotic behaviour are said to have a greater capacity for '*activation*' within this biological system. That is, they produce biochemical and electrophysiological activity in these structures more readily than those who are low in neuroticism. Finally, Eysenck and Eysenck (1976) proposed that a third concept (psychoticism) was needed to explain behaviours that seemed to lie along a dimension that ranged from normal through criminal and psychopathic to psychotic. The biological model for this dimension is less well developed. A substantial review of the status of the arousal/activation model of introversion/extraversion is given in Bullock and Gilliland (1993).

Gray's (1972, 1981) biological theory of personality

Gray's theory shares some similarity with Eysenck's proposals, however, he argues that the two dimensions of extraversion and neuroticism should be conceptually realigned as dimensions of *impulsivity* and *anxiety*. This proposition was based upon research on animal learning and physiology. It suggested that, in animals, individual differences exist in the susceptibility to punishment (the anxiety dimension), which is physiologically mediated by activity within a behavioural inhibition system composed of the septo-hippocampal system, monoamine-mediated afferents from the brain-stem, and neocortical projection in the frontal lobe. The psychometric vector defining this biological construct would extend from neurotic introvert to stable extravert. The axis sits at 45 degrees within the orthogonal space of Eysenck's extraversion and neuroticism factors. Individual differences in the susceptibility to reward (the impulsivity dimension) in animals are viewed as being related to an 'approach' system which is primarily mediated by the medial forebrain bundle and the lateral hypothalamus. In psychometric terms, this would equate to a vector with poles of neurotic extravert to stable introvert.

These two biological models briefly adumbrated above can be said to be the two most substantive attempts at a causal model of temperament/personality. Within the framework of these models, more specific models have been generated to explain certain behaviours within particular domains of interest. For example, within the clinical domain, Cloninger's (1986) model of adaptive personality traits, Raine's (1993) remarkable work on the biological bases of criminal behaviour, and Zuckerman's (1991) work on the biological factors associated with the production of sensation-seeking behaviour. However, both H.J. Eysenck's and Gray's models share many problems with regard to the evidence supporting the conceptualisation of anxiety/neuroticism as a unidimensional construct. M.W. Eysenck (1992, and in this book) outlines the sometimes disparate results found when looking for convergent evidence of a construct of anxiety at the biological, cognitive and psychometric levels of analysis. Of especial note here is the work by Fahrenberg (1988, 1992) who, after twenty years of investigation of the construct of anxiety at the *biological* level of analysis, found no evidence for a unidimensional construct of anxiety as posited by Eysenck and Gray. Myrtek's (1984) work on the evaluation of the concept of physiological responsiveness or lability of the nervous system (as espoused by H.J. Eysenck) also led him to conclude that the use of such terminology is not supported by the available empirical evidence. Fahrenberg (1992) has since hinted that an idiographic approach to the examination and measurement of the construct might be the only way forward. I will return to this issue later in this chapter.

Intelligence

Within the domain of intelligence there had been little or no substantive causal theory generated until the initial work of Hendrickson and Hendrickson (1980), who provided a biochemically based, observed, causal model for individual differences in psychometric measures of intelligence. Since then, much empirical work has attempted to replicate and extend their initial observations. Two recent empirically based reviews of the Hendrickson work have been recently provided by Robinson (1993, in press). Two other substantial reviews of the entire area are provided by Barrett and Eysenck (1992) and Deary and Caryl (1993). While much of this work has concentrated upon the mechanism of nerve conduction variability (Barrett and Eysenck, 1994) and cortical nerve conduction velocity (Reed and Jensen, 1993), there have been three other significant theoretical developments in this same area, each focusing upon different conceptualisations of explanatory theory at the biological level.

First, the work of Weiss (1986, 1989, 1992) has generated a theory which relies upon specific brain biochemistry and particle physics to provide prediction and theoretical support for empirical findings within both the electroencephalographic and psychometric realms of cognitive abilities. Essentially, Weiss has suggested a possible biochemical mechanism for the transmission and subsequent use of information within the brain that also explains why there is a relation between cerebral glucose metabolic rate and performance on IQ tests (Haier, 1993). Weiss also indicates that this biochemical functioning is the product of a hypothesised gene locus for intelligence. Related to this work is that of Lehrl and Fischer (1988, 1990) who have looked at individual differences in cognitive functioning in terms of information-processing capacity. They compute capacity directly (in bits per second) and find that this measure correlates in the order of +0.8 with verbal IQ scores. (Note however that Kline *et al.*, 1994, and Draycott and Kline, 1994, have demonstrated that the parameter may be more closely related to crystallised IQ and memory than to general intelligence *per se*.)

Secondly, there is the work of Robinson (1982, 1987, 1993) who has generated a cerebral arousability theory within the domains of neo-Pavlovian and Eysenckian personality theory. Robinson's work also provides an explanatory theory for the concept of biological intelligence and its measurement using electroencephalography. This is a model that has provided spectacular empirical results (correlations between psychometric measures of personality and physical system parameters between 0.63 and 0.95), yet has been largely ignored by the wider community of individual difference psychologists. Admittedly, some of the work on the intelligence theory has not met with complete replication to date (Barrett and Eysenck, 1992; although see Stough *et al.*, 1996), but nevertheless, this is a theory that has generated several testable hypotheses and awaits substantive examination by independent investigators.

Finally, a recent paper by Miller (1994) has put forward the hypothesis that myelinisation of cerebral nerve fibres is one of the major causal mechanisms that differentiates individuals in terms of intelligence and information-processing capacity. This is an integrative theory that draws upon empirical evidence from several fields of study, including behavioural genetics, psychometrics, biomedical imaging, electrophysiology, developmental biology, nutrition and brain biochemistry. The theory is tied very much to the concept of nerve transmission variability and speed of conduction, these transmission signal characteristics being mediated by the quantity of myelinated axons and the density of myelinisation of fibres within the brain.

In this brief discussion of the status of theory concerning intelligence, I have purposely not mentioned the various theories that may be said to remain more at the level of speculation than based upon any solid foundation of empirical evidence. The all-encompassing nature of such theories has tended to leave them metaphorically 'beached' in an academic cul-de-sac. They are of interest, but of little practical use for an investigator trying to tease out the causal mechanisms of individual differences in intelligence. For example, theories proposed by Howe (1988, 1989), Sternberg (1990) and Gardner (Gardner, Kornhaber and Wake, 1996) are all variously based at the cognitive and social level of process, yet, apart from elements of Sternberg's triarchic theory, all exist more as speculative descriptions of the causation of observed behaviours than testable, formal theoretical propositions. For example, much of Howe's theorising about the causes of individual differences in intelligence (and also giftedness) seems to be based more on the interpretation of the results from a few narrow areas of investigation than a broad overview of the entire range of empirical evidence that is now available. At the opposite end of this spectrum, Gardner's model of multiple intelligences is attractive in that it comprehensively addresses the issue of the behavioural width of the concept, but offers no solutions as to how an investigator might proceed to test certain propositions of the model. Although this particular area of investigation still lacks substantive process-based theory, it is my opinion that it is not to be found in models that rely solely on differences in cognitive processes, learning styles, or social learning processes, to explain individual differences in intelligence. With the quantity of empirical evidence becoming available concerning the biological correlates of psychometric intelligence, it is perhaps more optimal to view the behavioural outcome measures as the result of the interaction between the environment *and* an individual's biological make-up.

AN EVALUATION

The rather brief outline of the key models and theories that exist within the individual differences area shows that the nature of the theory being produced is changing. The advances in knowledge and understanding of individual differences is no longer the domain of the social scientist or psychometrician. Rather, explanatory theory has shifted in two ways: to the more fundamental level of biology in order to seek causal explanations of behavioural outcomes, and to the cognitive level, in order to determine the processes that define the behaviours being observed. This is not to deny the importance of purely social and psychometric levels of analysis, which are invaluable for identifying the phenomena whose processes then require explanation. However, I suspect that the primary cause of these phenomena will best be found at the biological level of explanation, using this knowledge simultaneously to seek behavioural-outcome explanations using cognitive process models.

This shift in focus towards biological and cognitive process models is not happening because researchers have arbitrarily decided that they will begin to seek explanation at this level. There is instead recognition that purely social and psychometric theories cannot fully explain the causes of individual differences, whilst any theory that ignores the many biological differences between organisms when attempting to describe individual and group behaviours is clearly incomplete. This is not an argument for nature over nurture or a crude attempt to explain behaviour directly by recourse to a particular biological structure, system or process. It is, however, a serious attempt to begin to explicate the role of an individual's biology in determining, to some degree, their motivation, personality, emotionality and intelligence. It is also accepted that there is constant interaction with the environment, which is also perhaps likely to be having an impact on an individual's cerebral physiology (Jacobs et al., 1993). Lynn's (1993) review of the evidence concerning the relationship between nutrition and intellectual functioning demonstrates the substantive interactive effect of this particular, albeit gross, feature of the environment.

In addition, it is significant that the models all deal with a level of process that is very detailed, but that can be linked through psychometric indices and empirical observation to real-world behaviours. Essentially, the biological approach needs to consider the extent to which mechanisms, structures, or processes can be altered by environmental factors (illness, learning, training, pharmacological intervention etc.). Some (e.g., nerve conduction variability) appear to be relatively fixed, whilst others may be modifiable. The recursive nature of the interaction between environment and biology has already been suggested in the field of behaviour genetics, with the Scarr and McCartney (1983) theory of the genotype/environment linkage. This states that genotypes determine to some extent the kind of environment and situations that an individual will choose (when possible). That is, the genotype can be seen to be restraining or promoting certain interactions with the environment. Attitudinal as well as personality and intelligence data show a significant genetic influence (Martin et al., 1986; Heath et al., 1989) suggesting that learning and social mobility tend to augment rather than erode the effects of the genotype on behaviour. This has obvious repercussions within biometric analyses for the specification of the environment as something that is independent from an individual's genotype.

A second feature of the new generation of models being produced is that they are all built upon a foundation of empirical work. Some is used indirectly in order to show that the models can predict a variety of specified outcomes, with other more direct evidence indicating that key features of the models can be empirically verified. This is especially true of Robinson's model (mentioned above). It is based initially on psychological observations and inferred psychological processes. Objective psychophysiological data are subsequently used to test the inferred biological substrate rather than relying on assumed physiological structures or processes (e.g., limbic reactivity). All such models extend beyond the domain of biology, relying upon evidence at both the psychometric/cognitive and social levels to aid and assist in the model-generation process. It is now becoming more apparent that research in individual differences requires a shift from the correlational analysis model to that of an experimental paradigm (a point made by Eysenck, 1994). Whilst the correlational model can assist in identifying substantive correlates, and to some extent can aid in the causal modelling of constructs (such as in the use of structural equation modelling based upon covariance structures), it is not sufficient as an experimental model for the elucidation and empirical analysis of individual processes. These are essentially cognitively based operations that require examination of dynamic systems rather than static 'concepts'.

A third feature of the models now being proposed is that they may break down artificial distinctions between personality, temperament and ability. They seek to explain both personality/temperament and intellectual functions. With the introduction of Goleman's (1995) concept of emotional intelligence (akin to Sternberg's, 1985, and H.J. Eysenck's, 1992, usage of the term *social/practical intelligence*), it is now clear that process models must begin to take into account the nature of behaviour as an integration of motive, personality, temperament and intellect. This might well be expected to have an impact on purely cognitive process models of cognition such as the SOAR model of Laird, Newell and Rosenbloom (1987) and Newell (1990). The implication is that the empirical testing of such models requires a careful approach that is sensitive to the possible interactions between processes. Further, it does lead one to question the adequacy of many of the psychometric and biological models of personality that have been put forward. For example, Eysenck's or Gray's theories of temperament invoke relatively few major concepts. They are parsimonious, 'broad brush' models. However, as has been noted above, the concept of N (anxiety) is probably too broad as currently conceived, with little or no evidence (Myrtek, 1984) for either a 'lability' or single behavioural dimension (even though the psychometric analysis of questionnaire data consistently indicates a single broad factor). If N is a more individualistic, cognitively based concept, with a differentiated response style within individuals, then Fahrenberg's argument concerning idiographic assessment may well prove relevant. That is, it will prove to be impossible to account for psychophysiological and behavioural differences in anxiety levels using essentially nomothetic measuring instruments. Such a research strategy would have profound implications for the whole area of individual differences research. However, the puzzling feature of this issue is why the questionnaire measurement of anxiety seems to point consistently to a single general measure (see Eysenck and Eysenck, 1985, for a review of this research literature), whereas psychophysiological and behavioural evidence appears multidimensional and fractionated, to use Haynes and Wilson's (1979) terminology.

THE FUTURE

So, where does all this take us? From the above, the reader may deduce that I consider the biological process models now being generated as the hotbed for future empirical work in individual differences research. Cognitive and social-process models, (e.g., the work of M.W. Eysenck and Hampson) will complement this approach. From the brief overview of models presented above, I think the reader will see that this whole area is on the verge of a change in research style that is simultaneously focusing on both the biological and cognitive levels of analysis, allied to a change in experimental paradigm that is becoming more deductive in design. However, Kline's (1995) statements at a recent conference on occupational testing should also be noted. He stressed the paucity of substantive developments within psychometric measures of personality, and the need to look at performance itself rather than continue to ask self-report questions about it. Perhaps the whole area of psychometrics should be regenerated within a more experimental and deductive framework, with self-report questionnaires being replaced by carefully developed performance measures. In a sense, Cattell and Warburton (1967) have already provided us with a foundation for many new 'objective' tests. Deductions from the models outlined above should enable a more precise and targeted psychometric/experimental approach to the creation of a new range of measures of both cognitive and affect variables.

However, I also feel that somewhere along the line, psychometricians have forgotten about motivation – a point also made by Pervin (1990). Although the social-cognitive area has addressed the concept with some vigour, psychometricians have largely ignored the concept (with the exception of Cattell, 1990; see also Boyle, 1988 for an excellent review of this area). This is perhaps the most difficult of all psychometric problems to solve, in that it requires the assessment of an essentially dynamic process. Cattell's Motivation Analysis Test is but one approach to this problem. Taking into account the biological models of temperament, personality and intelligence, the problem first requires an elucidation of what needs to be measured (if anything), over and above these three constructs. Perhaps motivation is simply some product of all three, that requires a form of dynamic calculus of the type initially presented by Cattell. Certainly, it is difficult to decide whether a concept such as Gray's susceptibility to reward is itself a causal motivating variable or should be targeted as a temperament variable – which is perceived differently from a hypothesised motivation variable such as 'need for achievement'.

In conclusion, I hope the reader now has developed an impression of both the excitement and challenge that faces individual differences research in the 1990s and beyond. With the advent of modern technology for the non-invasive measurement and imaging of many biological structures and processes, a new window has been opened into the functioning human being. In addition, with fifty years of psychometric work on the identification and measurement of behavioural phenomena, the time is now ripe for a new paradigm to take hold. Eysenck and Eysenck first put forward this possibility in 1985, Kline has repeatedly indicated in the intervening period that purely psychometric analyses are leading nowhere, and Revelle's (1995) recent review of the area of personality investigation has demonstrated that some research strategy change is underway. I hope I have added some additional impetus and focus to these calls for change.

REFERENCES

Abramson, L.Y., Seligman, M.E.P. and Teasdale, J.D. (1978) 'Learned helplessness in humans: critique and reformulation', *Journal of Abnormal Psychology* 87: 49–74.

Allport, G.W. (1937) *Personality: A Psychological Interpretation*, New York: Holt, Rinehart and Winston.

Bandura, A. (1986) *Social Foundations of Thought and Action: A Social-Cognitive Theory*, Englewood Cliffs, NJ: Prentice-Hall.

Barrett, P. T. and Eysenck, H.J. (1992) 'Brain electrical potentials and intelligence', in A. Gale and M.W. Eysenck (eds) *Handbook of Individual Differences: Biological Perspectives*, New York: McGraw-Hill.

—— (1994) 'The relationship between evoked potential component amplitude, latency, contour length, variability, zero crossings and psychometric intelligence', *Personality and Individual Differences* 16: 3–32.

Boyle, G. J. (1988) 'Elucidation of motivation structure by dynamic calculus', in J.R. Nesselroade and Cattell, R.B. (eds) *Handbook of Multivariate Experimental Psychology (2nd edn)*, New York: Plenum Press.

Bullock, W.A. and Gilliland, K. (1993) 'Eysenck's arousal theory of introversion-extraversion: a converging measures investigation', *Journal of Personality and Social Psychology* 4: 113–123.

Carroll, J.B. (1993) *Human Cognitive Abilities: A Survey of Factor-Analytic Studies*, Cambridge: Cambridge University Press.

Cattell, R.B. (1957) *Personality and Motivation Structure and Measurement*, New York: New World.

—— (1971) *Abilities: Their Structure, Growth and Action*, Boston: Houghton-Mifflin.

—— (1990) 'Advance in Cattellian personality theory', in L.A. Pervin (ed.) *Handbook of Personality Theory and Research*, New York: Guilford Press.

Cattell, R.B. and Warburton, F.W. (1967) *Objective Personality and Motivation Tests: A Theoretical Introduction and Practical Compendium*, Urbana, IL: University of Illinois Press.

Cloninger, C.R. (1986) 'A unified biosocial theory of personality and its role in the development of anxiety states', *Psychiatric Developments* 3: 167–226.

Cohen, R.L. (1994) 'Some thoughts on individual differences and theory construction', *Intelligence* 18: 2–13.

Deary, I. and Caryl, P. (1993) 'Intelligence, EEG, and evoked potentials', in P. A. Vernon (ed.) *Biological Approaches to Human Intelligence*, New Jersey: Ablex.

Draycott, S. and Kline, P. (1994) 'Further investigation into the nature of BIP: a factor analysis of the BIP with primary abilities', *Personality and Individual Differences* 17: 201–209.

Eysenck, H.J. (1947) *Dimensions of Personality*, London: Routledge.

—— (1957) *The Dynamics of Hysteria and Anxiety*, London: Routledge and Kegan Paul.

—— (1967) *The Biological Basis of Personality*, Springfield, IL: Charles C. Thomas.

—— (1970) *The Structure of Human Personality*, (3rd edn), London: Methuen.

—— (1988) 'The concept of "intelligence": useful or useless?', *Intelligence* 12: 1–16.

——(1992) 'The biological basis of intelligence', in P. A. Vernon (ed.) *The Biological Basis of Intelligence*, New Jersey: Ablex.

——(1994) 'Personality and intelligence: psychometric and experimental approaches', in R.J. Sternberg and P. Ruzgis (eds) *Personality and Intelligence*, Cambridge: Cambridge University Press.

Eysenck, H.J. and Eysenck, M.W. (1985) *Personality and Individual Differences: A Natural Science Approach*, New York: Plenum Press.

Eysenck, H.J. and Eysenck, S.B.G. (1976) *Psychoticism as a Dimension of Personality*, London: Hodder and Stoughton.

Eysenck, M.W. (1992) 'The nature of anxiety', in A. Gale and M.W. Eysenck (eds) *Handbook of Individual Differences: Biological Perspectives*, New York: Wiley.

Eysenck, M.W. and Calvo, M.G. (1992) 'Anxiety and performance: the processing efficiency theory', *Cognition and Emotion* 6: 409–434.

Fahrenberg, J. (1988) 'Psychophysiological processes', in J.R. Nesselroade and R.B. Cattell (eds) *Handbook of Multivariate Experimental Psychology (2nd edn)*, New York: Plenum Press.

—— (1992) 'Psychophysiology of neuroticism and anxiety', in A. Gale and M.W. Eysenck (eds) *Handbook of Individual Differences: Biological Perspectives*, New York: Wiley.

Försterling, F. (1986) 'Attributional conceptions in clinical psychology', *American Psychologist*, 41: 275–285.

Gardner, H., Kornhaber, M.L. and Wake, W.K. (1996) *Intelligence: Multiple Perspectives*, Texas: Harcourt Brace College Publishers.

Gergen, K.J. and Gergen, M.M. (1988) 'Narrative and the self as relationship', in L. Berkowitz (ed.) *Advances in Experimental Social Psychology (Vol. 21)*, New York: Academic Press.

Goleman, D. (1995) *Emotional Intelligence*, New York: Bantam Books.

Gray, J.A. (1972) 'The psychophysiological nature of introversion-extraversion: a modification of Eysenck's theory', in V.D. Neblitsyn and J.A. Gray (eds) *Biological Bases of Individual Behaviour*, London: Academic Press.

—— (1981) 'A critique of Eysenck's theory of personality', in H.J. Eysenck (ed.) *A Model for Personality*, New York: Springer-Verlag.

Haier, R.J. (1993) 'Cerebral glucose metabolisation and intelligence', in P. A. Vernon (ed.) *The Biological Basis of Intelligence*, New Jersey: Ablex.

Haig, B.D. (in preparation) *Detecting Psychological Phenomena*, University of Canterbury, NZ.

Hampson, S.E. (1992) 'The emergence of personality: a broader context for biological perspectives', in A. Gale and M.W. Eysenck (eds) *Handbook of Individual Differences: Biological Perspectives*, New York: Wiley.

—— (1995) 'The construction of personality', in S.E. Hampson and A.M. Coleman (eds) *Individual Differences and Personality*, London: Longman.

Haynes, S.N. and Wilson, C.L. (1979) *Behavioural Assessment*, San Francisco: Jossey-Bass.

Heath, A.C., Eaves, L.J. and Martin, N.G. (1989) 'The genetic structure of personality III: multivariate genetic item analysis of the EPQ scales', *Personality and Individual Differences* 10: 877–888.

Hendrickson, A.E. and Hendrickson, D.E. (1980) 'The biological basis of individual differences in intelligence', *Personality and Individual Differences* 1: 3–33.

Howe, M.J.A. (1988) 'Intelligence as an explanation', *British Journal of Psychology* 79: 349–360.

—— (1989) 'Separate skills or general intelligence: the autonomy of human abilities', *British Journal of Educational Psychology* 59: 351–360.

Jacobs, B., Schall, M. and Scheibel, A.B. (1993) 'A quantitative dendritic analysis of Wernicke's area in humans. II: Gender, hemispheric, and environmental factors', *The Journal of Comparative Neurology* 327: 97–111.

Jensen, A.R. (1964) *Individual Differences in Learning: Interference Factor.* Washington, DC: Office of Education, US Department of Health, Education, and Welfare.

John, O.P. (1990) 'The "Big Five" factor taxonomy: dimensions of personality in the natural language and in questionnaires', in L.A. Pervin (ed.) *Handbook of Personality Theory and Research*, New York: Guilford Press.

Kline, P. (1993) *A Handbook of Psychological Testing*, London: Routledge.

—— (1995) 'Personality questionnaires in occupational psychology: The big 5 and beyond', *Proceedings of the BPS Occupational Psychology Conference*, Leicester, UK: BPS Books.

Kline, P., Draycott, S. and McAndrew, V. (1994) 'Reconstructing intelligence: a factor analytic study of the BIP', *Personality and Individual Differences* 16: 529–536.

Laird, J.E., Newell, A. and Rosenbloom, P. S. (1987) 'SOAR: an architecture for general intelligence', *Artificial Intelligence* 33: 1–64.

Lehrl, S. and Fischer, B. (1988) 'The basic parameters of human information processing: their role in the determination of intelligence', *Personality and Individual Differences* 9: 883–896.

—— (1990) 'A basic information psychological parameter (BIP) for the reconstruction of concepts of intelligence', *European Journal of Personality* 4: 259–286.

Lynn, R. (1993) 'Nutrition and Intelligence', in P. A. Vernon (ed.) *The Biological Basis of Intelligence*, New Jersey: Ablex.

McCrae, R.R. and Costa, P. T. (1985) 'Updating Norman's adequate taxonomy: intelligence and personality dimensions in natural language and in questionnaires', *Journal of Personality and Social Psychology* 49: 710–721.

Martin, N.G., Eaves, L.J., Heath, A.C., Jardine, R., Feingold, L.M. and Eysenck, H.J. (1986) 'Transmission of social attitudes', *Proceedings of the National Academy of Sciences, USA* 83: 4,364–4,368.

Miller, E.M. (1994) 'Intelligence and brain myelination: a hypothesis', *Personality and Individual Differences* 17: 803–862.

Myrtek, M. (1984) *Constitutional Psychophysiology*, New York: Academic Press.

Neisser, U. and Fivush, R. (1994) *The Remembering Self: Construction and Accuracy in the Self-Narrative*, Cambridge: Cambridge University Press.

Newell, A. (1990) *Unified Theories of Cognition*, Cambridge, MA: Harvard University Press.

Pervin, L.A. (ed.) (1990) *Handbook of Personality: Theory and Research*, New York: Guilford Press.

Raine, A. (1993) *The Psychopathology of Crime: Criminal Behaviour as a Clinical Disorder*, New York: Academic Press.

Reed, T.E. and Jensen, A.R. (1993) 'Choice Reaction Time and visual pathway nerve conduction velocity correlate with intelligence but appear not to correlate with each other: implications for information processing', *Intelligence* 17: 191–203.

Revelle, W. (1995) 'Personality processes', *Annual Review of Psychology* 46: 295–328.

Robinson, D.L. (1982) 'Properties of the diffuse thalamocortical system and human personality: a direct test of Pavlovian/Eysenckian theory', *Personality and Individual Differences* 3: 1–16.

—— (1987) 'A neuropsychological model of personality and individual differences', in J. Strelau and H.J. Eysenck (eds) *Personality Dimensions and Arousal*, London: Plenum Press.

—— (1993) 'The EEG and intelligence: an appraisal of methods and theories', *Personality and Individual Differences* 15: 695–716.

—— (forthcoming) 'A test of the Hendrickson postulate that reduced EEG response variance causes increased AEP contour length: implications for the "neural transmission errors" theory of intelligence', *Personality and Individual Differences*.

Rotter J.B. (1966) 'Generalized expectancies for internal versus external control of reinforcement', *Psychological Monographs* 80: whole monograph.

Scarr, S. and McCartney, K. (1983) 'How people make their own environments: a theory of genotype environment effects', *Developmental Psychology* 54: 424–435.

Seligman, M.E.P. (1975) *Helplessness: On Depression, Development, and Death*, San Francisco: W.H. Freeman.

Seligman, M.E.P., Abramson, L.Y., Semmel, A., von Baeyer, C. (1979) 'Depressive attributional style', *Journal of Abnormal Psychology* 88: 242–247.

Spearman, C. (1927) *The Abilities of Man*, London: Macmillan.

Stagner, R. (1937) *Psychology of Personality*, New York, McGraw-Hill.

Sternberg, R.J. (1977) *Intelligence, Information Processing, and Analogical Reasoning: The Componential Analysis of Human Abilities*, Hillsdale, NJ: Lawrence Erlbaum.

—— (1985) *Beyond IQ: A Triarchic Theory of Human Intelligence*, New York: Cambridge University Press.

—— (1990) *Metaphors of Mind: Conceptions of the Nature of Intelligence*, Cambridge: Cambridge University Press.

—— (1992) 'Cognitive theory and psychometrics', in R.K. Hambleton and J.N. Zaal (eds) *Advances in Educational and Psychological Testing: Theory and Applications*, London: Kluwer Academic Publishers.

Stough, C., Brebner, J., Nettlebeck, T., Cooper, C.J., Bates, T. and Mangan, G.L. (1996) 'The relationship between intelligence, personality, and inspection time', *British Journal of Psychology* 87: 255–268.

Sweeney, P. D., Anderson, K. and Bailey, S. (1986) 'Attributional style in depression: a meta-analytic review', *Journal of Personality and Social Psychology* 50: 974–991.

Thurstone, L.L. (1938) *Primary Mental Abilities*, Chicago: Chicago University Press.

Tupes, E.C. and Christal, R.C. (1961) *Recurrent Personality Factors based upon Trait*

Ratings, Technical Report No. ASDTR-61–97, Lackland Air Force Base, TX: US Air Force.

Underwood, B.J. (1975) 'Individual differences as a crucible in theory construction', *American Psychologist* 30: 128–134.

Vernon, P. E. (1950) *The Structure of Human Abilities*, London: Methuen.

Weiss, V. (1986) 'From memory span and mental speed toward the quantum mechanics of intelligence', *Personality and Individual Differences* 7: 737–749.

—— (1989) 'From short-term memory capacity toward the EEG resonance code', *Personality and Individual Differences* 10: 501–508.

—— (1992) 'Major genes of general intelligence', *Personality and Individual Differences* 13: 1,115–1,134.

Wilson, G.D., Barrett, P. T. and Gray, J.A. (1989) 'Human reactions to reward and punishment: a questionnaire examination of Gray's personality theory', *British Journal of Psychology* 80: 509–515.

—— (1990) 'A factor analysis of the Gray-Wilson Personality Questionnaire', *Personality and Individual Differences* 11: 1,037–1,045.

Woodward, J. (1989) 'Data and phenomena', *Synthese* 79: 393–472.

Zuckerman, M. (1991) *The Psychobiology of Personality*, Cambridge: Cambridge University Press.

Chapter 2

Can personality study ever be objective? The role of experiment in discovering the structure of personality

Hans J. Eysenck

THE NATURE OF TAXONOMY IN SCIENCE

Science always needs *taxonomic studies* to assign its contents to meaningful groups, and causal theories to give theoretical substance to these groups. Taxonomists in the fields of flora and fauna devised *polythetic* groupings in the absence of a causal theory, i.e., arrangements which 'place together organisms that have the greatest number of shared features, and no single feature is essential to group membership or is sufficient to make an organism a member of the group' (Sokal and Sneath, 1963). They credit Adamson (1763) with the introduction of the polythetic type of system into biology, taking the place held previously by the *monothetic* system in which a unique set of features is both sufficient and necessary for membership of the group thus defined. Any monothetic system will always carry the risk of serious misclassification if we wish to make natural phenetic groups. Yet any polythetic system has great problems in that numerical solutions are essentially indeterminate in the absence of causal relations; hence the well-known ferocity of battles between taxonomists in biology, and between factor analysts in psychology.

The *analysis by phenetic relationship* which has become all but universal in biology received a set-back when *analysis by relation through ancestry* was reinstated after the publication of *The Origin of Species*. Suddenly Darwin's theory seemed to suggest the basis for the existence of natural systematic categories; their members were related because of descent from a common ancestor. Unfortunately, history has shown that this enthusiasm could only be short-lived; we cannot make use of phylogeny for classification since in the vast majority of cases phylogenies are unknown. Inviting as the argument from ancestry may appear, therefore, in its Darwinian guise, nevertheless it has to be rejected for reasons given by Sokal and Sneath already quoted. The reasons for this rejection are very similar to those which in due course will cause us to reject principles of classification derived from Freudian psychoanalysis, and prefer those from a factor analytic approach. Freud's description of personality is in terms of anal, oral or other stages of infantile development; it presupposes knowledge which is not available, just as classification by phylogeny is inapplicable because of ignorance. (The same argument applies to Sheldon's derivation of body types from the three main germinal layers – Eysenck, 1970.) In both cases we are thrown back on our power of description and on such mathematical computations as we may find useful in giving quantitative assessments of similarities and differences between the observed characters.

In recent years this potentially fundamental *causal* variable – evolution – has been reinstated by virtue of the success of genetic investigations of DNA and the methodological advances associated with the advent of molecular genetics. We can now measure the differences in genetic make-up of different phenetic groups, and thus establish their evolutionary relationship. This has authenticated the major results of polythetic research, while adjudicating in cases of differences on minor matters. Clearly polythetic methods have considerable value, but cannot by themselves create a fundamental system of classification.

How in fact does a biologist proceed? Sneath (1964) has set the procedures out according to the following four steps.

1 The organisms are chosen, and their characters are recorded as a table.
2 Each organism is compared with every other and their overall resemblance is estimated as indicated by all the characters. This yields a new table, a table of similarities.
3 The organisms are now sorted into groups on the basis of their mutual similarities. Like organisms are brought next to like, and separated from unlike, and these groups or *phenons* are taken to represent the 'natural' taxonomic groups whose relationships can be represented in numerical form.
4 The characters can now be re-examined to find those that are most constant within the groups that have emerged from the analysis. These can be used as diagnostic characters in keys for identifying specimens.

Sokal and Sneath (1963) discuss in great detail the many theoretical problems that arise as well as the mathematical formulae useful in the estimation of taxonomic resemblances. Much of what they have to say is of great value and importance for psychology as well as for botany and zoology, although of course a number of problems are specific to each of these different sciences.

This represents one method of analysing tables of similarities, which are usually expressed in terms of correlations in psychological research. It corresponds to analysing correlations between people, each of whom has filled in a personality questionnaire, or has been rated on a rating scale; this would bring together people similar in personality make-up. Or we can correlate tests (or test items), to tell us which traits, or behaviours, go together. The latter method results in *factors*, and these have overwhelmingly become the basis of our personality taxonomies. Factor analysis, of course, has not only been used in psychology. Physicists have found it invaluable in dissecting complex physical phenomena, such as the consistency (rheology) of cheese (Harper and Baron, 1951; Scott-Blair, 1951a, b; Harper *et al.*, 1950). It has also been applied in geology (Merriam, 1965). I have discussed the nature of factor analysis, its application to physical phenomena, and the question of validity elsewhere (Eysenck, 1969a).

Such factors have the usual advantages of polythetic research, and I have always advocated the potential usefulness of factor analysis (Eysenck, 1969b). But there clearly are difficulties with its use that make it a good servant, but a bad master. The worst fault is the *inevitable subjectivity* which runs through the whole procedure.

- Selection of items is inherently subjective, as is selection of tests.
- Selection of samples is inherently subjective; usually only students of identical nationality are sampled.
- Choice of method of analysis is subjective, there being no agreed rules.
- Choice of oblique or orthogonal rotation (or even retention of factors as extracted) is inherently subjective, as are suggested rules of procedure like Thurstone's simple structure.
- The number of factors extracted and/or rotated is subjective, as is the choice of different criteria (eigenvalues, scree, etc.); it is well known that these criteria seldom give identical answers. Even with the use of a single criterion, like the scree test, the answer often resembles a Delphic oracle, depending on the whims and predilections of the worker involved.
- Interpretation of the factors is highly subjective, and dependent on the content of high-loading items. Dreger *et al.* (1995) have illustrated that many different interpretations of a given factor may be made by different judges. Revenstorff (1978) has published an extensive critique of factor analysis from the same point of view as adopted here.

Clearly results of factorial studies require careful inspection before being accepted as meaningful and scientifically valuable.

IS THERE A PARADIGM IN PERSONALITY RESEARCH?

It has been claimed recently that the 'Big Five' constitutes a descriptive paradigm. I will argue that a *purely* descriptive system is *inevitably* subjective, and hence cannot assume the properties of a scientific paradigm. The simple fact that even on its own grounds the 'Big Five' model has been widely criticised (e.g., Ben-Porath and Waller, 1992a, b; Block, 1995; Brand, 1994; Cattell, 1995; Church and Burke, 1994; Coolidge et al., 1994; Draycott and Kline, 1995; Eysenck, 1991a, b, 1992a; Hough, 1992; Jackson et al., (1996); McAdams, 1992; Matthews and Oddy (1993); Mershon and Gorsuch, 1988; Tellegen, 1993; van Heck et al., 1994; Zuckerman et al., 1988; and Zuckerman et al., 1993) illustrates this point.

Many others could be quoted, but essentially rivals claim precedence for other models with three major dimensions (Eysenck, 1990, 1994; and Cloninger, 1986); a different five-factor set (Zuckerman et al., 1988); a set of six factors (Brand, 1994 or Jackson et al., 1996) a bigger set of seven factors (Benet and Waller, 1995); going up all the way to Cattell's famous 16 PF (1950). Not only is the number of dimensions of personality still up in the air, but so is the kind of factor involved. The existence of a paradigm implies (fairly) universal agreement on its essentials; clearly such agreement is completely missing.

Complex phenomena are evidently difficult to classify objectively in the absence of some theory providing a causal approach to the problem. What I shall be suggesting is that no paradigm is possible in the field of personality in the absence of such an embedment of the variables involved in a nomological network (Garber and Strassberg, 1991; Cronbach and Meehl, 1955). It is only through such embedment that correlational constructs such as factors can find a place in a properly hypothetico-deductive setting, a setting that allows theories with testable deductions to develop and prove (or fail to prove) their adequacy. Without such developments factors can only be tested for consistency, i.e., reliability; whether they possess validity is another question. Factor analysts have consistently avoided putting their factors to this fundamental test, and hence have consistently failed to discover the paradigm that philosophers of science endorse as being the necessary entrance fee to scientific respectability. We can cut nature any way we like, but to cut nature at the joints, as science demands, needs a good deal more.

It is sometimes suggested that any factor, such as factor A (agreeableness) or C (conscientiousness) in the Big Five constitutes a theoretical system which allows prediction. Thus it might be predicted that conmen and gigolos are likely to be agreeable, and that psychopaths will lack conscientiousness. But these are just predictions based on synonyms; psychopathy is defined and described in terms of the absence of conscientiousness, and gigolos and conmen are by definition agreeable. We need something going far beyond such exercises in reliability in order to approach the concept of validity. Experiments along these lines may convince us that the scales really do measure some aspects of agreeableness and conscientiousness, but not that they are major dimensions of personality. That would require a good deal more.

Figure 2.1 suggests the essential nature of what is required to turn a factor into a dimension of personality. We start with the extraction of a factor, such as extraversion. The factor itself has of course a long history of development, going back over two thousand years (Eysenck, 1970). There have also been attempts to find *causal* concepts, but psychophysiology was too little developed to make this possible. The discovery of a strong genetic basis for the factor (Eysenck, 1956), after decades of belief in a 100 per cent family-based environmental cause of individual differences, opened up the left side of the diagram. We have to start the development of individual differences with the genetic determination of an individual's DNA. Recent studies have greatly increased the precision of this genetic determination (Eaves *et al.*, 1989), and have added important additional information, such as the fact that between-families (shared) environment does not contribute to the development of individual differences in personality, thus invalidating traditional and psychoanalytic theories of personality. But at the moment let us pursue the establishment of a strong genetic determination of E.

Given that the importance of DNA for personality development is now widely recognised (Plomin and McClearn, 1993), it will be clear that an intermediary is required between DNA and the behaviour that

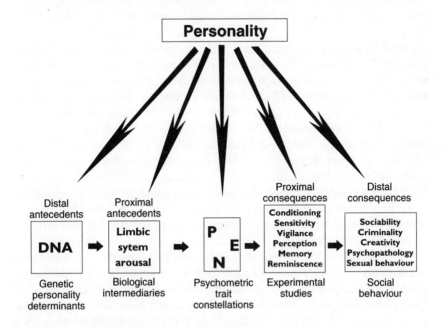

Figure 2.1 Model of personality paradigm

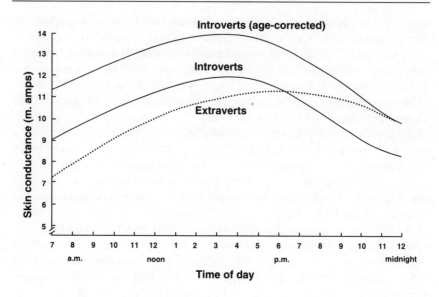

Figure 2.2 Skin conductance of introverts and extraverts as measures of cortical arousal (Wilson, 1990)

determines the observed psychometric trait constellations. DNA is copied onto RNA by a complementation process, and the RNA participates with various intracellular structures to produce peptides, which in turn compose proteins, including structural, transport and catalytic proteins (enzymes). These in turn facilitate the chemical reactions of life. Biological intermediaries are needed to translate *genetic potentials* and environmental pressures into behaviour; these intermediaries constitute the *proximal antecedents* of P, E and N in Figure 2.1. Some at least of these intermediaries have been identified, and a good deal of research is going on in this field (Eysenck, 1967, 1993; Eysenck and Eysenck, 1985; Zuckerman, 1991). The concept of *cortical arousal* (Eysenck, 1967, 1990; Strelau and Eysenck, 1987) has been particularly useful in suggesting a range of experimental studies of the psychophysiological intermediaries between DNA and extraversion. It is theories such as this that enable us to make testable predictions concerning the personality concept in question, and that provide the nomological network required for *validation* of personality concepts.

Such validation takes two forms. The first requires direct confirmation of the proposed link between E and cortical arousal; there is a large body of studies demonstrating that such a link exists (e.g., Stelmack, 1981; Gale, 1983; Gale and Edwards, 1986; Werre, 1987; Eysenck, 1994). A good example of work along these lines is an experiment reported by Wilson (1990), in which subjects' skin conductance was recorded automatically every hour, and they were asked to write down what they were doing at the time. Introverts (age-corrected) show greater skin conductance, i.e., greater arousal all the time until late evening. In the evening subjects were free to follow their inclinations, and as expected extraverts indulged in *arousing* activities like going to parties, dancing, etc., while introverts indulged in *disarousing* activities, like reading or watching television (Figure 2.2).

Of particular importance in this context is not only the fact that the great majority of studies have found in favour of the theory, but that we have discovered the requisite testing conditions that need to be fulfilled in order to obtain positive results. Thus in EEG studies very boring and very exciting testing conditions may lead to inconclusive results. As one might have expected from theory, middling arousing conditions are best here (Gale, 1983) as in many other types of study. This detailed investigation of situational variables is well in line with the interactive paradigm (personality plus situation → behaviour) that is now widely accepted in psychology.

THEORY, PREDICTION AND EXPERIMENTAL TESTING

I have dealt with the first way of testing the model shown in Figure 2.1, dealing with the distal and *proximal antecedents* of the psychometric trait constellation. The second way of testing the model deals with experimental studies of the *proximal consequences* of the theory, i.e., proper laboratory studies of conditioning, vigilance, memory, etc., where theory suggests a connection between the laboratory phenomenon and arousal-mediated personality factors (such as E). These predictions are based on the hypothetical arousal basis of E; in other words, they link proximal antecedents and proximal consequences via the personality construct in question.

As an example, consider the action decrement (Kleinsmith and Kaplan, 1963, 1964). They argued that high arousal would produce strong consolidation of the memory trace, thus leading to better recall in the long term. However, during consolidation the memory trace is not readily available for retrieval, so that in the short term highly arousable subjects would seem to have *poor* memory; this is called the *action decrement*. In their experiments arousal was produced artificially by various interventions. Howarth and Eysenck (1968) suggested that the personality-arousal theory would predict that extraverts (low arousal) would remember well in the short run, but decline over time, while introverts (high arousal) would show the opposite trend. Figure 2.3 shows the outcome of our experiment; the recall scores of extraverts and introverts show contrasting slopes, as predicted. This experiment is typical of a large number of experiments attempting to establish the link between arousal and extraversion through work with traditional laboratory phenomena (Eysenck and Eysenck, 1985).

This type of experiment embodies my belief in Cronbach's (1957) famous statement that unification of psychology was contingent upon a coming together of *correlational* and *experimental* psychology, the two scientific disciplines of psychology, as he called them. I have always been convinced of the truth of that statement, and have tried to follow this line of argument. Clearly, in this example of the use of the action decrement, personality theory has benefited considerably from an association with experimental psychology. However, the benefit is not one-sided. The experimental studies of the action decrement have not always been very successful, as indeed we might have anticipated. Neglect of personality variables in testing the Kleinsmith and Kaplan hypothesis means that unknown mixtures of extraverts, ambiverts and introverts enter into the experiment, and may give quite different results depending on the proportions involved. When we add the fact that Pavlov's law of trans-marginal inhibition is likely to make extraverts and introverts

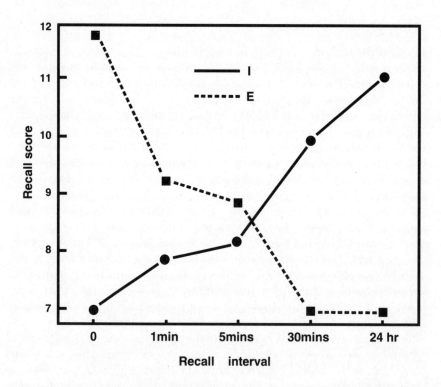

Figure 2.3 Recall scores of introverts and extraverts at different recall intervals (Howarth and Eysenck, 1968)

differentially responsive to the stimulation used to induce different degrees of arousal, we can see why *main effects* in a classical experimental test may become non-significant because interacting personality effects have been neglected, and thus assigned to the error term. No serious scientist would disregard theoretically important and relevant factors in such a cavalier fashion, but in psychology such disregard has been the custom rather than the exception.

This argument that both sides benefit from the coming together of the correlational and the experimental traditions is well illustrated by an experiment reported by Shigehisa and Symons (1973) and Shigehisa *et al.* (1973). They took up a theory dating back to Urbantschich (1883), to the effect that heteromodal stimulation would lower the threshold for a given sensory stimulus; i.e., manipulating the intensity of light would alter the threshold for sound, lowering it as the intensity of light increased, thus increasing arousal. Dozens of studies have had very different outcomes, some supporting the theory, others contradicting it, with others yet showing no effect. It was suggested that this was due to two effects not considered by the experimentalists. Pavlov's law of trans-marginal inhibition would suggest that there was a point where increases in the intensity of the heteromodal stimulation (the light) would begin to have a reverse effect, i.e., *heighten* threshold for sound. And this point of reversal would occur at a *lower* level of heteromodal stimulation for introverts (high arousal) than extraverts (low arousal).

This prediction agrees exactly with what was found; Figure 2.4 shows the results in diagrammatic form. Introverts (I) show the reversal at lower intensities than do ambiverts (A), with extraverts (E) showing little or no inversion at the largest intensity used. Shigehisa *et al.* (1973) found the same result when they looked at the effects of changing the intensity of sound stimulation on thresholds for light; again personality modulated the occurrence of the reversal. Clearly some experiments in classical experimental psychology give results that cannot be interpreted without inclusion of individual difference variables, and it is quite probable that the same is true of most, perhaps all, psychological experiments, though perhaps to a lesser degree. Subjects entering a psychological laboratory bring their personalities with them, and these personalities inevitably react differently to the experimental situation, in predictable fashion. Experimenters should always bear this self-evident truth in mind.

PERSONALITY AND SOCIAL BEHAVIOUR

The nomological networks outlined in Figure 2.1 should make it possible to make predictions also in the field of *distal consequences*, i.e., that of

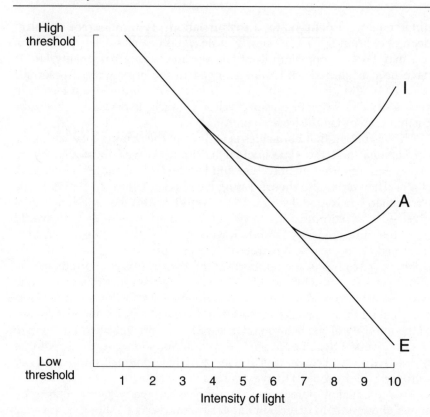

Figure 2.4 Sensory thresholds as a function of heteromodal stimulation for introverts, ambiverts and extraverts (Shegehisa and Symons, 1975)

social behaviour. I have listed a few directions in which such predictions have been made, usually with positive outcome. I have listed criminality (Eysenck and Gudjonsson, 1989), creativity (Eysenck, 1995), psychopathology (Eysenck, 1992b), sexual behaviour (Eysenck, 1976) and sociability (Eysenck and Eysenck, 1985). In the psychometric analysis sociability appears simply as a high-loading item (or set of items) in the factor of extraversion. But we have to *account* for social behaviour in *causal* terms, and clearly the hypothesised low cortical arousal of extraverts does just that: meeting with people is well known to increase cortical arousal, and thus fills the needs of the low-arousal extraverts. Conversely, the high-arousal introverts would be expected to avoid this arousing type of behaviour.

Another important area is marriage and marital satisfaction (Eysenck and Wakefield, 1981). Personality, directly or indirectly (i.e., by means of sexual attitudes, and behaviours, social behaviour, and the like, variables

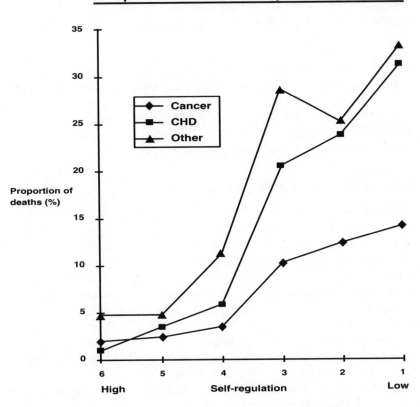

Figure 2.5 Mortality as a function of self-regulation (Grossarth-Maticek and
        Eysenck, 1995)

themselves largely caused by personality variables) accounted for a large
part of marital satisfaction. As predicted from theory, divorce and marital
dissatisfaction are mainly a function of neuroticism (Eysenck, 1980);
emotional instability disrupts the human relationship fundamental to a
happy marriage.

Another important set of distal consequences lies in the field of
psychosomatics. I have been associated with various oncologists (D.
Kissen; R. Grossarth-Maticek) in an endeavour to trace the personality
factors predisposing people to cancer and/or coronary heart disease, and
the outcome has been very satisfactory (Eysenck, 1991a). There is little
doubt that personality, particularly in its relation to coping behaviour in
response to stress, plays a large part in predisposing people to these
diseases, and it is also clear that neuroticism in particular is an important
ingredient in this disease-proneness. In relation to cancer, the dominant

personality trait is *suppression of emotional expression,* a characteristic that obviously makes measurement particularly difficult, although not impossible (Kissen and Eysenck, 1962). There is of course also a healthy type of personality, and we have shown in a prospective study that in large groups of healthy males and females, responding to an interviewer-administered questionnaire on self-regulation, or stable personality, fifteen years later mortality from cancer, coronary heart disease and other causes could be predicted with remarkable accuracy. Results are shown in Figure 2.5. These are just a few of the links of the nomological network outlined in Figure 2.1, and the distal consequences embedded in social behaviour; there are many more (Wilson, 1981).

SUMMARY AND CONCLUSIONS

A brief chapter like this cannot of course do more than touch on some of the problems involved in trying to construct a paradigm of personality. Perhaps the most intractable is the simple fact that questionnaires bear the major burden of concept construction, and that there are many reasons to be suspicious of self-ratings. There are two major sources of doubt here. In order to give truthful answers to often very intimate and personal questions, the subject has to have *trust* in the investigator, believing that the whole investigation has a worthwhile purpose in advancing science and perhaps helping people to improve the quality of their lives, and he has to *understand* exactly what the questions mean – misinterpretation in my experience is quite widespread, and frequent, particularly in below average IQ and education subjects. (Most questionnaires are validated on students!)

Grossarth-Maticek *et al.* (1993) and Grossarth-Maticek *et al.* (1995) have reported two experiments that showed quite clearly how important these two factors, *trust* and *understanding,* are in the validity estimates of questionnaire responses. Using four groups of randomised subjects, they found that in the group who were simply handed questionnaires without special care to establish either trust or understanding, validity was very low. Interviewer administration individually attempting to establish trust, or interviewer administration individually facilitating under-standing, gave very significant increases in validity. Finally, interviewer administration attempting to establish trust, and also understanding, gave far and away the best results. Unfortunately most questionnaires are administered under the worst condition, sometimes just sent out by mail, or administered over the phone. Much failure to replicate may be due to simple failure to administer the questionnaire with due regard to psychological factors like trust and understanding.

Given the many difficulties involved in working with personality, simple reliance on questionnaire responses or ratings is unlikely to suffice in the construction of a paradigm. I have always maintained that something much more theoretically sophisticated, involving the hypo-thetico-deductive method, is required, very much as suggested in Figure 2.1. The large body of work on the factors of psychoticism, extraversion and neuroticism suggests that this is a fruitful way of approaching the task of theory construction. Clearly, we are still at the beginning, not the end, of this quest, and there may be many important changes in the structure of the theories involved. But the success already achieved suggests that at least we are moving in the right direction.

REFERENCES

Adamson, M. (1763) *Familles des Plants*, Paris: Vincent.

Benet, V. and Waller, N. (1995) 'The Big Seven factor model of personality description: evidence for its cross-cultural generality in a Spanish sample', *Journal of Personality and Social Psychology* 69: 701–718.

Ben-Porath, Y. and Waller, N. (1992a) ' "Normal" personality inventories in clinical assessment. General requirements of the potential for using the NEO Personality Inventory', *Psychological Assessment* 4: 14–19.

Ben-Porath, Y. and Waller, N. (1992b) 'Five big issues in clinical personality assessment: a rejoinder to Costa and McCrae', *Psychological Assessment* 4: 23–35.

Block, J. (1995) 'A contrary view of the five factor approach to personality description', *Psychological Bulletin* 117: 187–215.

Brand, C. (1994) 'How many dimensions of personality – the "Big Five", the "Gigantic Three", or the "Comprehensive Six"?' *Psychologica Belgica* 34: 257–274.

Cattell, R.B. (1950) *Personality: a Systematic Theoretical and Factual Study*, New York: McGraw-Hill.

——(1995) 'The fallacy of five factors in the personality sphere', *The Psychologist* 28: 207–208.

Church, I. and Burke, P. (1994) 'Exploratory and confirmatory tests of the Big Five and Tellegen's three- and four-dimensional models', *Journal of Personality and Social Psychology* 60: 93–114.

Cloninger, C.R. (1986) 'A unified biosocial theory of personality and its role in the development of anxiety states', *Psychiatric Developments* 3: 167–226.

Coolidge, F., Becker, L., Di Rito, D., Durham, R., Kinlaw, M. and Philbrick, D. (1994) 'On the relationship of the five factor personality model to personality disorders: four reservations', *Psychological Reports* 75: 18–21.

Cronbach, L.J. (1957) 'The two disciplines of scientific psychology', *American Psychologist* 12: 671–684.

Cronbach, L.J. and Meehl, P. (1955) 'Construct validity in psychological tests', *Psychological Bulletin* 52: 281–302.

Draycott, S. and Kline, P. (1995) 'The Big Three or the Big Five in the EPQ-R vs. the Q-PI: a research note, replication and elaboration', *Personality and Individual Differences* 18: 801–804.

Dreger, R.M., Lichtenstein, D. and Cattell, R.B. (1995) 'Manual for the experimental edition of the personality questionnaire for pre-school children: Form A', *Journal of Social Behavior and Personality Monograph* 10: 1–50.

Eaves, L., Eysenck, H.J. and Martin, N. (1989) *Genes, Culture and Personality*, New York: Academic Press.

Eysenck, H.J. (1956) 'The inheritance of extraversion-introversion', *Acta Psychologica* 12: 95–110.

—— (1967) *The Biological Basis of Personality*, Springfield, IL: C.C. Thomas.

—— (1969a) 'The validity of the M.P.I. – negative validity', in H.J. Eysenck and S.B.G. Eysenck (eds) *Personality Structure and Measurement*, London: Routledge and Kegan Paul.

—— (1969b) 'Nature and history of human typology', in H.J. Eysenck and S.B.G. Eysenck (eds) *Personality Structure and Measurement*, London: Routledge and Kegan Paul.

—— (1970) *The Structure of Human Personality*, London: Methuen.

—— (1976) *Sex and Personality*, London: Open Books.

—— (1980) 'Personality, marital satisfaction and divorce', *Psychological Reports* 47: 1,235–1,238.

—— (1990) 'Biological dimensions of personality', in L.A. Pervin (ed.) *Handbook of Personality*, New York: Guilford Press.

—— (1991a) *Smoking, Personality and Stress: Psychosocial Factors in the Prevention of Cancer and Coronary Heart Disease*, New York: Springer Verlag.

—— (1991b) 'Dimensions of personality: 16, 5 or 3? Criteria for a taxonomic paradigm', *Personality and Individual Differences* 12: 773–790.

—— (1992a) 'Four ways five factors are not basic', *Personality and Individual Differences* 13: 667–673.

—— (1992b) 'The definition and measurement of psychoticism', *Personality and Individual Differences* 13: 757–785.

—— (1993) 'From DNA to social behaviour: conditions for a paradigm of personality research', in J. Hettema and I. Deary (eds) *Foundations of Personality*, Dortrecht: Kluwer Academic Publishers.

—— (1994) 'Personality: biological foundations', in P.A. Vernon (ed.) *The Neuropsychology of Individual Differences*, San Diego, CA: Academic Press.

—— (1995) *Genius: The Natural History of Creativity*, Cambridge: Cambridge University Press.

Eysenck, H.J. and Eysenck, M.W. (1985) *Personality and Individual Differences*, New York: Plenum Press.

Eysenck, H.J. and Gudjonsson, G. (1989) *The Causes and Cures of Criminality*, New York: Plenum Press.

Eysenck, H.J. and Wakefield, J. (1981) 'Psychological factors as predictors of marital satisfaction', *Advances in Behavioural Research and Therapy* 3: 151–192.

Gale, A. (1983) 'Electroencephalographic studies of extraversion and introversion: a case study in the psychophysiology of individual differences', *Personality and Individual Differences* 4: 371–380.

Gale, A. and Edwards, J. (1986) 'Individual differences', in M. Coles, E. Douchin and S. S. Parges (eds) *Psychophysiology: Systems, Processes and Applications*, New York: Guilford.

Garber, J. and Strassberg, Z. (1991) 'Construct validity: history and application to developmental psychopathology', in M. Grove and D. Ciachetti (eds) *Personality and Psychopathology*, Minneapolis: University of Minnesota Press.

Grossarth-Maticek, R. and Eysenck, H.J. (1995) 'Self-regulation and mortality from cancer, coronary heart disease, and other causes: a prospective study', *Personality and Individual Differences* 19: 781–795.

Grossarth-Maticek, R., Eysenck, H.J. and Barrett, P. (1993) 'The prediction of cancer and coronary heart disease as a function of the method of questionnaire administration', *Psychological Reports* 73: 943–959.

Grossarth-Maticek, R., Eysenck, H.J. and Boyle, G.J. (1995) 'Method of test administration as a factor in test validity: the use of a personality questionnaire in the prediction of cancer and coronary heart disease', *Behaviour Research and Therapy* 33: 705–710.

Harper, R. and Baron, M. (1951) 'The application of factor analysis to tests on disease', *British Journal of Applied Physics* 2: 35–41.

Harper, R., Kent, A. and Scott-Blair, G. (1950) 'The application of multiple factor analysis to identical test data', *British Journal of Applied Physics* 1: 1–6.

Hough, L. (1992) 'The "Big Five" personality variables – construct confusion: description versus prediction', *Human Performance* 5: 139–155.

Howarth, E. and Eysenck, H.J. (1968) 'Extraversion, arousal, and paired-associate learning', *Journal of Experimental Research in Personality* 3: 114–116.

Jackson, D.N., Paunonen, S.V., Fraboni, M. and Goffin, R.D. (1996) 'A five-factor versus a six-factor model of personality structure', *Personality and Individual Differences* 20: 33–45.

Kissen, D.M. and Eysenck, H.J. (1962) 'Personality in male lung cancer patients', *Journal of Psychosomatic Research* 6: 123–137.

Kleinsmith, L. and Kaplan, S. (1963) 'Paired associate learning as a function of arousal and interpolated interval', *Journal of Experimental Psychology* 65: 190–193.

—— (1964) 'Interaction of arousal and recall interval in nonsense syllable and paired-associate learning', *Journal of Experimental Psychology* 67: 124–126.

McAdams, D. (1992) 'The five-factor model in personality: a critical appraisal', *Journal of Personality* 60: 329–361.

Matthews, G. and Oddy, K. (1993) 'Recovery of major personality dimensions from adjective data', *Personality and Individual Differences* 15: 419–431.

Merriam, D.F. (1965) 'Geology and the computer', *New Scientist* 26: 513–515.

Mershon, B. and Gorsuch, R.L. (1988) 'Number of factors in the personality sphere: does increase in factors increase predictability of real-life criteria?', *Journal of Personality and Social Psychology* 55: 675–680.

Plomin, R. and McClearn, E. (1993) *Nature, Nurture and Psychology*, Washington, DC: American Psychological Association.

Revenstorff, D. (1978) 'Vom unsinnigen Aufwand', *Archiv für Psychologie* 130: 1–36.

Scott-Blair, G. (1951a) 'Some aspects of the search for invariants', *British Journal of the Philosophical Society* 1: 1–16.

—— (1951b) 'Possible industrial application of factor analysis', *Oil* 1: 14–16.

Shigehisa, P., Shigehisa, I. and Symons, J. (1973) 'Effects of intensity of auditory stimulation on photogenic visual sensitivity in relation to personality', *Japanese Psychological Research* 15: 104–172.

Shigehisa, I. and Symons, J. (1973) 'Effects of intensity of visual stimulation on auditory sensitivity in relation to personality', *British Journal of Psychology* 64: 205–213.

Sneath, P.H.S. (1964) 'Computers in bacterial classification', *Advancement of Science* 9: 572–582.

Sokal, R.R. and Sneath, P.H. (1963) *Principles of Numerical Taxonomy*, London: W.H. Freeman.

Stelmack, R. (1981) 'The psychophysiology of extraversion and neuroticism', in H.J. Eysenck (ed.) *A Model for Personality*, New York: Springer-Verlag.

Strelau, J. and Eysenck, H.J. (1987) *Personality Dimensions of Arousal*, New York: Plenum Press.

Tellegen, A. (1993) 'False concepts and psychological concepts of personality and personality disorders', *Psychological Inquiry* 4: 122–130.

Urbantschich, V. (1883) 'Über den Einfluss von Trigeminus-Reizen auf die Sinnesempfindungen insbesondere auf den Gesichtssinn', *Archiv für die gesamte Physiologie des Menschen und der Tiere* 30: 129–175.

Van Heck, G., Perugini, M., Caprara, V. and Foreger, J. (1994) 'The Big Five as tendencies in situations', *Personality and Individual Differences* 16: 715–731.

Werre, P. (1987) 'Extraversion-introversion, contingent negative variation and arousal', in J. Strelau and H.J. Eysenck (eds) *Personality Dimensions and Arousal*, New York: Plenum.

Wilson, G.D. (1981) 'Personality and social behaviour', in H.J. Eysenck (ed.) *A Model for Personality*, New York: Springer-Verlag.

—— (1990) 'Personality, time of day and arousal', *Personality and Individual Differences* 11: 153–168.

Zuckerman, M. (1991) *Psychobiology of Personality*, Cambridge: Cambridge University Press.

Zuckerman, M., Kuhlman, D. and Camac, C. (1988) 'What lies beyond E and N? Factor analyses of scales believed to measure basic dimensions of personality', *Journal of Personality and Social Psychology* 54: 96–107.

Zuckerman, M., Kuhlman, D., Joireman, J., Tefa, P. and Kraft, M. (1993) 'A comparison of three structural models for personality: the Big Three, The Big Five, and the Alternative Five', *Journal of Personality and Social Psychology* 65: 757–768.

Chapter 3

The genetic basis of personality

Jim Stevenson

This chapter will outline the developments that have taken place in the study of genetic and environmental influences on personality over the last twenty-five years. This time period can be specified this precisely since these rapid developments began with a landmark publication in 1970 by John Jinks and David Fulker. They demonstrated that human behaviour could be subjected to the rigorous quantitative analysis of genetic and environmental influences – a technique that had previously been applied to physical characteristics and to animal behaviour. This precise quantitative analysis of genetic and environmental influences has come to be applied to twin, adoption and family studies of both individual differences in cognitive ability and in aspects of behaviour that reflect personality differences. Examples of the major adoption studies are the Texas Adoption Project (Loehlin *et al.*, 1981) and the Colorado Adoption Project (Plomin and DeFries, 1985; Plomin *et al.*, 1988; DeFries *et al.*, 1995). There has been a larger number of twin studies of personality, amongst the most influential of which are those by Loehlin and Nichols (1976) and Eaves *et al.*, (1989).

Rather than review the findings from these diverse studies – a task that has recently been undertaken by John Loehlin (1992a) – this chapter will introduce the methods used in quantitative genetic research and then apply these procedures to a set of data on child and adolescent twins that measured three aspects of personality, namely sociability, antisociality and prosociality. The chapter will end with some reflections on where genetic approaches to individual differences are likely to develop next. This will introduce the major developments in molecular genetics that have also taken place over the last twenty-five years but which are only just starting to be successfully applied to complex characteristics such as personality.

A GENERAL FRAMEWORK FOR UNDERSTANDING QUANTITATIVE GENETIC RESEARCH

The quantitative genetic analysis of individual differences attempts to identify the relative magnitude of the influences of variation in genetic make-up and variation in environments experienced on aspects of personality. The results of such an analysis are limited by the population from which the samples of scores have been obtained. The estimates are therefore population specific. Their generalisability will be constrained by the extent to which the full range of genotypic and environmental variation has been sampled.

The extent of genetic variation is substantial although much of our DNA is held in common with other humans and indeed much is identical to that in other species. However, the extent to which we do vary in genetic make-up may affect variation in measured phenotypic characteristics. This genetic variability by and large acts additively – there are non-additive genetic effects such as dominance (interactions between pairs of genes at the same position on a chromosome) and epistasis (interactions between genes at different positions). For the present purposes we will only be concerned with additive genetic effects (A).

The environment is conceptualised as having effects that are divisible into two broad categories. These environmental effects or experiences may act to make siblings within a family resemble one another or to make people from different families distinct. For example, if the quality of housing affects a child's well-being this will tend to affect all children in the same family similarly. The push towards educational achievement encouraged by some parents is also likely to act in this manner. As such factors influence all members of a family, they are jointly referred to as the common or shared environment (C).

The second environmental component is one that may cause differences between members of the same family: it is called the unique or non-shared environment (E). Illnesses experienced by only one sibling, friendships outside the family and the quality of relationships with particular teachers are all examples of influences that are likely to make brothers and sisters different from one another. It must be remembered that brothers and sisters also differ *genetically* from one another (except for the special case of monozygotic twins, discussed below). Therefore differences within a family may be ascribed to both A (genetic differences) and E (the influence of the non-shared environment).

In its simplest form, the aim of quantitative genetic analysis is to obtain estimates of the relative magnitude of A, C and E. This can be achieved within a variety of genetically informative designs. These measure the resemblance in a given phenotypic characteristic – e.g., behaviour – between people with differing but known degrees of genetic resemblance. Some designs also consider variation in the extent to which a common environment has been shared (for example in biological siblings adopted into different families). For now I will simply illustrate the basic logic of deriving these estimates from data on twin pairs who have been raised together.

The total phenotypic variance in a measure is set to unity and the variance is partitioned into the three sources described above:

$$1 = A + C + E \qquad (1)$$

The basic information derived from a twin study is the similarity between members of two types of twin pair – genetically identical or monozygotic (MZ) and fraternal or dizygotic (DZ) pairs. The degree of resemblance is estimated using correlation between twin and co-twin across pairs giving r_{MZ} and r_{DZ}. The origin of resemblance within MZ pairs stems from their identical genetic make-up (A) and shared environment effects (C). Since the size of r_{MZ} is an index of MZ resemblance the following equation can be derived:

$$r_{MZ} = A + C \qquad (2)$$

The resemblance between DZ pairs arises again from the shared environment (C) but in this case only from half of A since DZ twin pairs on average only share half their genetic variability. The equation for r_{DZ} is therefore:

$$r_{DZ} = .5A + C \qquad (3)$$

The design therefore provides three simultaneous equations with three unknowns and these can be solved algebraically. Equations 2 and 3 can be subtracted and both sides multiplied by two to give

$$2(r_{MZ} - r_{DZ}) = A \qquad (4)$$

which is the well-known expression for heritability (h^2) from twin data. Equation 4 can be substituted in equation 2 and rearranged to provide an estimate of C:

$$2\,r_{DZ} - r_{MZ} = C \qquad (5)$$

Differences between MZ pairs are only influenced by non-shared environmental effects (E). The influence of the non-shared environment is indicated by the extent to which r_{MZ} is less than one. More formally, by substituting equation (2) into (1) and rearranging

$$E = 1 - r_{MZ} \qquad (6)$$

The logic of the classic twin study has two major caveats that need to be recognised. First, it is assumed that the shared environment acts equally on MZ and DZ pairs: that is MZ pairs are not more similar than DZ pairs for environmental (rather than purely genetic) reasons. This assumption needs to be tested for each phenotypic characteristic. Where it *has* been examined, the assumption has generally been found to be reasonable: when clear environmental differences have been found MZ twins are treated more similarly than DZ pairs on aspects of experience (e.g., being dressed more similarly) that do not affect the psychological characteristics being investigated.

Second, the non-shared environment (E) includes both systematic and random sources of dissimilarity between MZ pairs – e.g., measurement error. A separate estimate of reliability is therefore required in order to separate out non-shared environment effects from unreliability.

To summarise, the important principle is that variance in a personality measure can be analysed into a set of additive genetic and two environmental influences each indicated by a coefficient varying between 0 and 1. The magnitude of these coefficients is determined by the proportion of the variance in the personality measure that is accounted for by variation in each genetic or environment factor.

The above account shows that in principle it is possible to obtain estimates for A, C and E algebraically from the correlations for MZ and DZ pairs. Current methods of analysis of genetically informative designs use structural equation modelling to obtain these estimates from variances and covariances rather than correlations (Neale and Cardon, 1992). These methods allow more rigorous testing of the significance of the A, C and E components, and have been applied to adoption studies and data from more extended sets of family relatives. These methods can address more complex multivariate issues, such as the extent to which the associations between psychological characteristics arise from the action of common genetic or environmental influences.

With structural equation modelling approach the use of path diagrams is helpful: Loehlin (1992b) gives a useful introduction to the topic for those who are unfamiliar with this concept. In Figure 3.1 the basic model

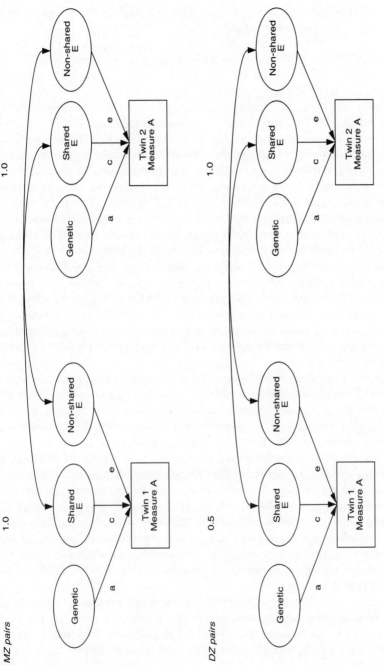

Figure 3.1 Path diagram for univariate ACE analysis

for the analysis of twin data has been represented in path diagram form. 'Measure A' simply represents any behavioural or psychological measure – e.g., a score on a personality questionnaire. This measure is obtained from each twin. There are slightly different versions of the model for MZ and DZ pairs since the twins differ in their degree of genetic relatedness. In the case of the MZ twins, the path coefficient for their genetic similarity is fixed at 1.0. For the DZ twins it will be 0.5, as each DZ pair will (on average) share half their genes.

As with the simultaneous equations used above we can derive expectations of the size of a correlation between two measures but now by the paths that link them. Compound paths are produced by multiplying path coefficients. For MZ pairs the size of the correlation (or covariance) is made up of path via genetic effects (a × 1.0 × a, or a^2) and via shared environment (c × 1.0 × c or c^2). The expectation of the correlation (covariance) between DZ pairs is (a × .5 × a) + (c × 1.0 × c). The model specifies that non-shared environments do not contribute to resemblance between twins and hence there is no link between twin and co-twin scores via the non-shared environment.

The structural equation modelling program will choose those values for a, c and e that will produce expected values for the covariances between MZ and DZ pairs that are as close as possible to the observed covariances. The diagram in Figure 3.1 simply represents equations 1 to 3, above. Having presented our genetic model in this form it becomes relatively straightforward to present more complex multivariate models in this format.

Figure 3.2 presents a model to explore the effects of genetic and environmental influences on two *different* personality measures. Here the matter at issue is the extent to which the *covariance between the two measures* is a product of common genetic or common shared and non-shared environmental factors. One set of general ACE terms is allowed to influence both personality measures and one set of ACE terms is specific to the second measure. This particular type of multivariate analysis is called a Cholesky decomposition. It partitions the covariance into orthogonal (i.e., uncorrelated) sets of ACE terms. In the example in the next section this model is extended to the three-variable case. There one ACE set affects all three measures, another just two of them and the final set is specific to just one of the measures. For a discussion of the issues that arise in interpreting the results of this form of analysis see Loehlin (1996).

As with the univariate example the squares of path values converging on a given measure add up to 1, as the total variance is being partitioned. In Figure 3.2 we can see that personality measure two has variance attributed to ag_2, cg_2 and eg_2 (all shared with measure 1) plus as_2, cs_2 and es_2 (specific factors). The bivariate diagram indicates the way in which

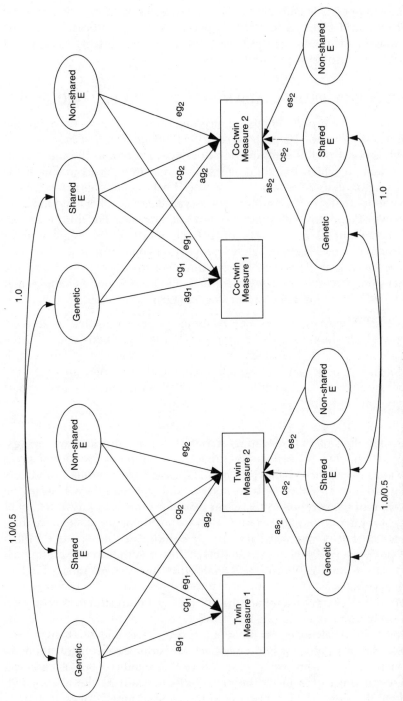

Figure 3.2 Path diagram for bivariate ACE Cholesky decomposition

quantitative genetic analysis can be extended to start to examine possible processes underlying differences in personality. This approach will now be illustrated in an analysis of aspects of personality and social behaviour in children and adolescents.

SOCIABILITY, PROSOCIAL AND ANTISOCIAL BEHAVIOUR

The study to be reported here is concerned with the origins of individual differences in various aspects of social behaviour. The first is sociability, which is construed as a component of temperament and is a measure of the extent to which the child seeks out and attempts to maintain the company of others. The second is prosocial behaviour. This is taken to be behaviours that show a concern for the well-being of others and includes displays of empathy, helping behaviour and altruism. The third is antisocial behaviour. This consists of behaviours that are aggressive or destructive, directed either against people or against property.

The basic issue is whether these three constructs represent a single dimension. The evidence is varied, and the issue is not as simple as it might at first appear. For as Zahn-Waxler (1986) concludes:

> Altruism and aggression may be either positively related, negatively related, or unrelated, depending on (1) the definitions used; (2) the particular types of altruism and aggression measured; (3) the cognitions, emotions and personality characteristics that mediate the behaviours; as well as (4) a host of other situational, biological and environmental influences.
>
> (p. 305)

Eron and Huesmann (1984) suggest that prosocial behaviour and aggression do form a single factor, albeit that the correlations between the two measures of prosocial behaviour and aggression were only -.29 and -.36. Several other variables are also known to affect the size and even the direction of the correlations between these three measures, or others that are conceptually similar. These include age (Steinberg, 1986), situation (Richman et al., 1988), familiarity of surroundings (Stanhope et al., 1987) and popularity (Eisenberg et al., 1988). Thus it is important to establish the relationships between the variables at several age ranges and in several situations.

Four studies have examined the extent of genetic influences on prosocial behaviour. In adults Rushton et al. (1986) found heritabilities of .56, .68 and .70 for altruism, empathy and nurturance, and Matthews et al., (1981) report significant heritability for empathic concern. Infants aged 14 months also seem to show significant heritability (.36) of prosocial behaviour (measured using the procedures of Zahn-Waxler et al., 1979), and modest heritability is also found in maternal reports of behaviour at

20 months (Zahn-Waxler *et al.*, 1992). Thus it seems that genetic influences on prosocial behaviour may be present in young infants but these are less marked than those acting on adults.

Sociability has been the subject of a larger number of twin studies. Buss and Plomin's (1984) review concluded that sociability was one of the temperament dimensions most consistently found to show a significant heritability.

Evidence from twin studies on antisocial behaviour, conduct disorder and criminality suggests that genetic factors may be less important than for other forms of maladjustment (Rutter *et al.*, 1990), and such genetic effects as are present may be less strong in adolescence than in adulthood: it is not known whether such age-related changes in heritability would be found in positive social behaviours.

The present study thus examines the environmental and genetic influences on sociability, prosocial behaviour and antisocial behaviour in a sample of children – a group for which such information is lacking. It also determines whether the same genes tend to influence all three behaviours.

A twin study on personality

Twins were recruited via their parents who volunteered to take part after being contacted initially through local Twin Club Association groups. Only those twins aged between 5 and 16 years were entered into the present analysis. The sample was further restricted to same-sex pairs. This produced a sample of 373 twin pairs (160 MZ and 213 DZ same-sex pairs) where both members of the pair provided data on antisocial behaviour, sociability and prosocial behaviour.

Parents of all the twins completed a Twin Similarity Questionnaire (TSQ: Cohen *et al.*, 1975). An earlier analysis on a large sample of British twins with zygosities established by blood typing had been used to derive a highly accurate scoring procedure for the TSQ (Stevenson *et al.*, 1987) that was used to compute scores for the present sample. Those obtaining a similarity score of more than 17 out of a maximum of 20 were designated as monozygotic and the remainder as dizygotic.

It was decided to measure the three facets of social behaviour through maternal report in the form of ratings made on standardised questionnaires. In the case of prosocial and antisocial behaviour, the behaviours in these categories do not occur very frequently, and because of their extended contact with the child, mothers are in the best position to observe and report on these infrequent behaviours.

Sociability was measured by the EAS Temperament scales (Buss and Plomin, 1984). This is a widely used standardised measure of temperament that is suitable for a wide range of ages from the pre-school period into adolescence. Sociability is one of the three sub-scales measured by the EAS and has been shown to have good test-retest reliability in adults ($r = .85$; Buss and Plomin, 1984) and to be relatively stable from age 12 to 24 months ($r = .57$; Plomin and DeFries, 1985).

Prosocial behaviour was measured using a novel parent questionnaire (Goodman, 1994) incorporating questions modelled on the Prosocial Behaviour Questionnaire, a teacher questionnaire developed by Weir and Duveen (1981). The original scale had been validated and shown to have good reliability ($r = .81$) when used by teachers with children aged 8 years (Weir et al., 1980). Although direct validation for this parent version is not available, Goodman (personal communication) has shown that the parent-derived prosocial scores correlate substantially more highly with teacher-derived prosocial scores ($r = .34$) obtained using the Weir and Duveen questionnaire than with teacher-derived behavioural deviance scores ($r = -.014$) or antisocial scores ($r = -.10$) obtained using the Rutter Teacher Scale (Rutter, 1967). A further justification for the use of a parent's version is the finding of Wahler and Sansbury (1990) that parent/observer agreement is greatest for positive social behaviours.

Antisocial behaviour was measured using the Rutter Parent Scale (Rutter et al., 1970). This is a standardised and widely adopted measure of behavioural deviance in school-aged children.

It is first necessary to establish that the twins' scores are comparable to those in the general population. It is also desirable to show that there are no significant mean differences between MZ and DZ pairs of twins. A multivariate analysis of variance (MANOVA) with sex and zygosity as factors and antisocial behaviour, sociability and prosocial behaviour as dependent variables produced a significant multivariate effect for sex ($F(3,756) = 16.57$, $p< .0001$) but not for zygosity ($F(3,756) = 0.25$, ns). There was a significant multivariate interaction between sex and zygosity ($F(3,756) = 3.88$, $p< .01$). The subsequent univariate analysis showed that the sex effect was significant for all three measures: antisocial behaviour ($F(1,758) = 8.11$, $p< .01$), sociability ($F(1,758) = 26.05$, $p< .0001$) and prosocial behaviour ($F(1,758) = 28.52$, $p< .0001$). The sex by zygosity interaction was significant only for prosocial behaviour ($F(1,758) = 6.97$, $p< .01$).

These findings indicate that girls are less antisocial and sociable but are more prosocial than boys. The sex difference in prosocial behaviour is less marked for DZ twins. The sex differences for antisocial and prosocial behaviour are in the expected direction. As there are no significant main effects of zygosity on the measures, these preliminary analyses indicate that it is appropriate to use these data to investigate genetic and environmental effects.

Using the pooled data from all twins in MZ and DZ pairs, antisocial behaviour, sociability and prosocial behaviour were found to be significantly but not strongly correlated (see Table 3.1).

Table 3.1   Correlations between prosocial behaviour, antisocial
behaviour and sociability (N=762)

	Prosocial	Antisocial	Sociability
Prosocial	1.000		
Antisocial	-.367	1.000	
Sociability	-.126	.278	1.000

All p < .001

Univariate model

The first genetic analysis fitted an ACE model to each of these three measures in turn (i.e., univariate analysis). The results are given in Table 3.2. These aspects of child and adolescent personality are seen to have distinctly different profiles of genetic and environmental influences. Individual differences in prosocial behaviour are mainly influenced by genetic variability between children. Just over half the variance was attributable to this source. The environmental influences are equally

Table 3.2 Univariate genetic analyses

	A	C	E	χ^2	d.f.	p	CFI[a]	AIC[b]
Prosocial	.54	.20	.27	1.91	3	ns	1.00	-4.01
Antisocial	.24	.54	.22	9.23	3	.03	0.98	3.32
Sociability	.67	–	.33	4.35	4	ns	0.99	-3.65

– parameter fixed to zero
a Comparative Fit Index
b Akiaike's Information Criterion

divided between shared and non-shared effects. Variation in antisocial behaviour is least influenced by genetic factors, and of the three is the only one to show a substantial effect of the shared environment. Sociability on the other hand shows no evidence of shared environmental effects, indeed the C term had to be set to zero to allow model fitting programme to converge on a solution. Individual differences in sociability are primarily determined by genetic differences.

These distinct univariate A, C and E values provide indirect support for the notion that the prosocial, antisocial and sociability measures on these children are not just influenced by a general parental view of the child's personality. The ratings indicate that the parents are identifying aspects of individual differences in personality that arise from different sets of biological and social influences.

Multivariate model

Although conceptually distinct, there is evidence from the correlations in Table 3.1 that these aspects of personality are related. It is therefore appropriate to ask what mechanisms produce these correlations. The correlations will arise if the characteristics have some common causes or possibly if they are causally related to each other. A multivariate genetic model can show whether two characteristics have shared genetic or environmental influences in common.

The results of applying a Cholesky decomposition to these three measures is shown in Figure 3.3. The genetic influences on these characteristics are largely specific. The genetic effects on prosociality ($.74^2 = .54$) have only minor influence on antisocial behaviour ($.19^2 = .04$) and sociability ($.15^2 = .02$). There are common genetic effects on antisocial behaviour and sociability that account for nearly all the correlation between these two measures. There are in addition substantial specific genetic effects on sociability ($.69^2 = .48$). The common shared environment mediates the association between prosociality and antisociality. There are no substantial effects from the common non-shared environment.

The smallest correlation in Table 3.1 was between prosociality and sociability, and this was almost entirely account for by shared genetic factors ($.74 \times .15/.126 = 88$ per cent). The correlation between prosociality and antisociality on the other hand arises both because of common shared environmental influences ($.44 \times .33/.376 = 39$ per cent) and common genetic effects ($.74 \times .19/.376 = 37$ per cent). The model slightly underestimates the size of the correlation between antisociality and sociability but the largest proportion of the covariance arises from common genetic effects ($.47 \times .41 = .193$) with common non-shared environment playing a minor role ($.43 \times .10 = .04$).

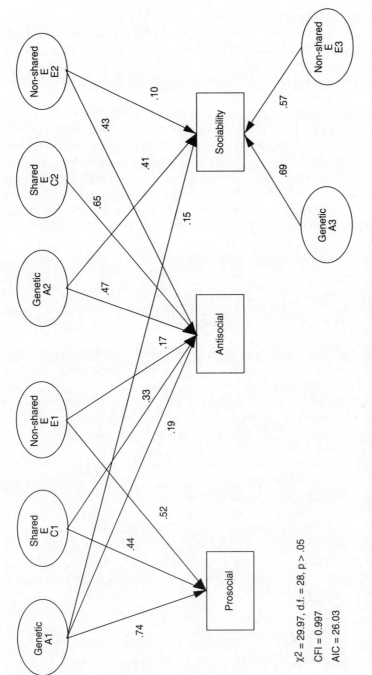

$\chi^2 = 29.97$, d.f. = 28, p > .05

CFI = 0.997

AIC = 26.03

Figure 3.3 Path diagram for trivariate ACE Cholesky decomposition of prosocial and anti-social behaviour and sociability (paths for only one twin included)

Discussion of results

The correlations between the scores on the sociability, prosocial and anti-social measure, although statistically significant, were not high, suggesting that individual differences in aspects of positive social behaviours are largely independent of each other. Nevertheless it is important that these findings should be replicated using measures other than maternal report.

The genetic effects on sociability and prosocial behaviour were two or three times greater than those on antisocial behaviour. This last was mainly influenced by shared or common environment effects. Previous studies suggest that these may include marital discord and parental criminality (Rutter and Giller, 1983). This pattern of results for antisocial behaviour is consistent with previous studies on delinquency, criminality and conduct disorder in adolescence and contrasts with the rather greater genetic influence on antisocial behaviour in adulthood (Rutter *et al.*, 1990).

Sociability was influenced by just genetic and specific environment effects. This replicates previous findings that sociability is one of the more strongly genetically influenced early-emerging behavioural traits (Buss and Plomin, 1984), and the influence of the non-shared environment will tend to make siblings different from one another in sociability (Plomin and Daniels, 1987).

For the first time it has been shown that prosocial behaviour in child-hood and adolescence is influenced by genetic differences between children. The results suggest that as for adults (Rushton *et al.*, 1986; Matthews *et al.*, 1981) and for infants (Emde *et al.*, 1992) genetic factors make a considerable contribution to child/adolescent prosocial behaviour. If individual differences in a behaviour have a significant genetic component then it is desirable to postulate some plausible biological mechanism that may mediate the genetic effect on behaviour. In the present case Panksepp (1986) has suggested that altruism has a basis in brain opiod activity in limbic circuits.

It should be emphasised that although genetic differences accounted for 55 per cent of the variance in prosocial behaviour scores, this means that nearly half the variance is produced by environmental effects and measurement error. About one fifth of the total variance is due to shared environmental effects, e.g., shared experiences within the family. In this respect prosocial behaviour is different from most personality dimensions where common environment effects tend to be minimal (Loehlin, 1992a).

A number of studies have shown that environmental events that affect prosocial behaviour include parental modelling (Krantz *et al.*, 1984; Tromsdorff, 1991), sibling behaviour (Dunn and Munn, 1986), parenting

style (Brody *et al.*, 1986; Brody *et al.*, 1987a; Grusec, 1991), marital relationships (Brody *et al.*, 1987b), maternal depression (Forehand and
McCombs, 1988) and even active parental limitations placed on children's altruism (Peterson *et al.*, 1984).

Most of the above influences are likely to be shared with other family
members. However the effects of non-shared environmental influences
(and measurement error) were somewhat greater (27 per cent). It is more
difficult to identify what these might be over and above differential
exposure to the previously mentioned features of parental behaviour.
However, Parmelee (1986) suggests that the experience of illnesses may
be one such potent influence on the development of individual differences in prosocial behaviour.

The finding of a substantial genetic basis for two of the three variables
studied here is in accordance with the main personality literature
reviewed by Loehlin (1992a). It is important to remember that these
genetic factors reflect genetic variability. For example, there is evidence
for variation in the degree of sociability being attributable to genetic
differences between people: this evidence is neutral as to whether the
average degree of sociability is biologically or socially determined.

It should also be recognised that the estimates of heritability reflect the
relative contribution of genetic and environmental influence as they are
currently experienced in the population. This does not preclude specific
types of special experience having a major impact on the prosocial
behaviour of individuals. Indeed there is accumulating evidence for the
efficacy of such special experiences in encouraging prosocial behaviour
either within therapy for children with behavioural deficits (Kazdin *et al.*,
1987; Kazdin *et al.*, 1989; Udwin, 1983) or within an educational context
for unselected children (Battistich *et al.*, 1989).

Finally, it is salutary to note that the finding that genetic/disposi-
tional factors are more strongly influential on *positive* aspects of
children's social behaviour is in keeping with mother's attributions
about their children's behaviour. In a study of sixty 4-year-old to 12-
year-old children, Gretarsson and Gelfand (1988) showed that positive
characteristics were seen as stable and inborn whilst negative ones were
transitory and tied to specific situations. Indeed the findings of the
present study are that individual differences in being 'nice' to people
are substantially influenced by genetic factors whereas those influ-
encing children to be 'nasty' to others mainly come from experiences
within the family.

The main conclusion from this analysis is that individual differences
in components of positive social behaviour in children and adolescents
are under contrasting systems of environmental and genetic effects. The
investigation of the development of sociability, prosocial behaviour and
antisocial behaviour needs to take account of these differences not least

by measuring these behaviours on separate indices and not subsuming them into a single underlying dimension.

THE WAY AHEAD

In order to discover how genetic variability can influence such a complex characteristic as personality what is needed is evidence of the biological *processes* that link genes and complex behavioural traits. There are several ways that this evidence may be found. One is to identify biological markers for personality differences. For example, if individuals high on a certain trait are different from others in a biochemical marker such as a neurotransmitter or in a physiological artifact such as an EEG trace, then it becomes possible to suggest a biological mechanism through which the genetic influences may operate. There is a long history of searching for such markers.

However this approach is indirect. It is now possible to examine directly linkages between variations in specific genes and variation in personality dimensions. The importance and intellectual challenge of understanding personality differences at this molecular genetic level is considerable. However the more medical science learns about the genetic complexity of diseases caused by single major genes the more daunting this enterprise becomes, and Alper (1996) is sceptical about the possibility of identifying genetic effects on complex behavioural characteristics such as personality differences.

By contrast, Cloninger *et al.*, (1996) suggest ways in which complex behaviours are amenable to genetic analysis. Indeed the publication of replicated findings on the association between a specific genetic locus in neurotransmitter regulation and novelty-seeking is a landmark vindication of this position (Ebstein *et al.*, 1966; Benjamin *et al.*, 1996). A theoretical formulation by Cloninger (1987) had predicted that dopamine was a major influence on novelty-seeking on the basis of experimental work with humans and animals. The Ebstein *et al.* and Benjamin *et al.* studies have shown that variation in the D4 dopamine receptor gene (D4DR) on chromosome 11 accounts for about 10 per cent of the genetic variation in novelty-seeking. Previous quantitative genetic analysis of novelty-seeking (Heath *et al.*, 1994) have identified a heritability of .41. Putting these two pieces of evidence together, it seems that variation in this locus on chromosome 11 accounts for 4 per cent of the total variance in novelty-seeking.

Where do genetic studies on personality go to next? It is clear from the overview provided by Loehlin that most of the Big 5 personality dimensions show evidence of genetic effects. What has yet to be fully explored is the architecture of these genetic and environmental influences. For example, are the shared environmental components producing an increased degree of Conscientiousness also acting to produce Culture? Are the same genes implicated in more than one personality dimension? These explanations are only plausible if the dimensions are non-orthogonal. Although these structural models need to be elaborated in a multivariate manner, a more psychologically interesting set of issues is the identification of the mechanisms and processes producing these effects. The A, C and E partitioning of variance does not identify how the effects are produced. However in a multivariate analysis, direct measures of environmental or indeed biological mediators could also be taken. The multivariate modelling could then identify whether these mediators carry a common genetic or environmental influence with the personality measure. Such research requires genetically informative designs coupled with direct measurements of these mediators. This strategy must lie at the heart of future behaviour genetic work on personality.

The examples discussed above framed genetic and environment effects as independent additive influences on personality. It has been recognised that important genetic effects on personality might be mediated by genetic influences on the environment. Genetically determined preferences and behaviours will result in the individual experiencing environments that differ from other people. There is therefore the possibility of both active and evocative effects of genes on the environment. Active effects arise when the individual seeks out particular experiences or elects to be a member of certain social groups. Evocative effects arise from people in the social environment responding to the person differently depending on how they are behaving. Both these processes can result in gene-environment correlation that arises from genetic influences on the environments experienced. This is an active area of research in child development (Plomin 1994) and one that is particularly suited to developmentally informative longitudinal twin studies.

Finally, the increasing use of molecular genetic techniques will revolutionise this field. To date much of this work has relied on single major genes. It is likely that the genetic effects on personality are created by the action of a large number of genes each with small or moderate effects. A central part of the genetic strategy for future personality research will be to identify these modest genetic influences using so called quantitative trait loci analyses, and the first such studies are just beginning to be reported.

REFERENCES

Alper, J.S. (1996) 'Genetic complexity in single-gene diseases – no simple link between genotype and phenotype', *British Medical Journal* 312: 196–197.

Battistich, V., Solomon, D., Watson, M., Solomon, J. and Schaps, E. (1989) 'Effects of elementary school program to enhance prosocial behaviour on children's cognitive-social problem-solving skills and strategies', *Journal of Applied Developmental Psychology* 10: 147–169.

Benjamin, J., Li, L., Patterson, C., Greenberg, B.D., Murphy, D.L. and Hamer, D.H. (1996) 'Population and familial association between the d4 dopamine-receptor gene and measures of novelty seeking', *Nature Genetics* 12: 81–84.

Brody, G.H., Stoneman, Z. and Burke, M. (1987a) 'Family system and individual child correlates of sibling behaviour', *American Journal of Orthopsychiatry* 57: 561–569.

—— (1987b) 'Child temperaments, maternal differential behaviour and sibling relationships', *Developmental Psychology* 23: 354–362.

Brody, G.H., Stoneman, Z. and MacKinnon, C.E. (1986) 'Contributions of maternal child-rearing practices and play contexts to sibling interactions', *Journal of Applied Developmental Psychology* 7: 225–236.

Buss, A.R. and Plomin, R. (1984) *Temperament: Early Developing Personality Traits*, Hillsdale, NJ: Erlbaum.

Cloninger, C.R. (1987) 'A systematic method for clinical description and classification of personality variants – a proposal', *Archives of General Psychiatry* 44: 573–588.

Cloninger, C.R., Adolfsson, R. and Svrakic, N.M. (1996) 'Mapping genes for human personality', *Nature Genetics* 12: 3–4.

Cohen, D.J., Dibble, E., Grawe, J.M. and Pollin, W. (1975) 'Reliably separating identical from fraternal twins', *Archives of General Psychiatry* 32: 1,371–1,375.

DeFries, J.C., Plomin, R. and Fulker, D.W. (1995) *Nature and Nurture During Middle Childhood*, Cambridge, MA: Blackwell.

Dunn, J. and Munn, P. (1986) 'Siblings and the development of prosocial behaviour', *International Journal of Behavioral Development* 9: 265–284.

Eaves, L., Eysenck, H.J. and Martin, N. (1989) *Genes, Culture and Personality: An Empirical Approach*, Oxford: Oxford University Press.

Ebstein, R.P., Novick, O., Umansky, R., Priel, B., Osher, Y., Blaine, D., Bennett, E.R., Nemanov, L., Katz, M. and Belmaker, R.H. (1996) 'Dopamine d4 receptor (D4DR) exon III polymorphism associated with the human personality trait of novelty seeking', *Nature Genetics* 12: 78–80.

Eisenberg, N., Cameron, E., Pasternack, J. and Tryon, K. (1988) 'Behavioral and sociocognitive correlates of ratings of prosocial behavior and sociometric status', *Journal of Genetic Psychology* 149: 5–15.

Emde, R. N., Plomin, R., Robinson, J., Corley, R., DeFries, J. C., Fulker, D. W., Reznick, J. S., Campos, J., Kagan, J. and Zahn-Waxler, C. (1992) 'Temperament, emotion and cognition at fourteen months: the MacArthur longitudinal twin study', *Child Development* 63: 1,437–1,455.

Eron, L.D. and Huesmann, L.R. (1984) 'The relation of prosocial behaviour to the development of aggression and psychopathology', *Aggressive Behaviour* 10: 201–211.

Forehand, R. and McCombs, A. (1988) 'Unravelling the antecedent-consequence conditions in maternal depression and adolescent functioning', *Behaviour Research and Therapy* 26: 399–405.

Goodman, R. (1994) 'A modified version of the Rutter Parent Questionnaire including extra items on children's strengths: a research note', *Journal of Child Psychology and Psychiatry* 35: 1,483–1.494.

Gretarsson, S.J. and Gelfand, D.M. (1988) 'Mothers' attributions regarding their children's social behavior and personality characteristics', *Developmental Psychology* 24: 264–269.

Grusec, J.E. (1991) 'Socialising concern for others in the home', *Developmental Psychology* 27: 338–342.

Heath, A.C., Cloninger, C.R. and Martin, N.G. (1994) 'Testing a model for the genetic structure of personality: a comparison of the personality systems of Cloninger and Eysenck', *Journal of Personality and Social Psychology* 66: 762–775.

Jinks, J.L. and Fulker, D.W. (1970) 'Comparison of the biometrical genetical, MAVA and classical approaches to the analysis of human behavior', *Psychological Bulletin* 73: 311–349.

Kazdin, A.E., Bass, D., Siegel, T. and Thomas, C. (1989) 'Cognitive-behaviour therapy and relationship therapy in the treatment of children referred for antisocial behaviour', *Journal of Consulting and Clinical Psychology* 57: 522–535.

Kazdin, A.E., Esveldt-Dawson, K., French, N.H. and Unis, A.S. (1987) 'Effects of parent training and problem-solving skills training combined in the treatment of anti-social child behaviour', *Journal of the American Academy of Child and Adolescent Psychiatry* 26: 416–424.

Krantz, M., Webb, S.D. and Andrews, D. (1984) 'The relationship between child and parental social competence', *Journal of Psychology* 114: 51–56.

Loehlin, J.C. (1992a) *Genes and environment in personality development*, Newbury Park, CA: Sage.

—— (1992b) *Latent Variable Models (2nd edn)*, Hillsdale, NJ: Lawrence Erlbaum Associates.

—— (1996) 'The Cholesky approach: a cautionary note', *Behaviour Genetics* 26: 65–70.

Loehlin, J.C., Horn, J.M. and Willerman, L. (1981) 'Personality resemblance in adoptive families', *Behavior Genetics* 11: 309–330.

Loehlin, J.C. and Nichols, R.C. (1976) *Heredity, Environment and Personality*, Austin, TX: University of Texas Press.

Matthews, K.A., Batson, C.D., Horn, J. and Rosenman, R.H. (1981) ' "Principles in his nature which interest him in the fortune of others . . . ": the heritability of empathic concern for others', *Journal of Personality* 49: 237–247.

Neale, M.C. and Cardon, L.R. (1992) *Methodology for Genetic Studies of Twins and Families*, Dordrecht: Kluwer.

Panksepp, J. (1986) 'The psychobiology of prosocial behaviours: separation distress, play, and altruism', in C. Zahn-Waxler, E. M. Cummings and R. Iannotti (eds) *Altruism and Aggression: Biological and Social Origins*, Cambridge: Cambridge University Press.

Parmelee, A.H. (1986) 'Children's illnesses: their beneficial effects on behavioral development', *Child Development* 57: 1–10.

Peterson, L., Reaven, N. and Homer, A.L. (1984) 'Limitations imposed by parents on children's altruism', *Merrill-Palmer Quarterly* 30: 269–286.

Plomin, R. (1994) *Genetics and Experience: The Interplay Between Nature and Nurture*, Thousand Oaks, CA: Sage.

Plomin, R. and Daniels, D. (1987) 'Why are children in the same family so different from one another?', *Behavioral and Brain Sciences* 10: 1–16.

Plomin, R. and DeFries, J.C. (1985) *Origins of Individual Differences in Infancy: The Colorado Adoption Project*, Orlando: Academic Press.

Plomin, R., DeFries, J.C. and Fulker, D.W. (1988) *Nature and Nurture during Infancy and Early Childhood*, Cambridge: Cambridge University Press.

Richman, C.L., Berry, C., Bittle, M. and Himan, K. (1988) 'Factors related to helping behaviour in preschool aged children', *Journal of Applied Developmental Psychology* 9: 151–165.

Rushton, J.P., Fulker, D.W., Neale, M.C., Nias, D.K. and Eysenck, H.J. (1986) 'Altruism and aggression: the heritability of individual differences', *Journal of Personality and Social Psychology* 50: 1,192–1,198.

Rutter, M. (1967) 'A children's behaviour questionnaire for completion by teachers: preliminary findings', *Journal of Child Psychology and Psychiatry* 8: 1–11.

Rutter, M. and Giller, H. (1983) *Juvenile Delinquency: Trends and Perspectives*, Harmondsworth: Penguin Books.

Rutter, M., MacDonald, H., Le Couteur, A., Harrington, R., Bolton, P. and Bailey, A. (1990) 'Genetic factors in child psychiatric disorders II: empirical findings', *Journal of Child Psychology and Psychiatry* 31: 39–84.

Rutter, M., Tizard, J. and Whitmore, K. (1970) *Education, Health and Behaviour*, London: Longman.

Stanhope, L., Bell, R.Q. and Parker-Cohen, N.Y. (1987) 'Temperament and helping behaviour in preschool children', *Developmental Psychology* 23: 347–353.

Steinberg, L. (1986) 'Stability (and instability) of Type A behaviour from childhood to young adulthood', *Developmental Psychology* 22: 393–402.

Stevenson, J., Graham, P.J., Fredman, G. and McLoughlin, V. (1987) 'A twin study of genetic influences on reading and spelling ability and disability', *Journal of Child Psychology and Psychiatry* 28: 229–247.

Tromsdorff, G. (1991) 'Child-rearing and children's empathy', *Perceptual and Motor Skills* 72: 387–390.

Udwin, O. (1983) 'Imaginative play training as an intervention method with institutionalised preschool children', *British Journal of Educational Psychology* 53: 32–39.

Wahler, R.G. and Sansbury, L.E. (1990) 'The monitoring skills of troubled mothers: their problems in defining child deviance', *Journal of Abnormal Child Psychology* 18: 577–589.

Weir, K. and Duveen, G. (1981) 'Further development and validation of the prosocial behaviour questionnaire for use by teachers', *Journal of Child Psychology and Psychiatry* 22: 357–374.

Weir, K., Stevenson, J. and Graham, P.J. (1980) 'Behavioural deviance and teacher ratings of prosocial behaviour', *Journal of the American Academy of Child Psychiatry* 19: 68–77.

Zahn-Waxler, C. (1986) 'Conclusions: lessons from the past and a look to the future', in C. Zahn-Waxler, E. M. Cummings and R. Iannotti (eds) *Altruism and Aggression: Biological and Social Origins*, Cambridge: Cambridge University Press.

Zahn-Waxler, C., Radke-Yarrow, M. and King, R. A. (1979) 'Child-rearing and children's prosocial initiation toward victims of distress', *Child Development* 50: 319–330.

Zahn-Waxler, C., Robinson, J.L. and Emde, R.N. (1992) 'The development of empathy in twins', *Developmental Psychology* 28: 1,038–1,047.

Chapter 4

Anxiety and cognitive processes

Michael W. Eysenck

One of the key issues in personality research is to identify the major factors of personality. As is well known, there are considerable differences among theorists in terms of the number and nature of the personality factors proposed. However, there is a growing consensus that there are only a few key factors, and there is even a fair measure of agreement concerning their identity (Digman, 1990; Kline, 1992). For reasons that are not altogether clear, several different theorists have argued that there are five major personality factors. Most theorists are agreed that trait anxiety or neuroticism is one of these five major factors. For example, McCrae and Costa (1985) used rating data to identify the five following factors: extraversion (vs. introversion); agreeableness (vs. hostility, jealousy); conscientiousness (similar to will to achieve); neuroticism (vs. stability); and openness (similar to intelligence or intellect).

Kline (1992) has discussed some of the relevant evidence, and concluded that trait anxiety or neuroticism is one of the few really well-established personality factors. As has been pointed out by several theorists (e.g., Gray, 1982), one of the main differences between trait anxiety and neuroticism is that the former (but not the latter) correlates negatively with the personality factor of extraversion. In spite of this difference, measures of trait anxiety and neuroticism typically correlate approximately +.6 or +.7 with each other (Watson and Clark, 1984). In view of this substantial correlation between them, trait anxiety and neuroticism will be considered together in this chapter. Many of the reasons for doing this are discussed by Watson and Clark (1984). They argued convincingly that the pattern of inter-correlations typically found among measures of trait anxiety, neuroticism and depression indicates that they are all basically providing an assessment of a dimension of negative affectivity.

Kline (1983) rightly emphasised the importance of sound measurement through his long-term interest in psychometrics. However, unlike most of those working in psychometrics, he has also been fully aware of the need to consider the processes underlying the dimensions of individual differences revealed by psychometric techniques. It has certainly been my firm view for many years that factor analysis and other statistical techniques are extremely useful for the purposes of describing major dimensions of individual differences. However, in order to proceed to explanation, it is necessary to move beyond the psychometric evidence. For example, we can only claim to have a good understanding of a personality dimension such as trait anxiety or neuroticism when we understand the underlying differences in cognitive, physiological and behavioural functioning of those who are high and low on that dimension. It is not clear that this point has been reached in terms of theory and research on trait anxiety and neuroticism, but relevant theoretical perspectives will be considered in the remainder of this chapter.

PHYSIOLOGICAL THEORIES OF ANXIETY

Several theories of trait anxiety and neuroticism (e.g., those of H.J. Eysenck, 1967 and Gray, 1982) have adopted a predominantly physiological approach. More specifically, it is assumed that each individual person's level of trait anxiety or neuroticism depends critically on the responsiveness of his or her physiological system. These individual differences in physiological responsiveness are claimed to depend to a large extent on heredity. According to H.J. Eysenck (1967), 'the evidence suggests fairly strongly that something like 50 per cent of individual differences in neuroticism and extraversion . . . is accountable for in terms of hereditary influences' (p.210). In similar fashion, Gray (1982) claimed that, 'studies of the personality traits of neuroticism and extraversion . . . estimate the contribution of heredity to these conditions at about 50 per cent of the variance' (p.438).

The most important evidence relating to the role of heredity in determining trait anxiety and neuroticism comes from twin studies. Jim Stevenson's chapter in this volume discusses the heritability of sociability: the findings regarding trait anxiety and neuroticism have been mixed. H.J. Eysenck and Prell (1951) found for neuroticism that the correlation between monozygotic twins was +.85, whereas it was only +.22 between dizygotic twins. These correlations suggest that neuroticism is almost totally determined by heredity. However, their reported correlation for monozygotic twins is considerably higher than that reported by any other researchers. Shields (1962) obtained a correlation of +.38 on neuroticism for monozygotic twins brought up together, compared with +.11 for dizygotic twins brought up together. Somewhat surprisingly, he also found a correlation of +.53 for monozygotic twins brought up apart. This high correlation probably occurred in part because many of the twins were brought up by different parts of the same family.

More recent studies indicate that the role of genetic factors in determining neuroticism is more limited than was suggested by previous research. Langinvainio *et al.* (1984) obtained a correlation of only +.25 for monozygotic twins brought up apart, +.32 for monozygotic twins brought up together, and +.10 for dizygotic twins brought up together. Similar findings were reported by Pedersen *et al.* (1984). They reported correlations of +.18, +.37, and +.18 for monozygotic twins brought up apart, monozygotic twins brought up together, and for dizygotic twins brought up together, respectively. There are clearly differences across studies, but the correlation for monozygotic twins brought up together is approximately +.35 if the anomalous figure of +.85 claimed by H.J. Eysenck and Prell (1951) is omitted. The only reasonable conclusion would appear to be the one put forward by Torgersen (1990): 'The development of the relatively normally distributed neuroticism or anxiousness may be modestly influenced by genetic factors.... However, by far the most important source of variance seems to be individual environmental factors' (p.285).

Some attempts have been made to identify the physiological system or systems underlying neuroticism or trait anxiety. H.J. Eysenck (1967) argued that individual differences in neuroticism depend upon the functioning of the so-called 'visceral brain', consisting of the hippocampus, amygdala, cingulum, septum and hypothalamus. In similar fashion, Gray (1982) argued that individual differences in trait anxiety depend upon the septo-hippocampal system, its neocortical projection in the frontal lobe, and its monoaminergic afferents from the brain-stem.

It has not been possible in most of the research to take direct measures of activity within the visceral brain or septo-hippocampal system. However, there have been numerous studies in which indirect psychophysiological measures of the alleged underlying systems were obtained. The relevant literature was reviewed by Fahrenberg (1987). He arrived at the following conclusion: 'Psychophysiological research on physiological correlates of the established emotionality (neuroticism) trait dimension has come to a standstill. Findings of questionnaire studies generally support the postulated psychophysiological relationship, but research that employs objectively measured physiological parameters in large-scale, methodologically well-controlled and replicated investigations has not substantiated these hypotheses' (p.117).

The almost complete failure of psychophysiological studies to find any differences between those high and low in trait anxiety is somewhat puzzling. Gray (1982) discussed the findings from two major strands of relevant research. First, a number of anti-anxiety drugs such as the benzodiazepines, barbiturates and alcohol have been found to have broadly comparable effects on behaviour. Second, lesions to the septo-hippocampal system in rats and other species produce several behavioural effects. As

Gray (1982) pointed out, there are nineteen different kinds of behavioural measure for which drug and lesion data are available, and on eighteen of them drugs and lesions have essentially the same effects. This similarity in patterning of effects provides powerful evidence that the septo-hippocampal system is centrally involved in anxiety.

The major reason why those high and low in trait anxiety or neuroticism do not generally differ on physiological measures is discussed more fully later. Those who score low on self-reported trait anxiety form a heterogeneous group. Weinberger *et al.* (1979) obtained measures of trait anxiety and of social desirability from their subjects. Those who scored low on both measures were categorised as truly low-anxious, whereas those who scored low on trait anxiety and high on social desirability were categorised as repressors. When the subjects were exposed to a moderately stressful situation, the repressors responded physiologically much more than the truly low-anxious; indeed, the repressors were more physiologically responsive than the high-anxious subjects on most of the measures. Thus, any relationship between trait anxiety and physiological responsiveness is obscured by the high responsiveness of repressors.

There is another reason why the findings discussed by Gray (1982) cannot readily be extrapolated to individuals high and low in trait anxiety. Gray focused on the findings from other species, and yet it is clear that the processes associated with anxiety are considerably more complex in the human species than in others. A crucial inter-species difference was identified by Hallam (1985): 'Even if the layman or clinician were to accept that perceiving events as, say, signals of punishment or non-reward brought forth biological responses that we have in common with other species one might still argue that the cause of complaints of anxiety was in perceiving events in this way, and not in possessing the biological mechanism of these responses' (p. 218). In other words, humans have a considerably more developed cognitive system than other species, and this difference must be taken into account when comparing other species with our own.

The main emphasis of Gray's (1982) theory is on the brain structures involved in anxiety. However, he has also focused on some of the cognitive processes involved. He argued that the septo-hippocampal system operates as a behavioural inhibition system. According to Gray (1975), the behavioural inhibition system is used '(a) to inhibit all ongoing behaviour ... and (b) to perform the maximum possible analysis of current environmental stimuli, especially activity in this system' (p. 354). The latter point was developed by Gray (1982). At a cognitive level, the behavioural inhibition system operates as a comparator. Information about the current state of the world and a prediction as to what that state should be are available to the comparator. If the comparator detects a mismatch between actual and predicted events, then there is increased activation of the behavioural inhibition system.

The major problem with the notion of a comparator is that it is by no means clear that the behavioural inhibition system is activated by mismatches between actual and predicted events. As M.W. Eysenck (1992) pointed out, 'There is surely a fundamental distinction between mismatches where the predicted event is preferable to the actual event and mismatches where the opposite is true. Mismatches of the former type may, indeed, produce anxiety, but mismatches of the latter type obviously produce more positive emotional states' (p. 17). Some relevant evidence was reported by Rachman and Lopatka (1986a, b), who studied the levels of predicted and experienced fear in snake phobics who were repeatedly exposed to a snake. The snake phobics reported increased fear following under-predictions of fear, which is as predicted by Gray (1982). However, when the snake phobics over-predicted fear, this led to a reduction in fear, a finding not in line with Gray's theory.

Additional problems

We have seen already that traditional theories such as those of H.J. Eysenck (1967) and Gray (1982) are inadequate in a number of ways. First, heredity plays a role in producing individual differences in trait anxiety and neuroticism, but it is smaller than is assumed by traditional theories. Second, while it is plausible to assume that individual differences in trait anxiety and neuroticism depend in part on differences in physiological responsiveness, there is little support for this view from the available evidence.

There are at least two other significant problems with traditional theories. First, it has been assumed that trait anxiety and neuroticism are semi-permanent personality characteristics which change very little over time. In fact, however, the test-retest reliability of these personality traits is often relatively low. As Conley (1984) pointed out, there are two reasons for this: (1) actual changes in personality over time; and (2) the intrinsic unreliability of the measures used to assess trait anxiety and neuroticism. Conley (1984) used statistical means to eliminate the effects of intrinsic unreliability. When he did this, he found that the level of consistency from one year to the next was .98. This figure is below that for intelligence, and means that levels of trait anxiety and neuroticism are not entirely stable over time.

The final problem with the traditional theories is the assumption that trait anxiety or neuroticism is unidimensional, in the sense that individuals are either generally high or generally low in their level of trait anxiety or neuroticism. This assumption is flawed because of the substantial evidence of specificity, with individuals being more anxious in some situations than in others. One of the more influential attempts to replace the unidimensional view of trait anxiety with a multidimensional conceptualisation was that of Endler (1983), who argued that there are five different dimensions of trait anxiety. According to his theoretical account, individuals high in trait anxiety will only show a greater increase in state anxiety than those low in trait anxiety when exposed to a threatening situation in which there is congruence between the nature of the threat and the dimension of trait anxiety possessed by the individual. This prediction of the theory has been confirmed on a number of occasions (see the review by Endler, 1983), but mainly when studies have considered the social evaluation and physical danger dimensions. Indeed, there is no compelling evidence for most of the other dimensions proposed by Endler (1983).

Summary

Individual differences in trait anxiety and neuroticism are partially determined by heredity, but the influence of heredity is smaller than was suggested within traditional theories. As a consequence, there was insufficient attention to the dynamic processes producing change in trait anxiety or neuroticism levels, especially to the cognitive processes. However, what is perhaps the greatest limitation of the traditional approach relates to issues which are discussed more fully in the rest of the chapter. The traditional approach was based on the implicit (or even explicit) assumption that there should be concordance or agreement among the cognitive, physiological and behavioural systems involved in anxiety. As we have seen, there is an almost complete lack of concordance between self-report and physiological measures of anxiety, and there are other systematic failures of concordance (see Weinberger, 1990). As a consequence, any adequate theory of trait anxiety or neuroticism will need to be based on a much more detailed consideration of the inter-relationships among the cognitive, physiological and behavioural systems than was the case with the traditional approach.

THE COGNITIVE APPROACH

As we have seen, traditional theories have failed for a variety of reasons. In essence, environmental influences and the role of learning were de-emphasised by H.J. Eysenck (1967) and Gray (1982). As a consequence of the failure to focus on changes over time, the significant role of the cognitive system was not fully appreciated, especially by H.J. Eysenck (1967). At a very general level, an individual's susceptibility to anxiety depends in part on the information stored in long-term memory. Schemata (coherent packages of inter-related information) are likely to play a key role, especially those schemata relating to danger and vulnerability (Beck and Clark, 1988). Schemata change dynamically over time when information is added to them as a result of experiences.

Failures of concordance

Most personality theorists who have considered trait anxiety or neuroticism have paid insufficient attention to the fact that there are three rather separate systems involved in anxiety (Lang, 1985); these systems are the behavioural, the physiological and the verbal or cognitive. It is especially important to consider all three systems because of the mounting evidence that measures of anxiety taken from each of the systems typically show failures of concordance or agreement. Consider, for example, a study on competent pianists performing in public (Craske and Craig, 1984). Several measures of anxiety were taken, and measures from within the same system generally correlated significantly with each other. However, measures of anxiety taken from different systems generally failed to correlate with each other.

There are several possible reasons for a lack of concordance among measures. One uninteresting reason is because some of the measures being used are insensitive or inappropriate ways of assessing anxiety. Another uninteresting reason was proposed by Thorpe (1989). According to him, 'It should not surprise us when different measures of anxiety do not agree with each other when we confound "question asked" with "response mode" ' (p. 192). The two reasons considered so far are based on the assumption that failures of concordance arise because of inadequate experimental procedures. However, another (and more interesting) reason for a lack of concordance stems from a detailed theoretical consideration of individual differences in the functioning of the cognitive system. This is discussed below.

As was pointed out earlier in the chapter, it is possible to divide those scoring low on trait anxiety into two categories: the truly low-anxious and repressors. Weinberger et al. (1979) found that repressors were very responsive physiologically in a stressful situation although their self-reported anxiety was low. Repressors have shown similar discrepancies between self-reported and physiological anxiety in several other studies (Weinberger, 1990).

In order to obtain a fuller understanding of repressors, it is necessary to consider their level of behavioural anxiety. The findings in the literature appear to be somewhat inconsistent, with repressors sometimes appearing to be more behaviourally anxious than others, but sometimes appearing to be non-anxious behaviourally (Weinberger, 1990). The author has recently carried out a series of unpublished studies to investigate this issue further. In some of the studies, repressors, the truly low-anxious, high-anxious individuals and defensive high-anxious individuals (i.e., with high scores on trait anxiety and on social desirability) were rated on trait anxiety by individuals who knew them well. It was found consistently that repressors were rated as low in trait anxiety, indicating that their behaviour is generally non-anxious. This finding tends to disconfirm the view that repressors are simply high-anxious individuals deliberately attempting on self-report measures to present themselves as non-anxious. That view is in any case disconfirmed by the fact that repressors practically never admit to experiencing high levels of anxiety even when they are led to believe that the experimenter has evidence of their true feelings.

Rather different findings were obtained in another unpublished study in which subjects were videotaped while describing their most undesirable personality characteristics. Detailed analyses of the videotapes indicated that the repressors were more behaviourally anxious than truly low-anxious, high-anxious and defensive high-anxious subjects, although they denied feeling more anxious than the other groups of subjects. The most plausible way of reconciling the various findings is as follows: repressors make use of a defensive coping style which permits them to minimise their underlying level of anxiety to themselves and to others; however, this defensive coping style is relatively ineffective in moderately or very stressful situations.

One important implication of the research on repressors is that the frequent approach of relying exclusively on self-report questionnaires in order to assess an individual's level of trait anxiety is inadequate. Repressors appear to be low in trait anxiety on such questionnaires, but their physiological responsiveness and their behavioural anxiety in stressful situations indicate that the reality is much more complex. In more general terms, the findings from repressors indicate the necessity of assessing the cognitive (self-report), physiological and behavioural systems concurrently if anxiety within individuals is to be understood fully.

Some progress has been made in the task of understanding the processes involved in producing the repressors' discrepancy between self-report measures on the one hand, and physiological and behavioural measures on the other. Fox (1994) used a negative priming paradigm, and found that repressors exhibited more inhibition for threat-related stimuli than did other anxiety groups. The implication is that repressors have inhibitory processes operating below the level of conscious awareness which prevent threat-related information from gaining access to conscious awareness. Presumably repressors have developed a defensive coping style over a period of years, and this eventually becomes relatively automatised and does not require the involvement of conscious processes.

A COGNITIVE THEORY OF TRAIT ANXIETY

Theoretical assumptions

M.W. Eysenck (e.g., 1992) has attempted to develop a cognitive theory of trait anxiety. The initial assumptions of the theory are that previous theories of trait anxiety have tended to downplay the role of the cognitive system, and that an adequate account would include cognitive processes and structures as central features. Another major assumption was that anxiety fulfils the function of facilitating the rapid detection of threat or impending danger, especially in environments that are potentially threatening. This is normally a valuable function. However, clinically anxious patients often substantially exaggerate the threateningness of the environment, and so the function of rapid threat detection becomes dysfunctional.

What processes are involved in threat detection? Obviously, the main processes involved are pre-attentive and/or attentional. As a consequence, the cognitive system is centrally involved with respect to the primary purpose of anxiety. More specifically, it is assumed that the attentional system in anxious individuals is selective, in the sense that threat-related stimuli are attended to at the expense of non-threatening stimuli. In order for threat-related stimuli to be detected rapidly, there must be almost constant attentional scanning of the environment.

M.W. Eysenck (1992) attempted to specify some of the main characteristics of attentional processing in high trait-anxious individuals in his hypervigilance theory. He argued that such individuals possess general hypervigilance, also known as distractibility, which is revealed by a tendency to attend to task-irrelevant stimuli. They also show specific hypervigilance, which involves the tendency to attend selectively to threat-related rather than to non-threatening stimuli. Those high in trait anxiety also show a high rate of environmental scanning, a broadening of attention during the period prior to the detection of a threatening or other significant stimulus, followed by a narrowing of attention while a threatening stimulus is being processed. It should be emphasised that all of these effects on the attentional system are assumed to be determined interactively by trait and state anxiety; that is to say, those high in trait anxiety will show the effects primarily when they are high in state anxiety.

Hypervigilance theory was mainly concerned with the effects of anxiety on attentional processes directed towards the environment. It seems probable that these processes are also directed towards internal sources of information (e.g., physiological processes). In other words, those high in trait anxiety selectively attend to threat-related stimuli, whether these stimuli are external or internal.

Empirical evidence

The evidence relating to hypervigilance theory was discussed by M.W. Eysenck (1992). The first study on selective processing of threat by anxious subjects was reported by M.W. Eysenck et al. (1987). They used a task in which pairs of words were presented concurrently, one to each ear. The subjects were instructed to shadow or repeat back aloud all of the words presented to the attended ear, while at the same time ignoring words presented to the non-attended ear. Some of the words presented to the attended ear were either socially or physically threatening, whereas all of the words presented to the non-attended ear were non-threatening. Information about the allocation of attention was obtained by requiring subjects to respond as rapidly as possible to a tone that was presented occasionally very shortly after a pair of words had been presented. It was assumed that subjects would respond faster to the tone when most of their attention was devoted to the ear on which the tone was presented than when most of their attention was allocated elsewhere.

The findings of M.W. Eysenck et al. (1987) were in line with the hyper-vigilance theory. Those who scored high on the Facilitation-Inhibition Scale (equivalent to high scorers on trait anxiety) tended to allocate atten-tional resources to the ear to which a threat-related word had just been presented. In contrast, inhibitors (equivalent to low scorers on trait anxiety) avoided allocating processing resources to the ear on which a threat-related word had just been presented.

MacLeod and Mathews (1988) used a visual analogue of the task utilised by M.W. Eysenck et al. (1987). They studied attentional bias towards or away from examination-relevant words several months before an important examination and in the week before the examina-tion. Subjects high in trait anxiety showed attentional bias towards the threat-related stimuli close in time to the examination but not several months before. Those low in trait anxiety had an attentional bias away from the same stimuli only on the second testing occasion. Thus, their feelings indicated that selective attentional bias is interactively deter-mined by trait and state anxiety.

It is assumed with hypervigilance theory that one of the ways in which anxiety facilitates threat detection is via a broadening of attention. Relevant evidence was reported by Shapiro and Lim (1989). They gave their subjects the task of responding to visual target signals as rapidly as possible, with the signal being presented either centrally or peripherally. On a small fraction of trials, central and peripheral target stimuli were presented concurrently. Anxious subjects were more than four times like-lier than non-anxious subjects to respond to the peripheral signal, suggesting that anxiety leads to greater sensitivity to peripheral stimuli and to a broadening of attention.

The prediction that anxiety leads to enhanced distractibility was tested by M.W. Eysenck and Graydon (1989). They asked neurotic introverts (high trait-anxious subjects) to perform a letter-transformation task on its own or in the presence of letter or meaningless blip distractors. The key finding was that the performance of the neurotic introverts was significantly impaired by the letter distractors, but that of the stable extraverts was not. In other words, the more anxious group was more susceptible to distraction than was the less anxious group.

As we have seen, there is substantial evidence that anxiety has several predictable effects on the attentional system. However, it is probable that anxiety has a number of other effects on the cognitive system. Of particular theoretical importance is the interpretive bias, which is the tendency to interpret ambiguous stimuli and situations in a threatening fashion. Interpretive bias was studied by M.W. Eysenck et al. (1987). Homophones having threat-related and non-threatening interpretations were presented auditorily, and subjects were simply instructed to write down the spelling of each word as it was presented. There was a correlation of +.60 between trait anxiety and the number of threatening homophone interpretations, demonstrating the existence of an interpretive bias in high trait-anxious individuals.

Further information on interpretive bias was reported by MacLeod (1990). Ambiguous sentences possessing a threat-related and a non-threatening interpretation were presented, with each sentence being followed by a word strongly associated with one of its possible interpretations. The task was to name the word as rapidly as possible. Those high in trait anxiety named words related to threatening interpretations faster when they were high in state anxiety, but named words related to non-threatening interpretations slower when high in state anxiety. The opposite pattern of findings was obtained from subjects low in trait anxiety. These findings indicate that interpretive bias is an interactive function of trait and state anxiety.

According to the theory, pre-attentive and attentional processes are the processes within the cognitive system which are of the greatest relevance to anxiety. However, those high in trait anxiety spend much more of their time worrying than those low in trait anxiety (M.W. Eysenck, 1992), and this suggests that they have facilitated access to threat-related information stored in long-term memory. Several studies have investigated negative memory bias, which is the tendency to recall threat-related rather than non-threatening information. The findings are rather inconsistent, but M.W. Eysenck (1992) drew the following conclusions from the evidence:

Negative memory bias is obtained most consistently when there is induction of an anxious mood state, or underlying danger or threat

schemata are activated. Since an anxious mood state probably facilitates activation of danger schemata, it is reasonable to conclude that
activation of such schemata may be a necessary precondition for a
negative memory bias in non-clinical anxious groups.

(M.W. Eysenck, 1992, p. 90)

Theoretical and practical implications

We have seen that those high in trait anxiety differ from those low in trait
anxiety in terms of a range of cognitive biases, including selective attentional bias, interpretive bias and negative memory bias. These biases
help to increase our understanding of the processes underlying the
personality dimension of trait anxiety. It is assumed that these biases are
affected in a top-down fashion by underlying schemata. Since these
schemata are susceptible to change as a result of experience, alterations
in the nature and extent of these biases over time can potentially be
accounted for within this theoretical approach.

There is as yet relatively little research on the existence of cognitive
biases in repressors. However, it is a reasonable theoretical assumption
that repressors will exhibit opposite cognitive biases to those shown by
high-anxious individuals. Some evidence supporting this assumption
was reported by Fox (1993). She discovered that repressors, but not truly
low-anxious individuals, showed a tendency to avoid allocating attention to socially threatening stimuli. In other words, repressors seem to
show an opposite selective attentional bias.

Perhaps the most convincing evidence of an opposite cognitive bias
in repressors was reported by Davis (1987). She found that repressors
had much longer latencies than other anxiety groups to recall
negative childhood memories, but not to recall positive ones. In other
words, repressors showed an opposite negative memory bias.

One of the major implications of the research on cognitive biases in
high-anxious and repressor groups is that it helps to elucidate the failures of concordance reported in the literature. In general terms, those
high in trait anxiety have relatively higher self-reported anxiety than
physiological or behavioural anxiety, whereas those low in trait anxiety
have relatively lower self-reported anxiety than physiological or
behavioural anxiety. It is assumed that these tendencies arise because of
the cognitive biases and opposite cognitive biases shown by high-
anxious individuals and repressors, respectively. Thus, failures of
concordance stem directly from individual differences in cognitive
biases.

CONCLUSIONS

At the practical level, there has been an almost universal tendency to rely on self-report questionnaire assessment of trait anxiety. In view of the widespread failures of concordance across the cognitive (self-report), physiological and behavioural systems involved in anxiety, this practice cannot be defended. Ideally, people who need an accurate assessment of susceptibility to anxiety (e.g., those involved in personnel selection) should obtain detailed measures of the functioning of the cognitive, physiological and behavioural systems. At the very least, much more consideration needs to be given to the interpretation of self-report measures. According to the cognitive theory of anxiety presented here, measures of self-reported anxiety are systematically distorted by various cognitive biases, and the prudent practitioner will take these distortions into account when assessing individual differences in anxiety.

REFERENCES

Beck, A.T. and Clark, D.A. (1988) 'Anxiety and depression: an information processing perspective', *Anxiety Research* 1: 23–36.

Conley, J.J. (1984) 'The hierarchy of consistency: a review and model of longitudinal findings on adult individual differences in intelligence, personality and self-opinion', *Personality and Individual Differences* 5: 11–25.

Craske, M.G. and Craig, K D. (1984) 'Musical performance anxiety: the three-systems model and self-efficacy theory', *Behaviour Research and Therapy* 22: 267–280.

Davis, P.J. (1987) 'Repression and the inaccessibility of affective memories', *Journal of Personality and Social Psychology* 53: 585–593.

Digman, J.M. (1990) 'Personality structure: emergence of the five-factor model', *Annual Review of Psychology* 41: 417–440.

Endler, N.S. (1983) 'Interactionism: a personality model, but not yet a theory', in M.M. Page (ed.) *Nebraska Symposium on Motivation: Personality – Current Theory and Research*, London: University of Nebraska Press.

Eysenck, H.J. (1967) *The Biological Basis of Personality*, Springfield, IL: C.C. Thomas.

Eysenck, H.J. and Prell, D.B. (1951) 'The inheritance of neuroticism', *Journal of Mental Science* 97: 441–465.

Eysenck, M.W. (1992) *Anxiety: The Cognitive Perspective*, London: Lawrence Erlbaum Associates Ltd.

Eysenck, M.W. and Graydon, J. (1989) 'Susceptibility to distraction as a function of personality', *Personality and Individual Differences* 10: 681–687.

Eysenck, M.W., MacLeod, C. and Mathews, A. (1987) 'Cognitive functioning and anxiety', *Psychological Research* 49: 189–195.

Fahrenberg, J. (1987) 'Concepts of activation and arousal in the theory of emotionality (neuroticism): a multivariate concept', in J. Strelau and H.J. Eysenck (eds) *Personality and Dimensions of Arousal*, New York: Plenum.

Fox, E. (1993) 'Allocation of visual attention and anxiety', *Cognition and Emotion* 7: 207–215.

——(1994) 'Attentional bias in anxiety: a defective inhibition hypothesis', *Cognition and Emotion* 8: 165–195.

Gray, J.A. (1975) *Elements of a Two-Process Theory of Learning*, London: Academic Press.
—— (1982) *The Neuropsychology of Anxiety*, Oxford: Clarendon.
Hallam, G. (1985) 'Anxiety and the brain: a reply to Gray', *Bulletin of the British Psychological Society* 3: 217–219.
Kline, P. (1983) *Personality: measurement and theory*, London: Hutchinson.
—— (1992) 'The factor structure in the fields of personality and ability', in A. Gale and M.W. Eysenck (eds) *Handbook of individual differences: biological perspectives*, Chichester: Wiley.
Lang, P.J. (1985) 'The cognitive psychophysiology of emotion: fear and anxiety', in A.H. Tuma and J. Maser (eds) *Anxiety and the Anxiety Disorders*, Hillsdale, NJ: Lawrence Erlbaum Associates Inc.
Langinvainio, H., Kaprio, J., Koskenvuo, M. and Lonnquist, J. (1984) 'Finnish twins reared apart, III: personality factors', *Acta Geneticae Mediacae et Gemmellologiae* 33: 259–267.
McCrae, R.R., and Costa, P.T. (1985) 'Updating Norman's "adequate taxonomy": intelligence and personality dimensions in natural language and in questionnaires', *Journal of Personality and Social Psychology* 49: 710–721.
MacLeod, C. (1990) 'Mood disorders and cognition', in M.W. Eysenck (ed.) *Cognitive Psychology: An International Review*, Chichester: Wiley.
MacLeod, C. and Mathews, A. (1988) 'Anxiety and the allocation of attention to threat', *Quarterly Journal of Experimental Psychology* 38A: 659–670.
Pedersen, N.L., Friberg, L., Floderus-Myrhed, B., McClearn, G.E. and Plomin, R. (1984) 'Swedish early separated twins: identification and characterisation', *Acta Geneticae Medicae et Gemellologiae* 33: 243–254.
Rachman, S. and Lopatka, C. (1986a) 'Match and mismatch in the prediction of fear I', *Behaviour Research and Therapy* 24: 387–393.
—— (1986b) 'Match and mismatch in the prediction of fear II', *Behaviour Research and Therapy* 24: 395–401.
Shapiro, K.L. and Lim, A. (1989) 'The impact of anxiety on visual attention to central and peripheral events', *Behaviour Research and Therapy* 27: 345–351.
Shields, J. (1962) *Monozygotic twins*, Oxford: Oxford University Press.
Thorpe, G.L. (1989) 'Confounding of assessment method with reaction assessed in the three systems model of fear and anxiety: a comment on Douglas, Lindsay and Brooks', *Behavioural Psychotherapy* 17: 191–192.
Torgersen, S. (1990) 'Genetics of anxiety and its clinical implications', in G.D. Burrows, M. Roth, and R. Noyes (eds) *Handbook of Anxiety, Vol. 3: The Neurobiology of Anxiety*, Amsterdam: Elsevier.
Watson, D. and Clark, L.A. (1984) 'Negative affectivity: the disposition to experience aversive emotional states', *Psychological Bulletin* 96: 465–490.
Weinberger, D.A. (1990) 'The construct validity of the repressive coping style', in J.L. Singer (ed.) *Repression and Dissociation: Implications for Personality Theory, Psychopathology, and Health*, Chicago: University of Chicago Press.
Weinberger, D.A., Schwartz, G.E. and Davidson, J.R. (1979) 'Low-anxious, high—anxious, and repressive coping styles: psychometric patterns and behavioural and physiological responses to stress', *Journal of Abnormal Psychology* 88: 369–380.

Chapter 5

The social psychology of personality

Sarah E. Hampson

Perhaps the first psychologist to explore the interpersonal nature of personality was William James (1890). He said that the self only exists in relation to other selves, and that a person has as many selves as people with whom he or she interacts. His insights have been adopted by psychiatrists, sociologists and social psychologists to generate several theoretical approaches to personality, all of which stress the interpersonal nature of personality. For Sullivan (1953), a psychiatrist, the individual cannot exist apart from his or her relation to others, and the study of personality *is* the study of interpersonal behaviour. Goffman, a sociologist, was influenced by symbolic interactionists such as Cooley (1902) and Mead (1934) in his development of the theatrical metaphor for interpersonal behaviour. He viewed people's interpersonal behaviour as a performance aimed at eliciting particular responses from the audience. Subsequently, Goffman's ideas were influential in the development of impression management theories in social psychology (e.g., Baumeister and Hutton, 1987; Schlenker and Weigold, 1992; Snyder, 1987), and organisational psychology (e.g., Rosenfeld *et al.*, 1995). This chapter presents another approach to personality originating from these ideas, the constructivist approach (Hampson, 1988, 1995). In common with other interpersonal theories, the constructivist approach is concerned with the processes that shape personality.

THE PROCESSES OF PERSONALITY CONSTRUCTION

According to the constructivist model of personality, personality is composed of three elements: the actor, the observer and the self-observer. The actor component refers to the characteristics the person brings to the social situation in which personality is constructed. These include genetic factors that may influence the kinds of behaviours of which a person is capable, or predisposed to perform, as well as the person's past learning history and present goals. Personality psychology is traditionally associated with the study of the actor component. According to this perspective, personality is located within the individual. The study of personality is the study of individual differences which can be conceptu-alised according to a variety of theoretical approaches (e.g., psychodynamic, learning theory, humanistic). These theories typically emphasise the stability of personality from about age 30 years, indicating that once formed, personality remains relatively fixed and unchanging (Costa and McCrae, 1994).

The observer component refers to the way the actor is perceived by other people. The actor's behaviour (using the term behaviour very broadly) is used by observers to construct an impression of the actor's personality. This is done by adding social significance and meaning to observed behaviour. The observer (or perceiver) is the audience in the interaction. For example, the observer might be making personality judgements about the actor in a job interview or on a date. However, the observer need not be physically present and the observer is often an imaginary audience.

The self-observer component is the direct consequence of the human capacity for self-awareness. The actor is aware that her or his behaviour is under observation. We attempt to observe ourselves in approximately the same way we can observe other people, to try to see ourselves as we think other people see us. Consequently, we infer the social significance of our actions and hypothesise about the impression we are making on others. We build theories about ourselves just as we build theories about other people.

The constructivist approach regards personality as more than the sum of its parts (Hampson, 1992). Personality consists of an actor's behaviour, which is overlaid with social meaning by the construal processes of observers and self-observers. It is the combination of the actor's behaviour and these construction processes that produces personality. The constructivist approach provides a theoretical frame-work for relating several distinct fields of psychology. The actor component subsumes much of traditional personality psychology (e.g., trait theories, psychodynamic theories). The observer component includes several areas of social psychology and social cognition (e.g., impression formation and person perception), and the self component includes aspects of social and clinical psychology (e.g., impression management, self-esteem).

So far, this description of the construction of personality is not that much different from a description of the construction that is part of our perception of most things in the world. For example, when we perceive that the object on the desk is a mug of coffee we are adding social significance to a concave object with a handle containing a steaming liquid. Both bottom-up (data-driven) and top-down (schema-driven) perceptual mechanisms are used to process the incoming data in a swift and efficient manner to warn us that the object is a mug of hot coffee and therefore is to be handled with care around the word processor. However, because of the dynamic nature of personality construction, the construction of personality is considerably more complex than the construction of perceptions of objects. The three components (actor, observer and self-observer) have reciprocal influences. The actor's behaviour is interpreted in a certain way by the observer, who then responds accordingly. The actor's subsequent behaviour is influenced by the observer's response. The actor's ability to be a self-observer will allow him/her to make some inference about the impression that is probably forming in the observer's mind, and the actor may wish to adjust his or her behaviour in order to modify this impression.

The dynamic aspect of personality construction sounds complicated and even calculating. However, these processes of perspective-taking are essential for communication, and we are all expert in them to at least some degree. Indeed, personality construction may be thought of as a form of communication. Together, the participants arrive at a mutually negotiated construction of this part of reality.

The constructivist approach to personality shares some of the features of social constructionism, which originated in an approach to sociology developed by Berger and Luckmann (1966), and has now as emerged as an alternative form of personality and social psychology (Burr, 1995). According to this view, the traditional empiricist approach to science adopted by psychology is wrong, particularly for social psychology. If social reality is viewed as entirely the creation of interpersonal processes, embodied in language, then the social world does not exist independent of our constructions of it. There is nothing out there against which to validate our constructions. Therefore, an objective, scientific approach to social psychology is impossible, and an explicitly subjective one is the only viable alternative (Potter and Wetherell, 1987).

In contrast, the constructivist approach to personality does not reject realism. It proposes that observers and self-observers construct personality by interpreting the actor's raw behaviour. Therefore, personality has an anchor in the real world. The constructivist view is supported by a recent realist philosophy of science (Greenwood, 1991). There is an important distinction between the terms constructivist and constructionist as they are used here. The term constructivist is taken from the early days of cognitive psychology, when the importance of top-down, schema-driven processing was being established (e.g., Neisser, 1976). Psychologists were investigating how cognitive processes construct our awareness of reality. In contrast, the term constructionist refers to a view of psychological phenomena as having no basis in reality, but instead as being the product of social processes.

To illustrate this argument, consider four positions with regard to the nature of the language of personality description. The first, we will call the traditional position. Trait theorists are converging on an agreement about the structure of personality, known as the Big Five (e.g., Digman, 1990). This structure has emerged from many studies of both self-ratings and observer ratings on traits. It can also be found in ratings of the semantic similarity of traits. As Jim Stevenson and Paul Barrett discuss in this volume, much research on the biological basis of personality now seeks to show the extent to which the Big Five traits have a genetic basis (Loehlin, 1992). In its most simplistic form, this approach equates the language of personality description (i.e., traits) with biological counterparts to be identified within the individual. This type of thinking gives rise to headlines in the newspaper such as 'Bad-tempered and extravagant? Blame it on the genes' (*The Times*, 2 January 1996). A more complex version of this position would view trait language as not necessarily mapping directly onto the biological basis of personality. Thus, although we perceive ourselves and others in terms of the Big Five structure, the underlying biological basis may be organised differently. However, it should be possible indirectly to map the one onto the other (McCrae and Costa, 1995).

A second view may be identified that is equally committed to the reality of personality. However, it is more sceptical about the language of personality description. From this perspective, our personality-descriptive language distorts the reality of personality. For example, observers perceive more consistency than is actually the case. This position sparked off a prolonged debate over the systematic distortion hypothesis (Shweder, 1982) which considered whether observers' perceptions of personality were accurate reflections of reality or biased perceptions with little or no correspondence with reality.

Both of the above positions fail to incorporate the socially constructed dimension of personality traits. They both rely on a strictly realist position in which it is assumed that personality exists independently of observer. Social constructionism adopts a different position with regard to personality language. Two constructionist positions may be identified: one strong position, which is not consistent with the constructivist approach to personality and one weak position, which is. The strong version of social constructionism would argue that personality language has no basis in reality (Burr, 1995). Personality is socially created and exists only in language. It is created by social processes and is not open to objective verification. The less extreme position, which is compatible with the constructivist approach, recognises that there are socially constructed aspects to personality language but also assumes that there is an independent reality to which the language refers. The mapping of the language on reality may not be straightforward.

THE OBSERVER IN PERSONALITY CONSTRUCTION PROCESSES

The emphasis in this chapter is on the role of the observer in the construction of personality. It is emphasised here because this chapter is concerned with the social psychology of personality, and because whereas other chapters in this book address topics that expand on the actor component, they do not address the observer. Kenny (1994) recently commented that person perception lies at the interface between social psychology and personality. The constructivist approach, with its inclusion of the observer as a key component of personality in personality construction, provides an integration of these two aspects of psychology.

The following discussion of the observer in personality construction is organised according to a three-stage model of personality perception (see Figure 5.1). In brief, the process of personality construction from the observer's perspective involves (1) the identification of behaviour, (2) the categorisation of behavioural acts, and (3) the attribution of personality. These three stages are usually, but not necessarily, sequential. Whether or not processing proceeds from stage 1 to stage 2, or from stage 2 to stage 3, depends upon the goals of the perceiver/observer. Many social inter-actions can take place without going beyond behaviour identification, and many more can be quite satisfactory without engaging in personality attribution.

Before developing the three-stage model, it is necessary to clarify the distinction between the two uses of traits. Personality traits can be used by observers/perceivers to describe (categorise) behaviour, or to describe personality. Each use of traits involves different processes. However, psychologists are not always clear on this distinction, and there can be confusion if a study of act categorisation is interpreted as if it were looking at trait attribution, or vice versa. In act categorisation (stage 2), traits are used to describe behaviour. Instead of identifying behaviour (e.g., Jane is carrying John's shopping bag), we use a descriptive category (a trait adjective) to describe it (e.g., Jane is being helpful). The behaviour

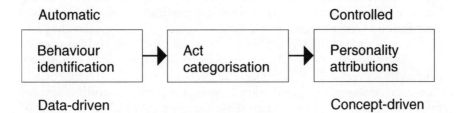

Figure 5.1 A three-stage model of personality perception

is categorised as an instance of a particular trait category. In person categorisation, the trait is applied to the person performing the behaviour,
not just the behaviour itself (e.g., Jane is helpful). In everyday language,
we may blur the distinction between the two uses of traits with no
adverse consequences. Indeed, the tendency to use traits to describe
persons when we really only mean to categorise behaviours may be
another manifestation of the fundamental attribution error, which is the
tendency to explain behaviour in dispositional terms and to ignore the
part played by the situation (Ross, 1977). However, as personality
psychologists it is important to keep this distinction straight, as will be
illustrated later.

Stage 1: Behaviour identification

The first step in person perception is to identify what it is that a person is
doing. Behaviour identification precedes either use of the trait concept.
For example, is the person running or walking? Is Jane carrying something? Behaviour identification probably relies to some extent on
data-driven (bottom-up) processes, as opposed to schema-driven (top-
down) processes. Research on the direct perception of behaviour has
shown that we can recognise several aspects of individuals automatically, from minimal information. Observers can identify the gait of a
person filmed in the dark wearing lights attached to the major joints of
the body so that they are seen only as a pattern of moving points of light
(e.g., Johansson, 1975), and both objects and the human profile are
perceived as ageing when certain standard transformations are
performed on drawings of them (Pittinger and Shaw, 1975).

One advantage of direct perception is that it involves automatic
processes that require little cognitive effort (Logan, 1989). Hence we can
comprehend many aspects of what people are doing without paying
conscious attention to the problem. Another advantage of automatic
processing is that it can take place in parallel with other more effortful
kinds of processing. Simply identifying at a concrete level what a person
is doing is sufficient for many purposes, and in these cases there is no
reason to proceed beyond this first stage of person perception. However,
we often progress to the next stage to provide a more informative
description of behaviour.

Stage 2: Act categorisation

Act categorisation can only occur after behaviour identification. It
involves further identification of the behaviour as a member of a trait
category. Models of act categorisation in personality perception have
been developed from models of categorisation in cognitive psychology

(Rosch *et al.*, 1976). According to the semantic category model, each trait is a category that refers to numerous superficially different behaviours, which have overlapping features that enable them to be categorised by the same trait term (e.g., Borkenau, 1986; Hampson *et al.*, 1986). Behaviours are composed of three kinds of features: behavioural (the actions that occur), situational (the context in which they occur) and motivational (the underlying motive they reflect), and these features vary in their prototypicality with regard to different trait categories. Motivational features are often key to categorising behaviour and, because motivations have to be inferred from the context and other information, they can be the cause of miscategorisations. A behaviour may appear to be a good member of one category (e.g., Jane carrying John's shopping is a good instance of the trait category helpful), however, if we knew more about the relationship between Jane and John, we might more correctly categorise Jane's behaviour as submissive.

Studies of traits categories have demonstrated that traits vary on a dimension of category breadth (Hampson *et al.*, 1987). That is, some traits (e.g., talkative) are relatively narrow in their range of application, categorising only a limited number of specific behaviours. Other traits are broader in their range (e.g., sociable), and still others are even broader (e.g., extraverted). Traits that describe the same aspect of personality at different levels of breadth form hierarchies. For example, talkative is viewed as a subset of sociable, which in turn is a subset of extraversion (Hampson *et al.*, 1986). Categorising a behaviour at different levels of breadth is a trade-off between bandwidth and fidelity. If too narrow a trait is used, it is less informative of other related behaviours this person may be expected to perform, whereas categorisation at too broad a level provides an ambiguous description of the behaviour.

Stage 3: Personality attribution

Personality attribution involves the application of the trait concept to the person performing the behaviour. For example, we describe people as helpful, submissive or altruistic. Within social psychology and social cognition, the process of using traits to describe people forms the study of dispositional attributions. Unlike act categorisation, we do not usually make personality attributions based on just one piece of behaviour (although we may). General attribution rules that govern dispositional inference have been proposed, such as Kelley's (1973) analysis of variance approach, or Jones and Davis' (1965) theory of correspondent inference.

In addition, more specific theories can be developed for the conditions under which particular traits will be attributed to persons. For example, Reeder and Brewer (1979) presented different attributional schema for different kinds of traits. For positive moral traits such as honesty, many behavioural instances are required to convince the observer that the person is truly honest, whereas for dishonesty, the observer may use just one behaviour to make a trait attribution. If you observe a pickpocket at work in a crowd, you are likely to make an immediate person categorisation (dishonest thief). This is an example of where a person categorisation is made simultaneously with the behaviour categorisation.

Broader traits encompass a greater variety of behaviour and therefore are less precise in their meaning. There are many ways of being extraverted, whereas being talkative is a more specific description of behaviour. At the very broadest level in trait hierarchies are traits such as good and nice, which have virtually no descriptive content. They are almost purely evaluative. In studies of people's preferences for particular levels of trait description, John *et al.* (1991) found that observers prefer to describe people at the broadest level possible that still retains descriptive informativeness (e.g., extraverted is preferred over talkative, sociable or nice). Traits at this level appear to maximise the trade-off between informativeness and specificity for the purposes of person description.

In addition to the three stages, the model is also characterised by two general characteristics. (1) The features are ordered in terms of a continuum of data-driven, automatic, spontaneous, bottom-up processing versus concept-driven, controlled, deliberate, top-down processing. Recently, there has been considerable interest in the extent to which people's social judgements are driven by automatic versus controlled processing (e.g., Uleman and Bargh, 1989), and this model assumes that both are used in person perception. (2) As a result of (1), the stages are ordered in terms of the amount of cognitive work involved in processing. Following Fiske and Taylor's (1991) principle of cognitive economy, observers are not expected to proceed further along the stages than is necessary for current processing needs. We do not make elaborate personality inferences about everyone we encounter. In general, we do not need to make personality attributions to buy a bus ticket or to pay for our groceries. However, as soon as one level of processing proves inadequate, then the next level will be used. Thus, an important implication of the three-stage model is that we need to study the conditions that prompt further processing. Unexpected or inconsistent behaviour (e.g., the check-out clerk comments on the unhealthy nature of your food purchases), is likely to prompt person categorisation (Wong and Weiner, 1981). Repeated exposure to the person will lead to accumulated knowledge, which is necessary for some trait attributions (Reeder and Brewer, 1979; Kelley, 1973). Expected future interaction, and instructions to form an impression of a target person, are typical instructional manipulations in social psychology experiments that prompt personality attributions (e.g., Bassili and Smith, 1986).

One complication to the simple one-directional path through the stages occurs when the observer and the actor are previously acquainted. Act categorisation and personality attribution may be different if the observer has already attributed traits to the actor. For example, if through extensive past acquaintance, the observer has already categorised the actor as ambitious (stage 3 personality attribution), then on seeing the actor chatting to a superior at work, the observer may categorise this behaviour as ingratiating instead of sociable (stage 2 act categorisation). The category selected at stage 2 can be affected by a category applied to the actor previously at stage 3.

Related theories

The three-stage model has features in common with several other theories of person perception. The two-stage model of dispositional judgement proposed by Trope and Liberman (1993) focuses on act categorisation and personality attribution without addressing the initial stage of behaviour identification. Both Fiske and Neuberg's (1990) continuum model, and Brewer's (1988) dual-process model are directed towards similar issues to the three-stage model described above. They both provide accounts of the processes involved in person perception. However, both of these theories have been concerned with the use of stereotypes (personality descriptive nouns) in person perception as opposed to the use of traits (personality descriptive adjectives). Stereotyping is a form of person categorisation in which the actor is categorised as a member of a social group. In the three-stage model described here, stereotyping could occur at any of the three stages. At stage 1, direct perception enables certain characteristics to be perceived automatically (e.g., gender), which may trigger the observer's stereotypes. If a stereotype has been triggered at stage 1, this may lead to the greater accessibility of stereotypic categories for describing behaviour at stage 2, and for attributing to the person at stage 3.

Another approach to person perception is represented by Smith (1988) and Smith and Zárate (1992). They based their theorising on an exemplar model that proposes that actual examples of previously encountered people (exemplars) are stored in memory. When categorising a new person, her or his perceived similarity with stored examples is examined. For example, by likening Saddam Hussein to Hitler, it can be inferred that he too is capable of ordering the mass extermination of an ethnic minority. The exemplar model provides an alternative to traits as the basis of representations of persons. However, it does not address issues of cognitive economy by providing for different levels of complexity of processing depending on the observer's current needs. Nevertheless, it is possible that an exemplar approach could be incorporated into a staged model of person perception.

ARE PERSONALITY INFERENCES SPONTANEOUS?

The three-stage model of person perception described above proposes that the most complex stage, stage 3 personality attribution, involves top-down processing that does not occur automatically. This proposition is in direct contradiction to the position taken by several social psychologists who have been studying what they call spontaneous trait inferences. On the basis of studies by Smith and Miller (1983) and by Uleman (1987) and colleagues (e.g., Newman and Uleman, 1989), it is argued that when people read sentences such as 'The secretary solves the mystery', they spontaneously make a personality inference about the actor in the sentence as they are processing the sentence (e.g., that the secretary is clever). Such inferences are made automatically and therefore with little cognitive effort. According to the proponents of spontaneous inference, stage 3 processing is as automatic as stage 1 behaviour identification. They have developed an ingenious experimental procedure to demonstrate the spontaneity of trait inferences.

A cued-recall paradigm was used in which participants read sentences such as 'The secretary solved the mystery' and their later memory for these sentences was tested using cued recall. The cues were either personality traits that are strongly associated with these sentences (e.g., clever), or a word that is a strong semantic associate of some aspect of the sentence (e.g., typewriter, detective). It was consistently found that participants' recall of these sentences was better when given personality traits as cues than when given semantic associates as cues. Using the encoding hypothesis (Tulving and Thomson, 1973), it is argued that the personality inference that takes place when a sentence is being read serves as a retrieval cue for the sentence at recall. Because personality traits and not semantic associates produce better recall, it is argued that personality inferences must be being made at the time that the sentences were first read.

Although the results of these studies are not in doubt, the interpretation of these findings may be questioned. Claeys (1990) observed that in the spontaneous trait inference experiment, participants are described as making a personality inference on the basis of one piece of behavioural information and yet research in attribution theory suggests that most personality inferences are the result of a laborious process of causal analysis. For example, Kelley's (1973) attribution theory assumes that the consistency with which a behaviour is performed over a number of occasions is taken into account when making an attribution, as well as several other variables.

Claeys (1990) concluded that these studies have demonstrated the spontaneous categorisation of behaviour (i.e., stage 2 processing), and not the spontaneous categorisation of personality (i.e., stage 3 processing). To test this, he conducted a version of the experiment in which no actors appeared in the sentences, thus ensuring that only behavioural information was available – e.g., 'Carries someone's luggage up the stairs', for which the trait cue was helpful and the semantic cue was banister. If under these circumstances participants showed the recall advantage with traits as cues, then it could not be concluded that this effect was due to making personality inferences about the actors in the sentences, since actors were not specified. Such a finding would strengthen his view that all the previous studies were also demonstrating behaviour categorisation, not person categorisation.

Recall of verbs, objects and circumstances was better with trait cues than with semantic cues. Thus, this study replicated the past studies even though no actors were provided in the sentences, which makes it unlikely that participants were making personality inferences in this or the previous studies. This study underscores the importance of being clear about which use of the trait concept is under investigation. Interpreted in light of this study, the research on supposed spontaneous trait inference suggests that whereas observers may spontaneously categorise behaviour in trait terms, they do not typically spontaneously attribute personality traits to actors.

CONSTRUCTING PERSONALITY COHERENCE

People's behaviour is responsive to the demands of the situation (we are more talkative at a party than when attending a lecture). Consequently, people can appear to behave inconsistently across different situations and across time. At one time, the empirical demonstration of behavioural inconsistency threatened the validity of the concept of personality (Mischel, 1968). In response, personality psychology became more sophisticated in its approach to consistency. Conceptual and empirical developments now support the notion of personality coherence (Heatherton and Weinberger, 1994). Coherence accommodates behavioural inconsistencies across time and across situations by looking for patterns of consistent and inconsistent behaviour. For example, it is coherent for a person to be dominant at work but submissive at home. It is coherent over the course of her life for a woman to become more nurturing during child raising and more assertive of her own needs in middle age.

Inconsistencies make for a multidimensional picture of a person instead of a one or two dimensional view. Real people and good fictional characters are a complex blend of attractive and less attractive qualities and, at times, they behave in conflicting and even contradictory ways. The challenge for the observer (and the self-observer), is to make sense of the inconsistencies. There are various methods for studying coherence. The narrative approach to the study of persons (McAdams, 1993) explores the way people make sense of their lives by constructing their life stories. This approach is concerned with coherence at a broad level (e.g., how does two years working as a waiter fit with my image as a career scientist?). At the other extreme, we can focus on very specific instances of inconsistencies and study how people resolve them. For example, how do people construct personality impressions from inconsistent trait information?

A series of studies of people's use of inconsistent traits in descriptions of themselves and others, and of their strategies for resolving inconsistent traits presented to them as target descriptions, indicates that the three-stage model of person perception may render trait inconsistencies coherent (e.g., Casselden and Hampson, 1990; Hampson, in press). These studies have shown that when people describe themselves or liked others using lists of traits, up to about 20 per cent of their trait attributions can be inconsistent. We have compared participants' use of different kinds of inconsistent pairs, and we have found that some types of inconsistency are more likely than others. Participants are more likely to use ones that are evaluatively consistent (both desirable qualities) but that refer to inconsistent actions (e.g., daring and cautious) than they are to use ones that are evaluatively inconsistent (one desirable and one undesirable) but describe similar actions (e.g., daring and reckless). Participants are least likely to describe themselves with inconsistent trait pairs that are both descriptively and evaluatively inconsistent (e.g., daring and timid, or cautious and reckless). When asked to explain why they used descriptively inconsistent traits in their descriptions, participants strongly favoured a situational account: people are different in different situations. Participants were not concerned about the contradictory behaviours that their inconsistent use of traits implied. These contradictions could be explained by situational determinants of behaviour. What mattered most was to maintain the overall integrity of the positivity of the impression. In terms of the three-stage model, participants were describing familiar targets (themselves and liked others) that previously they had processed to stage 3. They had constructed personality impressions that reflected their overall positive evaluation of themselves and their friends. From earlier research (John et al., 1991) we know that the broadest level of personality description is almost purely evaluative (e.g., good, nice). These traits are very imprecise for predicting specific behaviours, but they do tell us to expect socially desirable behaviours. Because of their imprecision, such extremely broad traits were not favoured in personality descriptions. Participants were more likely to use somewhat less broad traits that are more informative (i.e., basic level traits). However, this tendency to use basic level traits in descriptions was moderated when describing a negative aspect of the person. In this case, participants used an even more precise (narrow) trait that referred to a circumscribed aspect of behaviour (e.g., unpunctual or untidy). In this way, they minimised the impact of the inconsistent, negative trait that threatened the overall coherence of the impression. With regard to the studies of inconsistent trait use, participants aimed to maintain their overall positive evaluation of the target at the expense of some behavioural inconsistency. In effect, they were using the inconsistent traits as descriptions of behaviour (stage 2), which they explained were often determined by situational factors. In this way, these inconsistencies did not threaten the integrity of the overall positive view of themselves or their friends (stage 3). Their dispositional attributions of nice and good people remained intact. The interesting lesson from these studies is that observers and self-observers appear not to be particularly bothered by behavioural inconsistency. What does bother them is inconsistency in terms of evaluation. It is far more difficult to accommodate a person being both good and bad than it is to see coherence in a person being good in contradictory ways (daring and cautious), or bad in contradictory ways (reckless and timid).

SUMMARY AND CONCLUSIONS

This chapter began by describing a constructivist model of personality, in which personality is viewed as a construction based on three components: the actor, the observer and the self-observer. The similarities and differences between the constructivist view of personality and social constructionism were discussed. The constructivist view of personality integrates personality and social psychology by linking the social-cognitive processes of person perception to the concept of personality. This point was elaborated in a discussion of the observer component. A three-stage model of person-perception processes was proposed (behaviour identification, act categorisation and personality attribution), incorporating the two uses of traits (as descriptions of behaviours and as descriptions of persons). This distinction between using traits for act categorisation or dispositional attribution has been illuminating for at least two lines of research in person perception. It resolves the incompatibility between attribution theory and the claim that trait inferences are made spontaneously: the former is concerned with person description whereas the latter is concerned with behaviour description. It also explains how coherent impressions are maintained in the face of inconsistency. People are willing to use inconsistent traits to describe inconsistent behaviours, so long as the overall, evaluative, dispositional attribution is not threatened.

The focus has been on the observer in personality construction, with emphasis given to a model of the processes used by the observer in perceiving another person. In particular, this discussion has examined the use of traits in personality perception. Although concentrating on the observer, it is important not to lose sight of the other components in the construction of personality, the actor and the self-observer. Constructed personality is the product of all three. The actor provides the raw behaviour which forms the input for the observer to process via the three-stage model. The processes by which the self-observer constructs an impression of her or himself include stages two and three of the model: we categorise our own acts and we attribute dispositions to ourselves. However, the unique feature of the self-observer is our capacity to think about the impression the observer is forming of us, and to use this information to shape our actions. The unravelling of these complex processes involves integrating the concept of personality with other aspects of social and clinical psychology than those presented here.

ACKNOWLEDGEMENTS

The writing of this chapter was supported, in part, by a grant from the National Science Foundation of the United States of America, Grant Number SBR-9209986. Sections of the chapter are based on two invited lectures that I gave in honour of Willem Claeys, at the University of Leuven, Belgium in March 1993.

REFERENCES

Bassili, J.A. and Smith, M.C. (1986) 'On the spontaneity of trait attribution: converging evidence for the role of cognitive strategy', *Journal of Personality and Social Psychology* 50: 239–245.

Baumeister, R.F. and Hutton, R.F. (1987) 'Self-presentation theory: self construction and audience pleasing', in B. Mullen and G.R. Goethals (eds) *Theories of Group Behaviour*, New York: Springer-Verlag.

Berger, P. and Luckmann, T. (1966) *The Social Construction of Reality: A Treatise in the Sociology of Knowledge*, New York: Doubleday and Co.

Borkenau, P. (1986) 'Toward an understanding of trait interrelations: acts as instances of several traits', *Journal of Personality and Social Psychology* 51: 371–381.

Brewer, M. B. (1988) 'A dual process model of impression formation', in T.K. Srull and R.S. Wyer, Jr. (eds) *Advances in Social Cognition (Vol. 1)*, Hillsdale, NJ: Erlbaum.

Burr, V. (1995) *An Introduction to Social Constructionism*, London: Routledge.

Casselden, P. A. and Hampson, S. E. (1990) 'Forming impressions from incongruent traits', *Journal of Personality and Social Psychology* 59: 353–62.

Claeys, W. (1990) 'On the spontaneity of behaviour categorisation and its implications for personality measurement', *European Journal of Personality* 4: 173–186.

Cooley, C.H. (1902) *Human Nature and the Social Order*, New York: Scribner.

Costa, P.T., Jr and McCrae, R.R. (1994) 'Set like plaster? Evidence for the stability of personality', in T.F. Heatherton and J.L. Weinberger (eds) *Can personality change?*, Washington, DC: American Psychological Association.

Digman, J.M. (1990) 'Personality structure: emergence of the five-factor model', *Annual Review of Psychology* 41: 417–440.

Fiske, S.T. and Neuberg, S.L. (1990) 'A continuum of impression formation, from category-based to individuating processes: influences of information and motivation on intention and interpretation', in M.P. Zanna (ed.) *Advances in Experimental Social Psychology (Vol. 23)*, New York: Academic Press.

Fiske, S.T. and Taylor, S.E. (1991) *Social Cognition*, New York: McGraw Hill.

Greenwood, J.D. (1991) *Relations and Representations: An Introduction to the Philosophy of Social Psychological Science*, London: Routledge.

Hampson, S.E. (1988) *The Construction of Personality: An Introduction*, London: Routledge.

—— (1992) 'The emergence of personality; a broader context for biological perspectives', in A. Gale and M.W. Eysenck (eds) *Handbook of Individual Differences: Biological Perspectives*, London: Wiley.

—— (1995) 'The construction of personality', in S.E. Hampson and A.M. Coleman (eds) *Individual Differences and Personality*, London: Longman.

Hampson, S.E. (in press) 'When is an inconsistency not an inconsistency? Trait reconciliation process in personality description and impression formation' *Journal of Personality and Social Psychology*.

Hampson, S.E., Goldberg, L.R. and John, O.P. (1987) 'Category-breadth and social-desirability values for 573 personality terms', *European Journal of Personality* 1: 241–258.

Hampson, S.E., John, O.P. and Goldberg, L.R. (1986) 'Category breadth and hierarchical structure in personality: studies of asymmetries in judgements of trait implications', *Journal of Personality and Social Psychology* 51: 37–54.

Heatherton, T.F. and Weinberger, J.L. (eds) (1994) *Can Personality Change?*, Washington, DC: American Psychological Association.

James, W. (1890) *Principles of Psychology*, New York: Holt.

Johansson, G. (1975) 'Visual motion perception', *Scientific American* 232: 76–88.

John, O.P., Hampson, S.E. and Goldberg, L.R. (1991) 'The basic level in personality-trait hierarchies: studies of trait use and accessibility in different contexts', *Journal of Personality and Social Psychology* 60: 348–361.

Jones, E.E. and Davis, K.E. (1965) 'From acts to dispositions: the attribution process in person perception', in L. Berkowitz (ed.) *Advances in Experimental Social Psychology, Vol. 2*, New York: Academic Press.

Kelley, H.H. (1967) 'Attribution theory in social psychology', in D. Levine (ed.) *Nebraska Symposium on Motivation (Vol. 15)*, Lincoln, NB: University of Nebraska Press.

—— (1973) 'The process of causal attribution', *American Psychologist* 28: 107–128.

Kenny, D.A. (1994) *Interpersonal Perception: A Social Relations Analysis*, New York: Guilford Press.

Loehlin, J.C. (1992) *Genes and Environment in Personality Development*, Newbury Park, CA: Sage.

Logan, G.D. (1989) 'Automaticity and cognitive control', in J.S. Uleman and J.A. Bargh (eds) *Unintended Thought*, New York: Guilford Press.

McAdams, D.P. (1993) *Stories We Live By: Personal Myths and the Making of the Self*, New York: William Morrow.

McCrae, R.R. and Costa, P.T. (1995) 'Trait explanation in personality psychology', *European Journal of Personality* 9: 321–252.

Mead, G.H. (1934) *Mind, Self, and Society,* Chicago, University of Chicago Press.

Mischel, W. (1968) *Personality and Assessment,* New York, Wiley.

Neisser, U. (1976) *Cognition and Reality,* San Francisco: Freeman.

Newman, L.S. and Uleman, J.S. (1989) 'Spontaneous trait inference', in J.S. Uleman and J.A. Bargh (eds) *Unintended Thought,* New York: Guilford Press.

Pittinger, J.B. and Shaw, R.E. (1975) 'Ageing faces as viscal-elastic events: implications for a theory of non-rigid shape perception', *Journal of Experimental Psychology: Human Perception and Performance* 1: 374–382.

Potter, J. and Wetherell, M. (1987) *Discourse and Social Psychology: Beyond Attitudes and Behaviour,* London: Sage.

Reeder, G.D. and Brewer, M.B. (1979) 'A schematic model of dispositional attribution in interpersonal perception', *Psychological Review* 86: 61–79.

Rosch, E., Mervis, C.B., Gray, W.D., Johnson, D. and Boyes-Braem, P. (1976) 'Basic objects in natural categories', *Cognitive Psychology* 8: 382–439.

Rosenfeld, P., Giacalone, R.A. and Riordan, C.A. (1995) *Impression Management in Organisations: Theory, Measurement, Practice,* London: Routledge.

Ross, L. (1977) 'The intuitive psychologist and his shortcomings: distortions in the attribution process', in L. Berkowitz (ed.) *Advances in Experimental Social Psychology, vol.10,* New York: Academic Press.

Schlenker, B.R. and Weigold, M.F. (1992) 'Interpersonal processes involving impression regulation and management', *Annual Review of Psychology* 43: 133–168.

Shweder, R.A. (1982) 'Fact and artifact in trait perception: the systematic distortion hypothesis', in B.A. Maher and W.B. Maher (eds) *Progress in Experimental Psychology Research Vol. 11,* New York: Academic Press.

Smith, E.R. (1988) 'Category accessibility effects in simulated exemplar-based memory', *Journal of Experimental Social Psychology* 24: 448–463.

Smith, E.R. and Miller, F.D. (1983) 'Mediation among attributional inferences and comprehension processes: initial findings and a general method', *Journal of Personality and Social Psychology* 52: 653–662.

Smith, E.R. and Zárate, M.A. (1992) 'Exemplar-based model of social judgement', *Psychological Review* 99: 3–21.

Snyder, M. (1987) *Public Appearances, Private Realities: The Psychology of Self-Monitoring,* New York: W.H. Freeman.

Sullivan, H.S. (1953) *The Interpersonal Theory of Psychiatry,* New York: Norton.

Trope, Y. and Liberman, A. (1993) 'The use of trait conceptions to identify other people's behavior and to draw inferences about their personalities', *Personality and Social Psychology Bulletin* 19: 553–562.

Tulving, E.E. and Thomson, D.M. (1973) 'Encoding specificity and retrieval processes in episodic memory', *Psychological Bulletin* 30: 352–373.

Uleman, J.S. (1987) 'Consciousness and control: the case of spontaneous trait inferences', *Personality and Social Psychology Bulletin* 13: 337–354.

Uleman, J.S. and Bargh, J.A. (eds) (1989) *Unintended Thought,* New York: Guilford Press.

Wong, P.T.P. and Weiner, B. (1981) 'When people ask "why" questions, and the heuristics of attributional search', *Journal of Personality and Social Psychology* 40: 650–663.

Chapter 6

Mood processes

Colin Cooper

This chapter focuses on mood *states* rather than personality *traits*. The distinction between these two concepts is less than clear-cut, however it is generally accepted that personality traits reflect how an individual generally behaves – their *personal style* – whereas state measures focus on how an individual feels at a particular instant: for example, fleeting moods of depression or anxiety. Trait psychology has received far more attention than the psychology of mood for it is very *useful* to know how an individual will generally behave, or what cognitive operations they will generally be able to perform: applications of trait psychology range from personnel selection and guidance to educational and clinical assessment. This stability of traits also makes the researcher's life straightforward: characteristics such as general ability or extraversion are there 'on tap' and can be used to test models of cognitive, genetic, biological or social processes following a single assessment. Research into mood processes is much more complex, and so I have divided the chapter into two sections. The first spells out in some detail *why* it is so very difficult to define and assess mood, examines which aspects of mood merit attention, and discusses the unrecognised drawbacks of some commonly used experimental designs. Finally, I examine some of the processes that seem to influence various aspects of mood.

THE PSYCHOMETRY OF MOOD

Because of the constancy of personality and ability traits it is fairly straightforward to correlate measures of traits with other variables (trait scores of identical twins, neural conduction velocities or whatever) to develop and test hypotheses about the biological, social and psychological processes that may cause the traits to appear.

There is now substantial agreement about at least some aspects of trait theory.

- The concept of trait is well understood and generally agreed. For example, the distinction between ability and temperament traits is both well accepted and supported by the experimental literature.
- The structure of ability and personality is widely agreed, despite some skirmishes about the relationship between Costa and McCrae's three minor factors, psychoticism and ability. Thus it is fairly straightforward (in principle) to devise and test hypotheses about the origins and development of traits, and to check whether each has a genetic and/or biological underpinning.
- Techniques for developing measures of traits through factor analysis, item analysis and item response theory are well understood, although there are wide variations in the methods of devising test items.
- The correlational techniques that are generally used in trait psychology are based upon large samples of individuals who are measured in unexceptional surroundings, which will have the effect of minimising any contamination of trait scores by mood states.
- Only one variable of interest can be derived from a scale measuring a trait – an estimate of the person's *level* of this trait. This is the only sensible dependent variable to be considered when understanding the processes underpinning personality or ability.

There is no such consensus of opinion in the mood literature, which seems to be at the same stage of development that personality theory had reached forty years ago. Definitions of mood and emotion are imprecise. The nature and number of the main mood states is not at all well understood. The most common technique of constructing mood scales makes it likely that at least some items may measure personality traits rather than mood states, although better methods of mood-scale construction have been advocated for decades. And whilst it is fairly obvious that one should use the *level* of the trait as the dependent variable when examining process models, with mood one can choose to study either the level, the average level, the variability or the time course of moods – or even exotica such as *affect intensity* (Diener *et al.*, 1985).

Not all of these problems are widely recognised even amongst mood theorists, and so they merit some elaboration. In addition, Paul Barrett has argued in this volume that it is pointless attempting to construct process models until there is a general consensus about the nature and structure of what is being measured. Thus it is necessary to explore these measurement issues in a little more detail before summarising what is known about basic mood processes.

The concept of mood

The very definition of the term 'mood' is controversial, particularly when it is contrasted with 'emotion'. Many authors (e.g., Izard, 1991, p. 21) speculate that moods are 'emotion[s] that endure', perhaps for months (Plutchik, 1994, p. 113), are less intense than emotions and may be 'tonic and not centred about an object or event' (Frijda, 1986). Apart from the problem that one has to produce a fairly watertight definition of 'emotion' in order to draw such distinctions, it seems that such a view has four major defects. First, by defining mood as being long-lived, emotion theorists sometimes seem to be reinventing the personality trait. For example, Isen (1984, p. 186) views 'irritability' not as a personality trait but as a type of mood. Second, it is not obvious how emotions can be measured separately from moods. When one looks at the scales used in experimental studies of emotions, it comes as some surprise to see that the old familiar mood scales are almost invari-ably used. Thus it seems there is no obvious way of operationalising the term 'emotion'. Third, the fine distinctions between mood and emotion seem to be based on armchair speculation rather than empirical evidence. For example, none of the authors cited above offer any experi-mental evidence about the time course of moods and emotions. Hard data from longitudinal studies show that in contrast to the views expressed above, moods are short-lived, lasting anywhere between thirty minutes (in adolescents) and three hours (Larson et al., 1980). Finally, it is not hard to think of counter-examples that call into doubt these fine distinctions between 'mood' and 'emotion'. An anxiety attack is like a mood in that it is not necessarily tied to any object, but like an emotion in that it may be short-lived. Feelings of sadness following the death of a loved one are long-lived (like a mood) but linked to a life event (as with emotions). I therefore join Bower (1981) and Watson and Tellegen (1985) who prefer to wield Occam's razor and use the terms 'emotion' and 'mood' interchangeably.

The distinction between mood and motivation is also problematical. Cattell (e.g., Cattell and Child, 1975) argues that mood states correspond to groups of psychological, cognitive, affective, physiological and other variables that happen to rise and fall together. For example, it may be found empirically that a feeling of restlessness is associated with increased perceptual vigilance and increased heart-rate. Thus they corre-spond to a mood state, which might be named 'anxiety'. Drives, on the other hand, are thought to direct behaviour. They may be inferred by discovering how people choose to spend their time and money, the areas in which they are knowledgeable (corrected for general ability) and other techniques designed to reveal unconscious aspects of motivation. About twenty such drives have emerged from Cattell's work, although these have not all been replicated and may be difficult to measure (Cooper and Kline, 1982). Emotion theorists generally disregard such a distinction between emotions and drives (Izard, 1991; Frijda, 1986; and Plutchik, 1994) with Plutchik describing Cattell's drives as 'basic emotions'. However it is not entirely obvious that drives such as desire to please one's partner, need for security, gregariousness or the desire to live according to religious principles (four of Cattell's drives) correspond in any simple way to affective experiences.

It also seems at least possible that some theories of arousal, such as that of Thayer (1978) may tap moods. 'Energetic arousal' (inferred from self-descriptions such as 'energetic', 'lively' and 'active') certainly *sounds* like positive affect whilst the items used to tap 'tense arousal' ('tense', 'fearful' and 'jittery') are amongst those used in other scales of negative affect. Thus it is no great surprise that McConville and Cooper (1992b) found that these items loaded on the main mood factors, and so Thayer's work could perhaps be regarded as providing evidence for mood (rather than arousal) theory.

In summary   The conceptual distinction between mood and emotion is not clear. Nor is there much empirical evidence to support any such distinction. Emotion theorists' equating of emotion and motivation runs counter to Cattell's psychometric model, and there is again little empirical evidence to show whether this is appropriate.

The structure of mood

There is a bewildering range of mood scales available, many of which have been designed for clinical applications. Thus whilst many inventories have been designed to measure depression, anxiety, hopelessness, 'negative affect' and the like, rather few have attempted to assess more pleasant moods, such as sociability, or *joie de vivre*. There are two problems with this rather haphazard approach to mapping the main dimensions of mood. First, it means that different investigators may have devised scales that measure the same construct, but may have labelled these constructs differently. One person's 'anxiety' may be equivalent to another theorist's 'state neuroticism', 'tense arousal' or 'negative affect', and this can create enormous confusion until the scale items are jointly factored to reveal the extent of their overlap. The second problem is that this *ad hoc* approach to constructing mood scales may leave certain important aspects of mood unmeasured. Apart from the work of Storm and Storm (1987) – which did not use factor analysis – and a little early work by Cattell mentioned in Cattell (1973), there has been little attempt to ensure that mood scales – even supposedly comprehensive ones – actually measure the full range of possible moods. Different mood theorists tend to use different samples of items and so discover different numbers of factors. Re-analysis of the correlations between mood scales (Watson and Tellegen, 1985) and hierarchical factor analyses of mood items drawn from the major mood scales, such as McConville and Cooper (1992b) reveal five primary mood factors (depression, hostility, fatigue, anxiety and extraversion) and two main second-order factors, corresponding to the factors of 'negative affect' (or state anxiety) and 'positive affect' (state extraversion) but others might well emerge from studies where the sampling of mood items is better controlled.

In summary   There is a desperate need to map the overlap between various scales and to agree how to name the main mood states. Positive affect (state extraversion) and negative affect (state anxiety) seem to be pervasive mood factors. However it is quite possible that some important aspects of mood remain unexplored.

The choice of dependent variable

Whereas a single measurement of personality defines the only aspect of the trait of any interest (its level), several different measures can be used to describe an individual's mood.

An individual's mean level of mood

Cattell's (1973 Ch. 6) data suggested that many personality traits have a corresponding mood state: that is, personality traits essentially correspond to averaged scores on mood scales. It is difficult to argue with this premise: someone who claims to be highly anxious all the time (high trait anxiety) will, presumably, tend to show high state anxiety whenever this is measured. Indeed this is the basis of scales such as the State Trait Anxiety Inventory (Spielberger *et al.*, 1970). Factor-analytic studies such as Cooper and McConville (1989) show that Cattell's state-anxiety items load Watson and Tellegen's factor of *negative affect*, whilst items from Cattell's scale of state extraversion correspond to Watson and Tellegen's factor of *positive affect*. Thus negative affect corresponds to state anxiety (or neuroticism) and that positive affect corresponds to state extraversion, giving further support to the idea that the two main personality traits have corresponding mood states.

This implies that there is little point in examining correlates of people's average levels of such moods, since these scores will inevitably correspond to personality traits. Despite this, several studies do so – for example, correlating personality and average mood with entirely predictable results, as can be seen from any brief search of the literature.

Instead, I suggest that there are four other dependent variables that may be useful in determining the processes that underpin mood.

A single measure of mood from individuals

Whether such studies are useful depends entirely on what is done with the data. There are three main possibilities.

- The comparison of the once-measured mood scores of two or more groups of participants – e.g., the influence of drug vs. placebo on mood, using a t-test to compare the once-measured moods of two groups of individuals. Here individual differences in personality will not confound differences in mood, but will simply appear as error variance, and so the results will be meaningful.
- The correlation of once-measured mood with other things – e.g., the correlation between scores on a mood scale and neurotransmitter levels. If Cattell's argument that personality traits correspond to mean levels of mood is correct, any study that *correlates* once-measured mood with other variables is likely to show up any relationship between *personality* and these variables. Such designs may not be helpful in revealing the processes that underlie mood.
- Tables of norms are not useful for interpreting individual scores on mood scales – e.g., establishing whether a score of 20 on the State Trait Anxiety scale is in any sense 'extreme'. Cooper and McConville (1990) argue that such interpretations will inevitably be confounded by the very substantial individual differences in mood variability that are found. Furthermore, in many cases one would want to know whether an individual is more or less anxious *than usual* – an ipsatised measure.

Measures of mood change within individuals

Using measures of mood change in a repeated measures design (e.g., mood scores before and after a clinical intervention) will allow the influence of the independent variable(s) to be assessed without the confounding effect of personality traits. However, it may be advisable to consider just the sign of the change rather than its magnitude. The results will otherwise be confounded by individual differences in mood variability (discussed below).

Studies of mood variability

Many studies (e.g., Wessman and Ricks, 1966) have found that whereas some people's moods stay stable over time, others show substantial variability in mood levels. Furthermore, the degree of variability shown by an individual is similar for all moods (McConville and Cooper, 1992a), suggesting that mood variability is an important characteristic of the individual that accounts for at least 25 per cent of the variation in the day-to-day mood scores of people living unexceptional lives. Its correlates and underlying processes thus deserve examination.

The time course of moods

There are two obvious aspects of the time course of moods that merit study. First, time-series analysis may be used to detect periodic fluctuations in mood level that may be caused either by some 'biological clock', or by regular life events (such as relaxation at weekends). The second technique might involve the analysis of the latency of mood shifts following significant life events. For example, if an individual's habitual level of a mood is known and this mood is monitored frequently following some life event or intervention, statistics such as: the time for the mood to rise to half its peak level; and the time taken for a mood to return to a point halfway between its peak and its habitual value (or the integral of this value) might be useful as dependent measures. The former would show the latency between life events and mood change. The latter would show the rate at which the mood returns to its habitual level.

In summary   Mood researchers have several dependent variables and experimental designs to choose from. It is argued that several of these may say more about personality processes than mood processes, whilst others may be confounded by individual differences in mood variability. Dependent variables that merit study include the analysis of once-measured mood from groups of individuals, measures of mood change within individuals, mood variability, and the time course of mood change.

Measuring mood unconfounded by personality

Most mood scales are constructed by identifying groups of items that form a factor when administered on one occasion to a large sample of people. Since this is precisely the same technique that is used to develop scales measuring personality traits, it is entirely possible that the most popular mood scales may measure personality traits rather than states. Cattell (1973) identified this problem long ago, and suggested that mood scales should be developed using longitudinal studies. Here mood states are identified through noting which variables rise and fall together over time ('P-technique'), or by identifying items that tend to change together when a mood scale is administered on two occasions to a large sample ('dR technique') – two simple and entirely sensible suggestions that have been almost totally ignored.

The extension of multi-method-multi-trait designs to mood states has similarly been ignored in the literature: mood states should ideally be found in different types of data (e.g., those arising from behavioural ratings or physiological measures) as well as in self-report questionnaires to guard against the possibility that scale scores are artefacts (caused, for example, by the sampling of a very narrow sample of items with considerable semantic overlap, or by demand characteristics) rather than genuine measures of pervasive mood states.

More generally, it is not obvious that any mood scale can possibly measure mood unconfounded by personality. It may be useful to think of scores on mood scales as representing two quite distinct characteristics: the habitual level of mood (or level of personality) upon which is superimposed the mood proper. In other words, level of mood should be defined relative to an individual's habitual level. Doing so will allow the effects of mood to be disentangled from the effects of personality. Two individuals could have the same score on a mood scale yet one could be two standard deviations below and the other three standard deviations above their habitual level of mood. It is difficult to think of any circumstance in which these two individuals' scores should be treated as identical.

It was argued in the previous section that the trait and pure state components of mood can be disentangled through the use of repeated measures ANOVA, the computation of difference-scores, the use of mean-mood scores as covariates, or partialling out habitual mood (or trait) scores from correlations. For example, it would be a simple matter to regress scores on the Trait Anxiety scale of the STAI onto mean levels of state anxiety from the STAI (obtained through sampling moods on many occasions) for a large sample of people. Assuming that the multiple-R was acceptable this would allow mean state-anxiety scores (the 'trait component' of the STAI state score) to be estimated for each new individual who is given both the trait and state versions of the test. A lookup table could be provided to translate trait anxiety scores into estimates of mean levels of state anxiety. This could then be subtracted from the person's state anxiety scores to yield pure state scores.

The fundamental point is that *some* attempt should be made to remove the influence of personality from measures of mood. In choosing to measure mood (e.g., state anxiety) on one occasion, rather than a personality trait (e.g., trait anxiety), the assumption is that there is something rather interesting about the particular occasion upon which mood is measured. One should otherwise assess the trait, rather than the state. For example, a therapist may be interested in determining whether levels of anxiety are high following some intervention, and so will really be interested in determining whether the individual's level of anxiety is appreciably lower than normal. Using the tables of norms of conventional mood scales tells the investigator whether or not an individual's score is much different from those of most people in most situations – and it is not entirely obvious why anyone should ever wish to know this. This point may seem obvious (and is implicitly acknowledged in many experimental designs, such as those discussed above) but it does not appear to have been made before in the literature.

In summary Mood scales are rarely constructed by the most appropriate methods. The techniques that are usually used make it quite probable that scales that purport to measure moods may actually measure (or be contaminated by) personality traits. Nor is it clear that the mood states that are inferred from questionnaires are equivalent to those identified by other methods, such as the analysis of behavioural ratings or physiological/biochemical data. I finally suggest that moods can most usefully be defined in terms of deviations from an individual's habitual mood level, which will correspond to a personality trait.

Overall conclusions

It is clear from the above analysis that much psychometric groundwork needs to be undertaken – for example, to develop tests that will measure the whole 'mood sphere' and produce a replicable and adequate model for the structure of mood. Next, it is important to identify those aspects of mood that could most usefully be studied: the analysis given above suggests that it is necessary to understand what causes the time-course of moods, their natural variability, and the processes that lead to differences in mood either within individuals or between groups. Finally, it is important that studies into mood processes should not be contaminated by individual differences in personality or other traits, and this can be achieved through following some of the designs discussed above, or by statistically controlling for such traits (e.g., through analysis of covariance). Based on the above analysis, I believe that the interesting issues in mood research involve understanding:

- processes that determine the time course of mood change
- processes that cause individual differences in mood variability
- processes that mediate mood change within individuals, or between groups.

EMPIRICAL STUDIES OF MOOD PROCESSES

The time course of moods

One process model of moods suggests that they are essentially periodic in nature. Shifts in mood might be determined in part by the ticking of some biological clock(s) whose location, mechanisms of operation and synchronisation and evolutionary significance remain to be explored. Although the literature shows several studies that examine the time course of moods, many of these are based on medical or clinical groups (e.g., those suffering pain from chronic rheumatism, or those diagnosed with bipolar disorder) or involve very small samples. The experimental design has a direct impact on the results that can be obtained, since it is necessary to sample moods at frequent intervals in order to detect high-frequency mood shifts. Since this typically involves completing a brief mood scale when signalled to do so by a radiopager or other alarm, the high-frequency sampling of moods rapidly becomes intrusive when attempted with 'normal' volunteers attempting to lead their natural lives. There is another problem with studies based on self-reports of people living well-ordered lives. Time of day is generally confounded with time of waking, and it is by no means simple to disentangle these two effects. Thus it is not always obvious whether diurnal shifts in mood are due to the ticking of some neural clock, or whether they are caused by fatigue or other features related to the length of time since waking.

In the brief review that follows I shall consider some of the modern experimental evidence for biological rhythms of increasing periodicity. Most studies involve administering mood questionnaires to a few individuals on many regularly spaced occasions, followed by time-series analysis to detect any periodic variation in mood level. Since inspection of graphs of mood level over time generally shows little evidence for irreversible transitions in mood level – for example, a sudden shift to a qualitatively different level/frequency of mood – chaos theory may not be appropriate for mood data.

There is little evidence for periodicity in the order of 1.5 hours – the daytime 'ultradian rhythm' originally postulated by sleep researchers (Neubauer and Freudenthaler, 1995), and although a 12-cycle-per-day rhythm has been found in Japanese undergraduates (Hayashi *et al.*, 1994), detailed inspection of the results shows that this affected self-evaluation and performance measures rather than mood. Several studies in the depression literature examine diurnal mood swings, but the decision to focus on a morning–evening cycle generally appears to be based more on theory than hard data from time-series analyses. An exception to this is the work of Clark, Watson and Leeka (1989) who found evidence for diurnal variation in positive affect, which rose to a maximum shortly after waking (whatever time of day this was). Negative affect showed no such periodicity. Boivin *et al.* (forthcoming) varied subjects' day-length for a period of some weeks in order to unconfound the effects of prior wakefulness and time of day on happiness and cheerfulness (although details of how and why these particular moods were assessed are not reported). They found that happiness was more closely tied to the circadian rhythm than to the time since waking. Cheerfulness showed a non-significant trend. Time since waking did however interact significantly with circadian rhythms to affect levels of both moods. Thus it seems that positive affect and happiness are influenced by both circadian rhythms and time since waking.

Evidence for seven-day mood swings – the 'Monday blues' – has been found in many studies (e.g., Larsen and Kasimatis, 1990) although evidence for the *biological* basis of the seven-day rhythm seems less than compelling. Weekly variations in urine salts or blood biochemistry may reflect social consequences of *'le Weekend'* (e.g., changed social, eating, drinking or sleeping habits) rather than anything else. Larsen and Kasimatis' seven-day cycle seemed to account for some 40 per cent of the variation in daily 'hedonic tone', especially for introverts (because of their lower levels of sensation-seeking activities). Pies (1992) reached much the same conclusion, and Almagor and Ehrlich (1990) showed that both positive affect and negative affect varied according to a seven-day cycle with negative affect being approximately 150° out of phase from positive affect – though as intimated above such studies may say more about similarities in lifestyles than any biological control mechanisms. Studies of cyclicity in individuals whose lifestyle does not reflect the five-day working week (e.g., some shift-workers) may be useful in this regard.

The idea of a 28-day cyclical fluctuation in mood tied to the phases of the moon (hence 'lunatic') has its roots in antiquity. However Wilson and Tobacyk (1990) found that there was little evidence that such a cycle was substantially related to psychological distress as evidenced by the number of calls to a crisis centre helpline, a finding which is consistent with the other literature that they cite. The 28-day cycle explained only 1 per cent of the variation in the number of calls. Longer-term fluctuations in mood (e.g., Seasonal Affective Disorder) are generally assumed to reflect biochemical changes to seasonal changes, and so are not considered here as examples of pure biological processes.

In summary There is good evidence that moods such as positive affect vary according to a circadian rhythm. However the empirical literature does not offer compelling evidence for any other forms of cyclical variation in mood beyond those that may be caused by life events.

Mood variability

There is excellent evidence showing that the variability of mood is a stable characteristic of the individual (Emmons and King, 1989, Cooper and McConville, 1990, Wessman, 1979, Wessman and Ricks, 1966). Individual differences in this area can be extremely marked, as shown in Figure 6.1 (from McConville, 1992). This graph shows the level of positive affect (state extraversion) for two individuals who were tested each day for thirty days. One person shows quite dramatic mood swings from day to day, whereas the mood of the other individual is much more stable. Mood variability is typically estimated by calculating the standard deviation of each individual's daily scores. When several quite different moods are monitored in the same individuals, it is found that variability in one mood (e.g., positive affect) typically correlates over 0.5 with variability in other, quite different, moods – even before correcting for reliability, floor and ceiling effects, etc. (*ibid.*). Nor is it due to

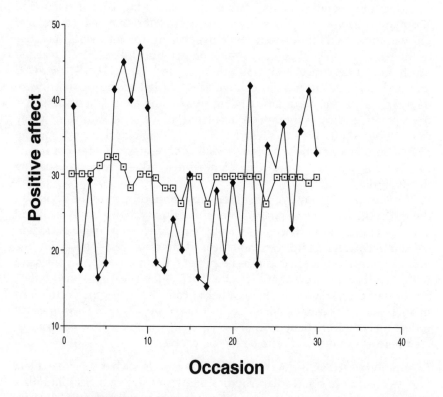

Figure 6.1 The daily positive-affect scores of a high-variability and a low-variability individual (McConville, 1992)

response-type artefacts such as the tendency to endorse extreme points on rating-scales (Cooper and McConville, 1990). Thus mood variability is an interesting characteristic of the individual – a trait whose origins should be investigated.

Diener *et al.*, (1985) have suggested that 'affect intensity' is preferable to the measurement of mood variability. This is a measure of 'the typical intensity with which individuals experience their emotions' (Larsen and Diener, 1987), which is supposed to be the same for all moods. Although this is a popular approach, Cooper and McConville (1993) showed that the whole concept is psychometrically flawed, and so it will not be discussed further.

Several studies have attempted to link individual differences in mood variability to personality, with rather inconsistent results. Eysenck and Eysenck (1985) suggest that high mood variability should be a consequence of high scores on neuroticism and extraversion, which is essentially what has been found by some researchers (Williams, 1990; Hepburn and Eysenck, 1989), although others (McConville and Cooper, 1992a; Howarth and Zumbo, 1989; Wessman and Ricks, 1966) could not discern such a relationship. McConville and Cooper (1992a) instead suggested that psychoticism affects mood variability – possibly because of its relation to impulsiveness, which Hepburn and Eysenck (1989) also found to be related to mood variability.

Levels of depression are associated with high mood variability in both normal (Larsen and Kasimatis, 1990; McConville and Cooper, 1996) and clinically depressed groups (Hall *et al.*, 1991) which is in strange contrast to the DSM definitions that would seem to suggest that flattening of affect (i.e., low variability) is a concomitant of depression. Lithium seems to both stabilise mood and reduce levels of depression in clinical and normal groups and so it seems likely that levels of depression and mood variability are linked, but it is not at all clear which (if either) of these variables is causal. The literature showing that mood stabilising drugs can also be effective in alleviating depression (e.g., Lynn, 1995) suggests that studies into the links between mechanisms that influence mood variability and mood level may be of some clinical interest.

Rather than trying to explain mood variability in terms of personality processes, a more parsimonious explanation may be that life-events affect mood variability. Some individuals may actively seek out intensely stimulating situations of every kind, and for this reason may show a higher degree of mood variability than those who lead ordered, uneventful lives. Experience-sampling techniques ask volunteers to carry a palmtop computer (or a radiopager and a stack of questionnaires) with them whilst carrying on their normal lives. They complete mood scales and some sort of behavioural log, such as the Experience Sampling Form (Csikszentmihalyi and Larson, 1987) when signalled to do so, allowing the impact of situation on mood to be determined. McConville (1992) reports one such study that was performed to determine whether individuals who showed highly variable moods simply led more varied lives than those whose moods remained stable. Seventeen volunteers were each paged seven times on each of five days, and thirty times on one day. The results showed that each person's variability of negative affect stayed more or less constant across the situations when these collapsed into three categories as recommended by Csikszentmihalyi and Larson (1987). Positive affect, on the other hand, varied appreciably more when taking part in 'maintenance activities' such as washing, eating, travelling to/from work and queuing than when working (attending lectures, reading, writing etc.). The other comparisons were not significant. Thus it seems probable that situational effects will be unable to explain fully individual differences in mood variability.

In summary   Mood variability seems to be a stable characteristic that describes how individuals habitually experience emotion: if this is reflected in behaviour then it seems reasonable to regard mood variability as a type of personality trait, perhaps reflecting some regulatory mechanism. Trait descriptors such as 'fiery', 'controlled' 'emotional' or 'constant' would seem to describe mood variability, and so it might be expected that this characteristic should have clear roots in the personality system. Much of the evidence is, however, inconclusive, with each of Eysenck's three main superfactors being found by some researchers (but not by others) to be related to mood variability. Quite why this is so is less than clear: differences in the statistical power of the various studies are unlikely to explain their divergence. It might be that a factor of mood variability exists, but that self-report measures cannot adequately measure it. This seems unlikely, given the trait descriptors discussed above. There seem to be no major technical flaws in the studies cited above which could account for this lack of correspondence. Or mood variability may perhaps be controlled by some physiological mechanism which is completely independent of those whose behavioural manifestations result in extraversion, neuroticism and psychoticism.

Mood change within individuals and between groups of individuals

A bewildering variety of substances and events can produce changes in mood. The onset or offset of life-events, clinical interventions, a huge range of chemicals when ingested, neurotransmitter levels, thoughts, perceptions, electrical stimulation of brain centres, exercise . . . the list is almost endless. Even a superficial review would require far more space than is available here, and such a review would also not be particularly useful for understanding mood *processes*, since to do so requires not just a list of mood-inducing events but some understanding of their interrelationship. Although biochemical assays before and after interventions such as exercise or drug therapy have been invaluable in identifying some mood processes (such as the role of the endorphins and catecholamines) it should be noted that:

- it will be difficult to formulate a comprehensive model until there is good agreement about the main factors of mood, especially when some otherwise elegant research is based on rather unsatisfactory measures of mood
- there may be problems in generalising from animal studies (in which the dependent variable is necessarily behavioural or physiological) to human studies, where self-reports of emotional states will be important
- it is not always clear which metabolic product(s) of a particular chemical influence mood
- since so many factors can influence moods, univariate or multivariate experiments in this area must control or assess a very large number of potentially confounding variables.

What *is* clear from the literature is that there are not just a few neurochemical pathways, corresponding to the main mood factors. Thus one cannot say that one experiences positive affect (for example) as a necessary consequence of some biochemical changes in some brain mechanism, as with Eysenck's biological model of personality (Eysenck, 1967).

There is little doubt about the impact of naturally occurring life-events on mood in 'normal' individuals (Warr *et al.*, 1983; Emmons *et al.*, 1986). 'Hassles theory', too, shows that apparently trivial life-events (such as missing a train or forgetting an umbrella) can have a profound effect on mood. The Velten technique and its variants (using depressing phrases, music or video-clips to induce negative moods) is effective in some – but not all – people (Martin, 1990). It is also frequently claimed that psychological mechanisms can ameliorate the effect of these stressors – e.g., theories of threat appraisal and coping (Folkman and Lazarus, 1980), and that self-regulation of mood is possible (Thayer *et al.*, 1994). The very fact that such a huge range of cognitively mediated life-events can influence mood is a partial explanation of the phenomenon of mood change: what is not always clear is how, precisely, such cognitions and appraisals lead to changes in affect as the huge bulk of research into the physiological correlates of mood has concentrated (for obvious reasons) on depressed mood, and various clinical groups.

Morris (1985) has suggested that it may be possible to regard mood disorders such as clinical depression as being quantitatively rather than qualitatively different from 'normal' moods (the *continuity hypothesis*). Clinical depression is like depressed mood, only more so: it may thus share at least some of the same underlying physiological and psychological mechanisms. This wonderfully parsimonious suggestion has some empirical support from studies showing that the mood-altering drugs prescribed for clinical groups frequently show similar effects in 'normal' volunteers (e.g., Calil *et al.*, 1990).

Although a bewildering variety of agents are implicated in mood change (ranging from elements such as selenium to neurotransmitters) the clinical models would at least provide a starting-point to explore the mechanisms of normal mood change. For whilst the biological basis of mood change has also been examined in non-clinical samples (e.g., Vaernes and Darragh, 1982), the great bulk of evidence is – for obvious reasons – based on clinical samples. We have found that the very mention of the continuity hypothesis can reduce reviewers almost to apoplexy, which seems a shame, since it would be useful to be able to draw on the clinical literature when investigating 'normal' mood processes. It would be invaluable if psychopharmacologists could reach some conclusion about the merits of the continuity hypothesis for various mood states.

CONCLUSIONS

Several methodological issues bedevil attempts to understand the processes that underpin mood. These include little agreement about the number and nature of the main dimensions of mood in normal people, problems in defining precisely what a mood *is*, and difficulties in assessing moods independently of personality traits. I have suggested that three main aspects of mood should be studied (their time course, their variability, and mechanisms of mood change) and comment that several experimental designs are singularly unsuited to the study of mood processes.

Given all these methodological and definitional problems, it is hardly surprising that our understanding of the basic mood processes is rudimentary in the extreme. The literature suggests little evidence for periodic changes in mood other than those caused by a 24-hour cycle: hypotheses about cyclic variation in moods due to biological clocks of other periodicities are less well supported by data. And whilst there is good evidence that the variability of moods is a stable feature of the individual – a trait – there is remarkable disagreement about the processes that may underpin such variations. Each of Eysenck's three main personality factors has been implicated by some researches, and found to be unrelated to mood variability by others.

The main problem encountered when reviewing the empirical

evidence concerns the utility of clinical models of mood disorder for explaining 'normal' mood processes – the continuity hypothesis. For there seems to be both a paucity of data about the biological concomitants of mood level in normal individuals and a reluctance to assume that processes that underlie mood disorders might also be involved in normal mood swings. In addition, although a huge range of cognitive variables are known to influence mood, the psychological and/or biochemical processes by which they operate are not always clear.

As intimated at the start of this chapter, the psychology of moods is not one of the better understood branches of individual differences, perhaps because of its lack of obvious relevance to applied psychology. Since there is little consensus about the nature of mood, let alone its structure, it is perhaps a little premature to expect any detailed model of normal mood processes to have emerged. Nor has it done so. Thus as well as examining the literature on mood processes, I have made some suggestions about how mood process research could usefully go forward. In particular, I have identified some dependent variables that could usefully be studied, and have drawn attention to the problems involved in assessing mood states independently of personality. It is to be hoped that some of these suggestions may be useful in clarifying and extending this intriguing field of study.

REFERENCES

Almagor, M. and Ehrlich, S. (1990) 'Personality correlates and cyclicity in positive and negative affect', *Psychological Reports* 66: 1,159–1,169.

Boivin, D.B., Czeisler, C.A., Dijk, D.-J., Duffy, J.F., Folkard, S., Minors, D.S., Totterdell, P. and Waterhouse, J.M. (forthcoming) 'Complex interaction of the sleep-wake cycle and circadian phase modulates mood in healthy subjects', *Archives of General Psychiatry*.

Bower, G.H. (1981) 'Mood and memory', *American Psychologist* 36: 129–148.

Calil, H.M., Zwicker, A.P. and Klepacz, S. (1990) 'The effects of lithium carbonate on healthy volunteers: mood stabilization?', *Biological Psychiatry* 27: 711–722.

Cattell, R.B. (1973) *Personality and Mood by Questionnaire*, San Francisco: Jossey-Bass.

Cattell, R.B. and Child, D. (1975) *Motivation and dynamic structure*, London: Holt, Rinehart and Winston.

Clark, L.A., Watson, D. and Leeka, J. (1989) 'Diurnal variation in the positive affects', *Motivation and emotion* 13: 205–234.

Cooper, C. and Kline, P. (1982) 'The internal structure of the Motivation Analysis Test', *British Journal of Educational Psychology* 52: 228–233.

Cooper, C. and McConville, C. (1989) 'The factorial equivalence of state anxiety: negative affect and state extraversion: positive affect', *Personality and Individual Differences* 10: 919–920.

—— (1990) 'Interpreting mood scores: clinical implications of individual differences in mood variability', *British Journal of Medical Psychology* 63: 215–225.

Cooper, C. and McConville, C. (1993) 'Affect intensity: factor or artifact', *Personality and Individual Differences* 14: 135–143.

Csikszentmihalyi, M. and Larson, R. (1987) 'Validity and reliability of the Experience Sampling Method', *Journal of Nervous and Mental Disease* 175: 526–536.

Diener, E., Larsen, R.J., Levine, S. and Emmons, R.A. (1985) 'Intensity and frequency: dimensions underlying positive and negative affect', *Journal of Personality and Social Psychology* 48: 1,253–1,265.

Emmons, R.A., Diener, E. and Larsen, R.J. (1986) 'Choice and avoidance of everyday situations and affect congruence: two models of reciprocal interactionism', *Journal of Personality and Social Psychology* 51: 815–826.

Emmons, R.A. and King, L.A. (1989) 'Personal striving differentiation and affective reactivity', *Journal of Personality and Social Psychology* 56: 478–484.

Eysenck, H.J. (1967) *The Biological Basis of Personality*, Springfield, IL: Charles C. Thomas.

Eysenck, H.J. and Eysenck, M.W. (1985) *Personality and Individual Differences*, New York: Plenum Press.

Folkman, S. and Lazarus, R.S. (1980) 'An analysis of coping in a middle-aged community sample', *Journal of Health and Social Behavior* 21: 219–239.

Frijda, N.H. (1986) *The Emotions*, Cambridge: Cambridge University Press.

Hall, D.P., Sing, H.C. and Romanowski, A.J. (1991) 'Identification and characterisation of greater mood variance in depression', *American Journal of Psychiatry* 148: 1,341–1,345.

Hayashi, M., Sato, K. and Hori, T. (1994) 'Ultradian rhythms in task performance, self-evaluation, and EEG activity', *Perceptual and Motor Skills* 79: 791–800.

Hepburn, L. and Eysenck, M.W. (1989) 'Personality, average mood and mood variability', *Personality and Individual Differences* 10: 975–983.

Howarth, E. and Zumbo, B.D. (1989) 'An empirical investigation of Eysenck's typology', *Journal of Research in Personality* 23: 343–353.

Isen, A.M. (1984) 'Towards understanding the role of affect in cognition', in R.S. Wyer and T.K. Srull (eds) *Handbook of Social Cognition*, Hillsdale, NJ: Erlbaum.

Izard, C.E. (1991) *The Psychology of Emotions*, New York: Plenum.

Larsen, R.J. and Diener, E. (1987) 'Affect intensity as an individual difference characteristic: a review', *Journal of Research in Personality* 21: 1–39.

Larsen, R.J. and Kasimatis, M. (1990) 'Individual differences in entrainment of mood to the weekly calendar', *Personality and Individual Differences* 58: 164–171.

Larson, R., Csikszentmihalyi, M. and Graef, R. (1980) 'Mood variability and the psychosocial adjustment of adolescents', *Journal of Youth and Adolescence* 9: 469–490.

Lynn, D.J. (1995) 'Lithium in steroid-induced depression', *British Journal of Psychiatry* 166: 264.

Martin, M. (1990) 'On the induction of moods', *Clinical Psychology Review* 10: 669–697.

McConville, C. (1992) 'Personality, motivational and situational influences on mood variability'. Thesis for the degree of Doctor of Philosophy, University of Ulster, Coleraine, County Londonderry, UK.

McConville, C. and Cooper, C. (1992a) 'Mood variability and personality', *Personality and Individual Differences* 13: 1,213–1,221.

—— (1992b) 'The structure of moods', *Personality and Individual Differences* 13: 909–919.

—— (1996) 'Mood variability and depression', *Current Psychology* 14: 329–338.

Morris, W.N. (1985) *Mood: The Frame of Mind*, New York: Springer-Verlag.

Neubauer, A.C. and Freudenthaler, H.H. (1995) 'Ultradian rhythms in cognitive performance: no evidence for a 1.5-h rhythm', *Biological Psychology* 40: 281–298.

Pies, R. (1992) 'Seven-day mood cycles', *American Journal of Psychiatry* 149: 418–419.

Plutchik, R. (1994) *The Psychology and Biology of Emotion*, New York: Harper Collins.

Spielberger, C.D., Gorsuch, R.L. and Lushene, R.E. (1970) *STAI Manual for the State Trait Inventory*, Palo Alto, CA: Consulting Psychologists Press.

Storm, C. and Storm, T. (1987) 'A taxonomic study of the vocabulary of emotions', *Journal of Personality and Social Psychology* 53: 805–816.

Thayer, R.E. (1978) 'Towards a psychological theory of multidimensional activation (arousal)', *Motivation and Emotion* 2: 1–34.

Thayer, R.E., Newman, J.R. and McClain, T.M. (1994) 'Self-regulation of mood', *Journal of Personality and Social Psychology* 67: 910–925.

Vaernes, R.J. and Darragh, A. (1982) 'Endocrine reactions and cognitive performance at 60 metres hyperbaric pressure: correlations with perceptual defense reactions', *Scandinavian Journal of Psychology* 23: 193–199.

Warr, P., Barter, J. and Brownbridge, G. (1983) 'On the independence of positive and negative affect', *Journal of Personality and Social Psychology* 44: 644–651.

Watson, D. and Tellegen, A. (1985) 'Towards a consensual structure of mood', *Psychological Bulletin* 98: 219–235.

Wessman, A.E. (1979) 'Moods: their personal dynamics and significance', in C.E. Izard (ed.) *Emotions in Personality and Psychopathology*, New York: Plenum.

Wessman, A.E. and Ricks, D.F. (1966) *Mood and Personality*, New York: Holt, Rinehart and Winston.

Williams, D.G. (1990) 'Effects of Psychoticism, Extraversion and Neuroticism in current mood: a statistical review of six studies', *Personality and Individual Differences* 11: 615–630.

Wilson, J.E. and Tobacyk, J.J. (1990) 'Lunar phases and crisis center telephone calls', *Journal of Social Psychology* 130: 47–51.

Chapter 7

The neurophysiology of *g*

Arthur R. Jensen

Although the origin of the idea that human mental ability has a physical substrate is lost in antiquity, scientific interest in the biological basis of mental ability was part of the Darwinian revolution in the mid-nineteenth century and coincident with the beginning of empirical psychology as a branch of natural science. Paul Broca (1824–80) discovered the localisation of functions in the cortex and actually *measured* individual differences in cranial capacity and brain size; Hermann von Helmholtz (1821–94) *measured* the velocity of nerve impulses in animals and humans. Francis Galton (1822–1911) *measured* individual differences in reaction time, simple sensory capacities and anthropometric variables, and sought their relation to variation in general mental ability, which then was only roughly estimated from educational and occupational attainments as the psychometric assessment of intelligence had to await Alfred Binet's (1857–1911) invention of the 'IQ test' in 1905.

Each of these lines of investigation has continued to the present, with a notably widening interest and a positively accelerating rate of research in recent years. The proliferation of scientific books and articles in the last decade alone is so overwhelming as to rule out a comprehensive review of specific studies within the limits of a single chapter. Fortunately, references to the many recent and fairly comprehensive reviews of the major topics in this field obviate having to cite a great many individual studies. Therefore, I shall attempt, not a review of research, but rather a broad overview of the whole domain and some of its main problems. The details of fact and argument are lost in this wide-angle picture, of course, but key references are cited to help readers pursue these at will. My particular overview, obviously, is but one of many possible ways of mapping this problem territory, each of which may perhaps have some heuristic value.

Although we already have a great many empirical facts, and neuroscience research is rapidly advancing, the field is still far from having anything like a consensus theory of the neurophysiology of higher mental processes. At present, no single theory of intelligent behaviour is capable of encompassing neurophysiological knowledge, the knowledge of cognitive processes gained in experimental cognitive psychology, and the structure of mental abilities provided by psychometrics and factor analysis. Our aerial view of this imposing domain resembles a huge, complex jigsaw puzzle; few of the pieces are assembled, most are unattached to any of the others, and the general chaos suggests some unknown number of pieces are probably missing.

Can all these separate pieces of this puzzle be fitted together to make a coherent picture? The science of relating intelligence to brain processes does not seem yet to have had its Linnaeus (to systematise the many disparate pieces), much less its Darwin (to explain their causal connections). The separate pieces of the brain/intelligence puzzle consist of the correlations between the diverse biological variables and IQ. Their causal connections are at best obscure and mostly unfathomed. Until a unified theory begins to take shape, we may go on adding separate new pieces to the puzzle – that is, new physical variables that are correlated with IQ – without being able to assess their functional significance.

DIVIDING THE DOMAIN

One way of simplifying the problem is to divide it conceptually into two distinct realms. The first realm deals with mental abilities in the structural (factor analytic) sense as sources of individual differences. Without reliable individual differences (or variance) in the human characteristics of interest, there can be no structure (in the psychometric sense). The science of this realm obviously has a purely behavioural base, consisting of people's conscious, intentional and overt responses to mental test items. Assuming there is a great deal of reliable (or true-score) variance in these responses, the correlations among a great many such responses made by large numbers of people, when the correlations are subjected to factor analysis, give rise to what psychometricians call the factor *structure* of mental abilities. As such, the whole operation need have no connection with neurophysiology or the workings of the brain. Its validity can be determined completely at the level of psychometrics. The results obtained at this level, though they may form a technically satisfying structural model with possibly useful validity for predicting behavioural outcomes such as scholastic or occupational achievement, are purely descriptive and not in the least explanatory. A structural model cannot by itself explain the *functional mechanisms* (neural structures and processes) of the observed abilities or the *cause of variance* in the observed abilities (or their covariances with one another). The crucial distinction I want to make is that the neurophysiological basis of *variance* in abilities might well involve researching different aspects of the brain than the discovery of the brain *mechanisms* responsible for the cognitive operations and behavioural manifestations we think of as constituting 'intelligence'. In other words, my working hypothesis is that whatever aspects of the brain are responsible for *individual differences* (and group differences) in 'intelligent' behaviour between all biologically normal *Homo sapiens* are causally different from those aspects of brain structure and function that constitute the essential neural design features of the brain that make intelligent behaviour possible in the first place. This conjecture, however, is no more than barely suggested by empirical evidence or theoretical preconceptions; it is proposed only as a possibly heuristic hypothesis.

Because a given phenomenon cannot explain itself, but must appeal for its explanation to another realm of phenomena, the explanation of many psychological behaviours is sought in correlated biological structures. Such biologically based explanations of psychological phenomena, often called *reductionism*, are often resisted (and even more often misunderstood) by psychologists and social scientists. This misunderstanding is a legacy of the mind–body dualism that bedevilled the prehistory of psychology. A lingering anti-reductionism still obscures and obstructs the scientifically worthy aim of attempting to relate brain and behaviour. The most common misconception about reductionism is that the recognition of phenomena observed at the 'lower' levels in the causal chain of reduction tends to diminish, negate or 'explain away' the phenomena of interest at the 'higher' levels, or the end products of the causal chain, which are usually of greatest interest to psychologists. Such crude reductionism is clearly seen as false, given the reality of unique emergent phenomena as we move from lower (or less complex) to higher (or more complex) levels of the explanatory hierarchy. An emergent phenomenon is every bit as real and at least as important as its constituent elements and underpinnings. A plane triangle, for example, though composed of three straight lines, is not *just* three lines, but has emergent properties that are unique to triangles (e.g., the trigonometric functions) that cannot be discovered (or even conceptualised) from a knowledge of unidimensional lines *per se*. Reducing water to its constituent elements results in two distinct gases, each with quite different properties from which the emergent properties of water could hardly be inferred. A general rule is that while elements and operations at a 'higher' level cannot violate the laws of a 'lower' level, they obey new laws that apply only to that higher level.

On a vastly greater scale, the elements of the brain have emergent properties. The functional units of the human brain are some 100 to 200 billion neurons with perhaps a trillion synaptic connections between them, constituting multiple systems, or systems within systems, and hierarchies of systems, each with unique emergent properties at each level of greater complexity. I refer to the properties dependent on higher levels of complexity as 'emergent' in order to emphasise that they need not be introduced into the system from somewhere outside the system.

Rather, they are intrinsic to the system, emerging uniquely from the hierarchy of increasing complexity of relationships among the elements of the system itself. The philosophic doctrine of dualism posits distinct entities, matter and mind (or soul), that supposedly interact with each other in producing the phenomena of consciousness, cognition, intelligent behaviour and other psychological phenomena. I regard this as anathema to the development of a natural science of brain–behaviour relationships. This point does not in the least imply that the system and its emergent properties in the individual are developmentally isolated from the influence of the physical environment and the behaviour of others. Early in individual development, neuronal systems, conceived statistically in terms of vast populations of neurons, are shaped to some extent by external influences and by truly random events, internal and external, as well as by genetic instructions – a quasi-stochastic process likened to Darwinian natural selection. The Nobel laureate Gerald Edelman (1987) coined the term 'neural Darwinism' to refer to neural explanations of behaviour that depend upon understanding the actions of neurons in terms of population sampling concepts involving the actions of countless numbers of neurons to produce any single outcome that could be characterised as behavioural. The intrinsic randomness implied by neural group selection from the populations of neurons during the developmental process insures variability and individuality in neural systems beyond that contributed by polygenic inheritance and learning. Thus even the brains of monozygotic twins, with identical heredity, do not have functionally identical 'wiring'.

The neurophysiological postulate

During mammalian evolution the Darwinian process of random variation and natural selection has shaped the physical characteristics of the organism, including the nervous system and the brain. This led to the emergence of any phenotypic characteristics, expressed as behavioural capacities, which under the conditions of the natural habitat have promoted survival of individuals. The anatomical and physiological underpinnings that made possible the behavioural characteristics favoured by natural selection were passed on genetically to successive generations. There is a remarkable continuity of essential structures and functions across all mammalian species. Many brain structures responsible for basic behaviour capacities are common to all normal members of every mammalian species. Among the most conspicuous characteristics of human beings is their great capacity for the modification of behaviour through individual experience, that is, learning and problem solving. This allows humans, more than any other species, far greater variation in the behaviour of individuals and of groups than could ever be predicted strictly from their biological heritage.

Yet, because of evolution, all mammalian brains are remarkably alike in their essential structure and physiology. The average between-species correlation (Pearson r) of the ten main structural divisions of the mammalian brain across 131 species is +.96 (Finlay and Darlington, 1995). This largest common factor in mammalian brains is therefore simply the difference in overall brain size. Variation in the relative sizes of the different structures accounts for only 8 per cent of the total variance. This implies that among biologically normal members of the human species, variation in brain structures and their *relative* sizes must be virtually nil. There is some variation in overall brain size, which in *Homo sapiens* has an approximately normal distribution with a mean of about 1,350 cm^3 and a standard deviation of about 150 cm^3. (About 5 per cent of this variance in individual brain sizes is associated with differences in body size.)

From an evolutionary perspective, it is most unlikely that there are intraspecies differences in the basic structural design and operating principles of the brain. If these main structural and functional units of the brain were studied only in one normal human being, the results would be validly generalisable to all other normal humans. That is to say, the processes by which the brain perceives, learns, remembers, and the like, are the same for everyone, just as are the essential structures and functions of every organ system in the entire body. Individual differences in normal brain processes exist at a different level, superimposed, as it were, over and above the common structures and operating principles.

My working hypothesis is that individual differences in behavioural capacities do not result from differences in the brain's structural operating mechanisms per se, but result entirely from other aspects of cerebral physiology that modify the sensitivity, efficiency and effectiveness of the basic information processes that mediate the individual's responses to certain aspects of the environment.

A crude analogy would be differences in the operating efficiency (e.g., miles per gallon, horsepower, maximum speed) of different makes of automobiles, all powered by internal combustion engines (hence the same operating mechanisms) but differing in, say, the number of cylinders, their cubic capacity and the octane rating of the petrol they use. Electric motor cars and steam-powered cars would have such different operating mechanisms that differences in their efficiency would need to have entirely different explanations.

I have therefore divided the study of the neurophysiology of intelligence into two parts. One part deals with the brain structures and neural processes that make possible the kinds of behaviour that we call intelligent. The other part examines the physical conditions that cause individual differences in intelligent behaviour. The first involves the structural modularity of specific brain functions; the second consists of some highly general brain functions that would account for the correlations among all the modular functions, that is, the correlations that are the basis of psychometric *g*. Dividing the problem this way has two worthwhile implications for research:

- the first part of the problem does not have to be completely solved before we can begin to answer the second
- a division of investigative labour can focus simultaneously on each of these two classes of brain phenomena. I suspect that the first aspect of the problem will prove to be much more difficult than the second.

BRAIN STRUCTURES AND NEURAL PROCESSES

Although the tremendous boom in brain research is making new and important discoveries almost daily, when it comes to explaining the psychological phenomena of thinking, problem solving and the mental abilities that especially distinguish what we call intelligence, the brain remains a seemingly inscrutable black box. All talk about the higher mental processes in terms of the brain and neurons remains hardly more than metaphorical. The precise localisations in the brain of various sensory and motor functions are well established, as are several mental functions associated with language (involving predominantly the left hemisphere) and certain other elemental functions related to intelligence, for example, attention and short-term memory (the prefrontal cortex and cortical association areas) and long-term memory (a subcortical structure at some distance, the hippocampus). Many brain modules serving more highly specialised functions, such as face recognition (localised in the right hemisphere) have been discovered (see Gazzaniga, 1989 and Posner *et al.*, 1988).

But localisation does not tell us what goes on in the brain to produce thinking, reasoning and the like, though many speculative models in the form of flow-charts, wiring diagrams, cell assemblies, neural networks, computer simulations and entities analogous to computer components have been suggested.

The prevailing and guiding hypothesis of modern neuroscience has been stated by Posner *et al.* (1988):

elementary operations forming the basis of cognitive analyses of human tasks are strictly localised. Many such local operations are involved in any cognitive task. A set of distributed brain areas must be orchestrated in the performance of even simple cognitive tasks. The task itself is not performed by any single area of the brain, but the operations that underlie the performance are strictly localised. This idea fits generally with many network theories in neuroscience and cognition.

But that

> most neuroscience network theories of higher processes provide little information on the specific computations performed at the nodes of the network, and most cognitive network models provide little or no information on the anatomy involved.
>
> (p. 1,627)

Research on the physiology of neurons, synapses and the working principles of neural circuitry is exceedingly far from explaining conscious thought, although a major aim of this line of research is to be able to express any theory of information processing in neural terms. This problem is now conceived of as requiring formulation in terms of population sampling of functional units among the brain's estimated 100 to 200 billion neurons that must interact with one another to produce even the simplest of mental phenomena. The problem is made even more complicated by the fact that, unlike a telephone switchboard or a digital computer, the neural system is not entirely 'hard-wired' but is shaped in part by early experience and neural action always retains a large amount of randomness. As Edelman (1988) has explained:

> In many ways, the brain does indeed behave like these systems (i.e., a telephone exchange or a computer). But when we look at certain detailed structural features and certain functional behaviours of the nervous system, the analogy breaks down, and we confront a series of problems the mutual implications of which amount to a series of interpretative crises for neuroscience. The *structural crises* are those of anatomy and development. Although the brain looks like a vast electrical network at one scale, at its most microscopic scale, it is not connected or arranged like any other natural or man-made network. The network of the brain is made during development by cellular movement, extensions, and connections of increasing numbers of neurons . . . It is an example of a self-organising system. *An examination of this system during its development and at its most microscopic ramifications after development indicates that precise point-to-point wiring cannot occur.* In general, therefore, uniquely specific connections cannot exist. If one numbered the branches of a neuron and correspondingly numbered the neurons it touched, the numbers would not correspond in any two individuals of a species – not even in identical twins or in genetically identical animals.
>
> (p. 182; italics Edelman's)

Edelman's (1987, 1993) theory of 'neuronal group selection' represents a major attempt to formulate the basic operating principles of neuronal action that could eventually explain the higher-order functions of the brain that are related to intelligence (such as perception, learning and memory) in empirically testable terms. Like every important new theory, however, it is still regarded as controversial and has been perhaps most trenchantly (but respectfully) criticised by another Nobel laureate, Francis Crick (1989). Edelman's theory is a structural one concerned with generalisable basic neural processes; it is not formally concerned with explaining individual differences at the behavioural level.

NEUROPHYSIOLOGICAL CAUSES OF INDIVIDUAL DIFFERENCES IN *G*

As I have argued elsewhere (Jensen, 1987a, 1994a), in considering individual differences in mental ability we should look at the structure of ability rather than puzzling over the nature of 'intelligence', which, from a scientific standpoint, has proved to be an exceedingly poor concept. After some 100 years, psychologists have not been able to reach agreement on a definition of it. So we should focus instead on the independent sources of variance among individuals revealed by the factor analysis of a wide variety of tests of mental abilities. The results of such analyses have been delineated in the three-strata hierarchical factor model of human abilities, which has been comprehensively explicated by John B. Carroll (1993). This factor model is the best way of viewing all the existing psychometric data.

In most large batteries of diverse tests, the *g* factor is usually the one independent source of variance that, by definition, is common to all the tests and is typically the single largest source of variance in the battery. Unlike all the group factors (also called primary factors, or first-order factors), the *g* factor cannot be described in terms of the type of information content of a test (e.g., verbal, spatial, numerical or mechanical). It is reflected by every kind of cognitive test that permits responses that can be scored or measured according to an objective standard (e.g., number of correct responses, response time). Also, *g* is a remarkably robust factor, in the sense that it is highly stable across different methods of factor analysis that allow extraction of a general factor from a correlation matrix (Jensen and Weng, 1994), and it is also consistent across different test batteries, provided they are composed of numerous and diverse subtests (Thorndike, 1987).

The most important reason for focusing on *g* in the present context, however, is that, of all psychometric factors, *g* has the largest number of anatomical and physiological correlates (Jensen, 1993; Jensen and Sinha, 1993).

Correlated vectors

One method that can be used to discover physical correlates of *g* specifically (rather than just some amalgam of various abilities) is the method of correlated vectors. This consists of extracting the g factor from a battery of at least ten or more diverse subtests (e.g., the Wechsler scales) and obtaining the column vector of the g loadings of each of the subtests, Vg. This essentially shows the size of the correlation between each test and g. Another vector is created by the correlations of each of the same subtests with some physical variable, P; call this vector VP. A significant correlation between Vg and VP unambiguously proves that the physical variable is related to g. (To ensure that differences in subtest reliabilities, which would similarly affect both the subtests' g loadings and the subtests' correlations with the physical variable, are not responsible for the correlation between Vg and VP the vector composed of the subtests' reliability coefficients, Vr_{xx} is partialed out.) This method of correlated vectors shows whether the physical variable is correlated with g independently of differences in the various subtests' reliability coefficients. This is a highly stringent test statistically, because the significance level of the correlation coefficient is based on the number of *subtests*. (Subject sample size affects the sampling error in the vectors.) The obtained correlation between Vg and VP, of course, does not itself indicate the magnitude of the relationship between *individual differences* in g and the physical variable, but it does prove the existence of a relationship between g and the physical variable with greater specificity and certainty than any other feasible method. Also, the upward sloping linear regression line of VP on Vg can be extrapolated out to the point on the abscissa where $g = 1$, as an estimate of the correlation between the physical variable and a hypothetical pure measure of g. To estimate the degree of relationship between the obtained measures themselves, one must resort to correlating individuals' g factor scores with the physical variable. The IQ obtained from standard test batteries is so highly correlated with g factor scores that, for most purposes, the IQ can be used instead of g factor scores.

Two types of correlation

Correlation between a physical variable and a psychological variable may be either *intrinsic* (and *functional*) or *incidental*. (This essential distinction and its methodology have been explicated in detail elsewhere: Jensen, 1980; Jensen and Sinha, 1993). The primary screening test for an intrinsic correlation is to determine whether it exists *within* families (i.e., among full siblings) rather than only *between* families (i.e., between the means of siblings across different families).

A *within*-families correlation is identified by calculating the correlation r_{ab} between (a) the signed differences between siblings' scores on a psychometric test (using age-standardised or age-regressed scores) and (b) the signed differences between siblings on age-regressed measures of the physical variable of interest. If the correlation is significant, it means that the psychometric variable and the physical variable co-vary among full siblings. That is, the sib with the higher IQ also has the higher physical trait, on average. The cause of this intrinsic covariance (or correlation) can be environmental (e.g., nutrition), or genetic, or both. (If the within-family correlation is genetic (or partially genetic), it is the result of *pleiotropy* – two phenotypically distinct traits being influenced by the same genes.) Whatever its cause, an intrinsic correlation indicates a functional connection between the mental and physical traits. If the physical × psychological correlation exists only between, and not within, families, it is *incidental*, and therefore does not represent a functional connection between the physical and psychological variable.

The between-families correlation (r_{cd} is the correlation between (c) the sum of siblings' (age-standardised) scores on the psychometric test and (d) the sum of the (age-standardised) measures on the physical variable. This kind of correlation, if not accompanied by a within-family correlation, is usually due to genetic heterogeneity of both the physical and the mental trait. Through cross-assortative mating for the two traits, the genes have become associated together within families in the population. But the two traits have no functional connection with each other and are not correlated genetically within families (i.e., among siblings). Many physical traits are correlated between families, but not within families. Among Europeans, for example, there is a between-families genetic correlation between eye colour and height, though there is no within-family correlation and no causal connection between these traits. Within-individual correlations between two traits (i.e., the usual correlation based on the measurements of unrelated individuals) can thus be decomposed into two components: between-families and within-families.

Before expending further research effort on a particular physical variable that is correlated with individual differences in a psychological trait, such as *g*, it should first be established that the correlation is intrinsic. The causal origins of incidental or non-pleiotropic genetic correlations between physical and behavioural traits may be of interest to evolutionists, anthropologists and sociologists, but such correlations are the most unlikely material for discovering the physical causes of individual differences in *g* or any other psychological variables. Even certain attributes of the brain itself, though showing individual differences that may be incidentally correlated with psychological differences, are not useful leads for research on the causal connections between brain and behaviour. On the other hand, a physical variable that is intrinsically or pleiotropically correlated with a psychological variable affords clues and leverage for research aimed at discovering the physiological basis of individual differences in the psychological trait.

Many studies of twins, adoptions and other kinships used in behavioural genetics to estimate the heritability of traits have shown that IQ is highly heritable (i.e., in the range of .60 to .80): see, for example, Nancy Pedersen's chapter in this volume. Recent research has shown that g, far more than any other factor, is responsible for the high heritability of IQ. When the method of correlated vectors was applied in one large twin study of the heritability of thirteen diverse subtests, the correlation between the vector of the subtests' g loadings, $\mathbf{V}g$, and the vector of the thirteen subtests' heritability coefficients was +.77; the g factor scores had a heritability of .81 (Pedersen et al., 1992). The higher heritability of g, as contrasted with that of other factors, indicates that it is a product of biological evolution and that it is this aspect of individual differences in human ability that is the most strongly linked to a physical substrate and therefore the most potentially fruitful for research on brain–behaviour connections in the cognitive domain. The high heritability of g also means that g cannot be explained solely in terms of knowledge and skills, which are a product of the interaction between an individual's experience and the brain mechanisms involved in conditioning and learning. In fact, as best as we can determine, the general factor in individual differences in learning is the same factor as psychometric g (Jensen, 1989).

Physical correlates of g: incidental or unknown status

Studies of virtually all of the known physical correlates of IQ and of g in normal persons are discussed in detail elsewhere (Eysenck, 1993; Eysenck and Barrett, 1985; Jensen and Sinha, 1993; Johnson, 1991; Vernon, 1990, 1993; Vernon and Mori, 1990). Most of the physical correlates of IQ have never been investigated with respect to the intrinsic–incidental distinction, so their importance as clues to brain processes that are causally related to IQ variance cannot yet be evaluated. The (within-individuals) correlations between these variables and IQ, though significant, are generally quite small, mostly in the range of .15 to .30. Variables showing positive correlations with IQ are: lighter eye colour, ability to curl one's tongue to form a tube, blood serum uric acid level (low correlation with IQ but much higher correlation with scholastic and occupational achievement), basal metabolic rate in children, vital capacity (the amount of air that can be inhaled), asthma and other allergies, inability to taste the synthetic chemical phenyl thiocarbamide, body's left-right midline symmetry, lower age of menarche. Also, several different blood groups and the Rh factor show significant correlations (either positive or negative) with IQ. (Studies reviewed by Jensen and Sinha, 1993.)

Stature is the only physical correlate of IQ that is quite certainly not an intrinsic correlation; there is no significant within-families correlation even in enormous and heterogeneous population samples, although a meta-analysis of virtually all studies shows a within-individuals correlation of +.23, which necessarily consists entirely of between-families variance.

Intrinsic physical correlates

These variables are determined to be intrinsic correlates of *g* either by their showing a significant within-family correlation or where a relationship has been demonstrated by manipulating the physical variable, either experimentally or through natural or accidental conditions such as brain pathology or trauma. Every one of the physical correlates listed below will eventually have to be integrated into a theory of the physical basis of individual differences in *g*.

a. Myopia   Near-sightedness, which is highly heritable, is a well-established correlate of IQ ($r \approx .25$) and appears to be a pleiotropic correlation (Cohn *et al.*, 1988). Beyond pleiotropy, the nature of the connection between myopia and IQ is as yet unknown. But the value of discovering that any physical variable is a pleiotropic correlate of *g* is that identification of the gene(s) for the physical trait also identifies a gene that contributes to variance in *g*; hence research on the ramifications of that gene's developmental effects can reveal its causal connection with mental ability.

b. Brain size and head size   Head size is not only a within-family correlate of IQ (Jensen and Johnson, 1994), but the method of correlated vectors has shown that the magnitudes of any subtest's *g* loadings predict ($r = +.64$) that subtest's correlation with head size (Jensen, 1994b). As external head size is correlated about +.50 with actual brain size, it has been used as a proxy for brain size in many studies of the IQ–brain relationship. But such indirect estimates of brain size are now being replaced by more accurate techniques such as magnetic resonance imaging (MRI). A meta-analysis of ten studies of the correlation between *in vivo* MRI-measured brain volume and IQ showed an overall correlation of +.36 (Rushton and Ankney, 1996). Why brain size is correlated with IQ is not yet known. It could be due to the total number of neurons, the amount of arborisation or dendritic branching, or the amount of non-neural structures, such as the myelin that covers the axons and the glial cells involved in the formation of myelin and the regulation of chemical neurotransmitters. (Einstein's brain was unusually rich in glial cells [Diamond *et al.*, 1985].) Any one, or a combination, of these features could account for the proportion of the variance in IQ that is associated with brain size.

c. Glucose metabolic rate   Glucose, a simple sugar, is the main fuel of brain metabolism. In positron emission tomography (PET) scans a small amount of radioactive glucose is injected into a person's vein. That person then engages in some form of mental effort for a definite period of time, such as taking a test. The PET scan then measures the brain's glucose metabolic rate (GMR) in different locations of the brain during the period of mental activity. Studies by Richard Haier and co-workers (Haier, 1993; Haier *et al.*, 1988, 1992; Larson *et al.*,1995) reveal the following: (1) Within individuals, GMR increases as a function of task difficulty, going from the easy to the more difficult items of a test of *g* (e.g., the Raven matrices). (2) Between individuals, high IQ subjects use less glucose to solve a particular problem compared with low IQ subjects. This suggests that IQ is related to the brain's *efficiency*. (3) Under the test condition, GMR is more localised in specific cortical regions in higher IQ subjects and is more diffusely spread over the cortex in lower IQ subjects. (4) When cognitive tasks of a particular type show improvement with prolonged practice, there is a corresponding decrease in the GMR while performing the task. (5) The method of correlated vectors applied to the eleven subtests of the Wechsler Adult Intelligence Scale shows that the column vector composed of the subtests' correlations with GMR is highly related ($r = -.79$) to the column vector of the subtests' *g* loadings. (The correlation is negative, because performance on each subtest is negatively correlated with GMR.)

d. Neuropsychology of mental speed   Mental speed, measured by a subject's median response time (RT) to an elementary cognitive task (ECT) over a number of trials, is now a well-established correlate of *g* (Jensen, 1993; Vernon, 1987). An even stronger correlate than average RT is intraindividual variability in RT, measured by the standard deviation of the subject's RTs over a given number of trials (Jensen, 1992). (This kind of mental speed is decidedly *not* the same as the speed of test-taking and clerical speed factor that emerges in the factor analyses of conventional psychometric tests.) Any theory of individual differences in the neurophysiology of mental ability must account for these facts. One approach to this goal is afforded by techniques for measuring the brain's electrical potentials.

e. Average evoked potential   There is a vast literature (reviewed by Deary and Caryl, 1993; Eysenck and Barrett, 1985; Haier *et al.*, 1983; Polich and Kok, 1995) on the average evoked potential (AEP). It shows that the latency and amplitude of the brain's electrical response to a visual or auditory stimulus are negatively correlated with IQ. Intraindividual variability in the latency of the AEP is also negatively correlated with IQ, while the complexity of the wave-form following the evoking stimulus is positively correlated with IQ. The method of correlated vectors shows that *g* is almost exclusively the active ingredient in these correlations; tests' *g* loadings are highly predictive (r between .80 and .95) of their correlations with AEP measurements (Jensen, 1987b). Moreover, AEP latencies parallel the subject's overt RTs to different ECTs (Schafer *et al.*, 1982).

f. Nerve conduction velocity   The centrality of mental speed indicated by the chronometric analysis of individual differences in mental ability suggests that the most elemental mechanism of mental speed, namely, nerve conduction velocity (NCV), might account for a part of *g* (Reed, 1984, 1988). Tests of this hypothesis based on NCV in peripheral nerves (the median nerve in the arm) have yielded contradictory findings, with two studies showing substantial positive correlations (r ≈ .40) between NCV and IQ (Vernon and Mori, 1992; Wickett and Vernon, 1994) and two studies showing near-zero correlations (Reed and Jensen, 1991; Rijsdijk *et al.*, 1995). The cause of the discrepant results of these technically sound studies remains obscure. A study of NCV in the visual tract from retina to the visual cortex, however, showed a significant correlation with fluid *g* (+.27, or +.36 after correction for range restriction) in 147 college males (Reed and Jensen, 1992). The further finding that both NCV and median RT to elementary cognitive tasks (ECTs) were both significantly correlated with fluid *g* but were not correlated with each other is theoretically problematic. One hypothesis is that there are individual differences in the particular neural pathways involved in performance on particular ECTs, some pathways being more efficient (e.g., shorter) than others, thereby attenuating the effect of NCV on the RT performance (Reed and Jensen, 1993). On the basis of a computer simulation of a quite simple neural model, Anderson (1994) has argued that individual differences in RT and its correlation with IQ cannot be explained in terms of differences in NCV. The relation of NCV to *g*, however, could yet prove to be a key element in the neurophysiological explanation of individual differences in mental ability; its promise calls for further research.

g. The myelination hypothesis   This is the most impressively comprehensive attempt I have yet seen to integrate many empirically established behavioural and physiological facts that could explain individual differences in *g*. Originally proposed by Edward M. Miller (1994), it relates a host of empirical facts of individual differences in cognition and brain anatomy and physiology to individual differences in the degree of myelination of axons in the brain. For example, we know that NCV is positively related to the amount of myelination. Fluid ability, mental speed and myelination together increase from infancy to maturity, and both decline in old age. A larger part of the brain's volume consists of myelin (and its supporting glial cells) than consists of neurons, and brain volume is positively correlated with IQ. Myelin insulates nerve impulses from 'neural noise' and 'cross-talk', which have been hypothesised as the basis of intraindividual variability in RT, a substantial correlate of g. The lipids and fatty acids of which myelin is composed (measured by blood cholesterol levels) are positively correlated with g. Miller also indicates many other physical phenomena related to g via myelin (including possible survival advantage throughout human evolution of genes for low intelligence), the explanations for which are beyond the scope of this chapter. The myelin hypothesis has yet to be tested directly, for example by showing an intrinsic correlation between individual differences in the ratio of myelin (and glia) to neural tissue in the brain and psychometric g.

Whether or not Miller's myelination hypothesis eventually proves true, his integrative review of the empirical relationships between physiological and cognitive functions will stand as one of this decade's important contributions to research on the neurophysiology of g.

Future research on g

Since its discovery by Spearman in 1904, the g factor has become so firmly established as a major psychological construct in terms of psychometric and factor analytic criteria that further research along these lines is unlikely either to disconfirm the construct validity of g or to add anything essentially new to our understanding of it. In fact, because g, unlike any of the primary or first-order factors revealed by factor analysis, cannot be described in terms of knowledge of mental test items, or in terms of skills, or even in terms of theoretical cognitive processes, it is not essentially a psychological or behavioural variable, but a biological one. It reflects certain properties of the human brain, as shown by its correlations with individual differences in a number of brain variables such as size, metabolic rate, nerve-conduction velocity, and the latency and amplitude of evoked electrical potentials. Some brains function better than others with respect to g. The new frontier of g research is the discovery of the anatomical and physiological structures of the brain that cause g. Research on g has finally reached the stage at which the only direction to go is that presaged by Spearman himself, who wrote that the final understanding of g 'must needs come from the most profound and detailed direct study of the human brain in its purely physical and chemical aspects' (1927, p. 403).

REFERENCES

Anderson, B. (1994) 'Speed of neuron conduction is not the basis of the IQ–RT correlation: Results from a simple neural model', *Intelligence* 19: 317–324.

Carroll, J.B. (1993) *Human Cognitive Abilities: A Survey of Factor-Analytic Studies*, Cambridge: Cambridge University Press.

Cohn, S.J., Cohn, C.M.G. and Jensen, A.R. (1988) 'Myopia and intelligence: a pleiotropic relationship?', *Human Genetics* 80: 53–58.

Crick, F. (1989) 'Neural Edelmanism', *Trends in Neurosciences* 12: 240–248.

Deary, I.J. and Caryl, P.G. (1993) 'Intelligence, EEG, and evoked potentials', in P.A. Vernon (ed.) *Biological Approaches to the Study of Human Intelligence*, Norwood, NJ: Ablex.

Diamond, M.C., Scheibel, A.B., Murphy Jr., G.M. and Harvey, T. (1985) 'The brain of a scientist: Albert Einstein', *Experimental Neurology* 88: 198–204.

Edelman, G.M. (1987) *Neural Darwinism: The Theory of Neuronal Group Selection*, New York: Basic Books.

——(1988) *Topobiology: An Introduction to Molecular Embryology*, New York: Basic Books.

——(1993) 'Neural Darwinism: selection and re-entrant signalling in higher brain function', *Neuron* 10: 115–125.

Eysenck, H.J. (1993) 'The biological basis of intelligence', in P.A. Vernon (ed.) *Biological Approaches to the Study of Human Intelligence*, Norwood, NJ: Ablex.

Eysenck, H.J. and Barrett, P. (1985) 'Psychophysiology and the measurement of intelligence', in C.R. Reynolds and P.C. Willson (eds) *Methodological and Statistical Advances in the Study of Individual Differences*, New York: Plenum.

Finlay, B.L. and Darlington, R.B. (1995) 'Linked regularities in the development and evolution of mammalian brains', *Science* 286: 1,578–1,584.

Gazzaniga, M.S. (1989) 'Organization of the human brain', *Science* 245: 947–952.

Haier, R.J. (1993) 'Cerebral glucose metabolism and intelligence', in P.A. Vernon (ed.) *Biological Approaches to the Study of Human Intelligence*, Norwood, NJ: Ablex.

Haier, R.J., Robinson, D.L., Braden, W. and Williams, D. (1983) 'Electrical potentials of the cerebral cortex and psychometric intelligence', *Personality and Individual Differences* 4: 591–599.

Haier, R.J., Siegel Jr., B.V., Nuechterlein, K.H., Hazlett, J.C., Wu, J.C., Browning, H.L. and Bucksbaum, M.S. (1988) 'Cortical glucose metabolic rate correlates of abstract reasoning and attention studies with positron emission tomography', *Intelligence* 12: 199–217.

Haier, R.J., Siegel, B., Tang, C., Abel, L. and Buchsbaum, M.S. (1992) 'Intelligence and changes in regional cerebral glucose metabolic rate following learning', *Intelligence* 16: 415–426.

Jensen, A.R. (1980) 'Uses of sibling data in educational and psychological research', *American Educational Research Journal* 17: 153–170.

——(1987a) 'Psychometric *g* as a focus of concerted research effort', *Intelligence* 11: 193–198.

——(1987b) 'The *g* beyond factor analysis', in R.R. Ronning, J.A. Glover, J.C. Conoley and J.C. Witt (eds) *The Influence of Cognitive Psychology on Testing*, Hillsdale, NJ: Erlbaum.

——(1989) 'The relationship between learning and intelligence', *Learning and Individual Differences* 1: 37–62.

——(1992) 'The importance of intraindividual variability in reaction time', *Personality and Individual Differences* 13: 869–882.

——(1993) 'Spearman's *g* links between psychometrics and biology' in F.M. Crinella and J. Yu (eds) *Brain Mechanisms*, New York: Annals of the New York Academy of Sciences.

——(1994a) 'Phlogiston, animal magnetism, and intelligence', in D.K. Detterman (ed.) *Current Topics in Human Intelligence: Vol. 4, Theories of Intelligence*, Norwood, NJ: Ablex.

——(1994b) 'Psychometric *g* related to differences in head size', *Personality and Individual Differences* 17: 597–606.

Jensen, A.R. and Johnson, F.W. (1994) 'Race and sex differences in head size and IQ', *Intelligence* 18: 309–333.

Jensen, A.R. and Sinha, S.N. (1993) 'Physical correlates of human intelligence', in P.A. Vernon (ed.) *Biological Approaches to the Study of Human Intelligence*, Norwood, NJ: Ablex.

Jensen, A.R. and Weng, L.-J. (1994) 'What is a good *g*?', *Intelligence* 18: 231–258.

Johnson, F.W. (1991) 'Biological factors and psychometric intelligence: a review', *Genetic, Social, and General Psychology Monographs* 117: 313–357.

Larson, G.E., Haier, R.J., LaCasse, L. and Hazen, K. (1995) 'Evaluation of a "mental effort" hypothesis for correlations between cortical metabolism and intelligence', *Intelligence* 21: 267–278.

Miller, E.M. (1994) 'Intelligence and brain myelination: a hypothesis', *Personality and Individual Differences*, 17: 803–832.

Pedersen, N.L., Plomin, R., Nesselroade, J.R. and McClearn, G.E. (1992) 'A quantitative genetic analysis of cognitive abilities during the second half of the life span', *Psychological Science* 3: 346–352.

Polich, J. and Kok, A. (1995) 'Cognitive and biological determinants of P300: An integrative review', *Biological Psychology* 41: 103–146.

Posner, M.I., Petersen, S.E., Fox, P.T. and Raichle, M.E. (1988) 'Localization of cognitive operations in the human brain', *Science* 240: 1,627–1,631.

Reed, T.E. (1984) 'Mechanism for heritability of intelligence', *Nature* 311: 417.

——(1988) 'A neurophysiological basis for the heritability of intelligence', in H.J. Jerison and I. Jerison (eds) *Intelligence and Evolutionary Biology*, Berlin: Springer.

Reed, T.E. and Jensen, A.R. (1991) 'Arm nerve conduction velocity (NCV), brain NCV, reaction time, and intelligence', *Intelligence* 15: 33–47.

——(1992) 'Conduction velocity in a brain nerve pathway of normal adults correlates with intelligence level', *Intelligence* 16: 259–272.

——(1993) 'Choice reaction time and visual pathway nerve conduction velocity both correlate with intelligence but appear not to correlate with each other: implications for information processing', *Intelligence* 17: 191–203.

Rijsdijk, F.V., Boomsma, D.L. and Vernon, P.A. (1995) 'Genetic analysis of peripheral nerve conduction velocity in twins', *Behavior Genetics* 25: 341–348.

Rushton, J.P. and Ankney, C.D. (1996) 'Brain size and cognitive ability: correlations with age, sex, social class and race', *Psychonomic Bulletin and Review* 3: 21–36.

Schafer, E.W.P., Amochaev, A. and Russell, M.J. (1982) 'Brain response timing correlates with information mediated variations in reaction time', *Psychophysiology* 19: 345.

Spearman, C. (1904) '"General intelligence" objectively determined and measured', *American Journal of Psychology* 15: 201–293.

——(1927) *The Abilities of Man*, London: Macmillan.

Thorndike, R.L. (1987) 'Stability of factor loadings', *Personality and Individual Differences* 8: 585–586.

Vernon, P.A. (ed.) (1987) *Speed of Information-Processing and Intelligence*, Norwood, NJ: Ablex.

——(1990) 'The use of biological measures to estimate behavioral intelligence', *Educational Psychologist* 25: 293–304.

——(ed.) (1993) *Biological Approaches to the Study of Human Intelligence*, Norwood, NJ: Ablex.

Vernon, P.A. and Mori, M. (1990) 'Physiological approaches to the assessment of intelligence', in C.R. Reynolds and R. Kamphaus (eds) *Handbook of Psychological and Educational Assessment of Children: Intelligence and Achievement*, New York: Guilford Press.

——(1992) 'Intelligence, reaction times, and peripheral nerve conduction velocity', *Intelligence* 16: 273–288.

Wickett, J.C. and Vernon, P.A. (1994) 'Peripheral nerve conduction velocity, reaction time, and intelligence: an attempt to replicate Vernon and Mori (1992)', *Intelligence* 18: 127–131.

Chapter 8

Biometric analyses of human abilities

Nancy L. Pedersen and Paul Lichtenstein

The purpose of this chapter is to provide the reader with an overview of findings concerning the causes of individual differences in cognitive abilities. The chapter will start with a short primer of biometric analyses because some readers may not be familiar with the principles, terminology and techniques used in this discipline; other readers may choose to scan it quickly. Presentation of a summary of findings will proceed in order of complexity, from univariate to developmental to multivariate issues.

A PRIMER

Quantitative genetic (or biometric) analyses delineate the aetiology of individual differences, that is, the extent to which variation reflects genetic and environmental differences among people. These sources of variation are broadly categorised into various anonymous components of variance. In order to estimate the relative importance of genetic and environmental variance, biometricians and behaviour geneticists apply quantitative genetic principles in comparing the similarity of individuals who share environments and genes to differing degrees. For example, because identical (MZ) twins share 100 per cent of their genes and fraternal (DZ) twins share half of their segregating genes, the importance of genetic effects is indicated when intraclass correlations for pairs of identical twins are greater than those for fraternal pairs. Comparisons of similarity among other pairs of relatives may also be used, such as parents and offspring (who share 50 per cent of their genes), half-sibs (25 per cent) or cousins (12.5 per cent).

However, in both twin and family studies, such correlations for abilities may reflect not only genetic similarity, but also similarity resulting from sharing the same familial environment. Thus, adoption designs are generally recognised as the most appropriate techniques for providing accurate estimates of the relative importance of genetic and environmental influences. The extent to which adoptees are similar to their biological parents reflects genetic similarity, whereas similarity between adoptees and their adoptive parents estimates the importance of shared family environments. Differences within identical pairs must be due to environmental differences because identical twins reared together share their complete genome and the same family environment. Thus, environmental effects that contribute to within-family differences are known as non-shared environmental influences.

UNIVARIATE FINDINGS

The nature of individual differences in cognitive abilities is one of the most frequently studied domains of behaviour genetics. Indeed, Plomin (1985) suggested that 'the relative importance of both nature and nurture in the development of mental ability [is] the oldest continuously researched question in the behavioural sciences'. In their widely cited review of the world's literature on behavioural genetic studies of IQ, Bouchard and McGue (1981) noted over 140 studies of this domain. Their analysis, as well as reanalyses of the data they provided (Chipuer *et al.*, 1990; Loehlin, 1989), led to the generally consistent conclusion that approximately half of the variation in general cognitive abilities, or IQ, results from genetic variation. In other words, when the data are pooled over age groups, samples and various configurations of relatives, approximately half of the individual differences we see are due to genetic differences among individuals. Although once considered highly controversial, most social scientists now accept that individual differences in IQ scores are at least partially inherited (Snyderman and Rothman, 1987).

Developmental issues

But the picture is not quite so simple. The results presented above are pooled over a wide range of ages. At the very least, measurement issues make generalisations across cohorts difficult. Furthermore, the structure of cognitive abilities and the genetic and environmental influences on the structure may change with age (see 'Multivariate issues' below). None the less, one of the most basic developmental questions is whether the relative importance of genetic variance (heritability) differs with age. The relative importance of genetic and environmental factors could change throughout the life span for a number of reasons. Although we are born with a full complement of genes, not all are operating at any one point in time. Genes may be 'turned on' only at specific stages during the life span while others may be inactivated. Temporal genes may be involved in the timing of specific age-related events (Paigen, 1980). Thus, changes in the activity of genes could result in differences in genetic variance at various points during the life span.

It is perhaps more obvious that environmental influences vary throughout the life span. Some life span developmental theorists predict that total variance increases as one accumulates experiences: that is, individual differences become more pronounced with age. Thus, it would be reasonable to assume that heritability decreases late in life as experiences accumulate and hence environmental influences become increasingly important (Baltes *et al.*, 1980) with the accumulation of wounds from life's 'slings and arrows of outrageous fortune'. The net effect on heritability estimates (i.e., the relative importance of genetic variance), will of course depend on whether total phenotypic variance is changing and whether the effects of genetic or environmental factors accumulate over time or are occasion-specific. If a single set of genes operates throughout development and information from the environment is 'stored over time', heritability will decrease over time (Eaves *et al.*, 1986). On the other hand, if environmental effects are occasion-specific, the heritability will increase with age.

Cross-sectional findings

Observations from early, cross-sectional studies of cognitive abilities led Plomin (1986) to conclude that heritability generally increases from infancy, through childhood and adolescence, up to adulthood. Research in early childhood suggested a steady increase in the heritability of IQ scores, at least until the early school years (Fulker *et al.*, 1988). Recent summaries of cross-sectional twin studies of intellectual performance (McCartney *et al.*, 1990; Boomsma, 1993; McGue *et al.*, 1993) conclude that heritability increases from 40 per cent in childhood to as high as 80 per cent in adulthood, possibly as a result of amplification of genetic effects existing early in development (Plomin, 1986).

Although most of the studies included in these summaries cover the first half of the life span, the results from several relatively recent ageing studies have now provided heritability estimates for cognitive abilities among older adults. Eighty per cent of the differences seen among adults (over 50 years of age) for general cognitive ability are due to genetic differences (Pedersen *et al.*, 1992). This value is somewhat higher than those found in adolescence and early adulthood, but is consistent with reports from middle-aged adults (Bouchard *et al.*, 1990; Tambs *et al.*, 1984). However, a further exploration into age differences in heritability estimates during the last half of the life span found some differences across age groups (Finkel *et al.*, 1995). Older Swedish twins (over 65 years) showed a significantly lower heritability for general cognitive abilities suggesting a possible inverted L-shaped function for the relationship between heritability and IQ later in the life span. If confirmed with longitudinal data and older samples, these results suggest that environmental influences become increasingly important for individual differences in cognitive ability late in life.

Longitudinal findings

Caution should be taken in drawing conclusions about development and ageing from cross-sectional analyses. Age differences found cross-section-ally may reflect cohort differences or historical effects, and not true developmental or ageing changes. In a longitudinal perspective, there are several types of stability that may be considered. Most familiar is pheno-typic stability, i.e., stability in the level (mean level stability) and interindividual stability as indicated by the correlation between the same measures at successive occasions. Structural stability is another concept of interest in developmental studies. Biometric analyses can contribute to the understanding of stability by elucidating the aetiology of phenotypic or structural stability in terms of genetic and environmental components. Thus, phenotypic stability is a result of the relative influence of genes and environments on two occasions as well as the stability of the genetic and environmental effects between those occasions. In a developmental perspective, the term genetic correlation refers to the extent to which genetic effects assessed on two occasions are correlated, i.e., the genetic continuity over time. Genetic effects may be highly stable, regardless of their relative importance at any two time points. Similarly, new or 'innova-tive' genetic effects may come into play at selected developmental stages. For a more detailed description of these concepts see Pedersen (1991).

Three studies stand out as pioneers in longitudinal analysis of the importance of genetic and environmental factors for cognitive abilities: the Skodak and Skeels adoption study (Skodak and Skeels, 1949), the Louisville Twin Study (Wilson, 1972, 1983, 1985), and the New York State Psychiatric Institute Study of Aging (Kallmann and Sander, 1948; Jarvik and Bank, 1983). The former two studies were concerned with infant and childhood development, while the Kallmann study focused on adult development and ageing. Both studies of early development found that genetic influences on mental abilities tended to increase longitudinally from infancy to early childhood. For example, Wilson's 1983 analyses of the pattern of spurts and lags in mental development (using repeated-measures analysis of variance) show that the MZ–DZ difference in infancy (three to twelve months) is only .07, but increases to .32 at age 8 to 15. Thus, the heritability for developmental profiles increases with age from three months to fifteen years. In contrast, patterns of changes in MZ and DZ intrapair differences across adulthood suggest that environ-mental influences may become more important in old age than in mid-adulthood (Jarvik and Bank, 1983).

The results from these important studies give general indications of a change in the relative importance of genetic effects with age. However, they do not reveal how genes operate throughout development. These early developmental studies have subsequently been built upon by several longitudinal studies started since the mid-1970s. In the Colorado Adoption Project (CAP), started in 1975, adopted away infants have been followed through adolescence (Plomin and DeFries, 1985). Similarly, longitudinal data are available on twins from infancy through age 7 from the MacArthur Longitudinal Twin Study (MALTS: Plomin *et al.*, 1990b) and the Twin Infant Project (TIP: DiLalla *et al.*, 1990). At the other end of the life span, the Swedish Adoption/Twin Study of Aging (SATSA: Pedersen *et al.*, 1991) has cognitive data from three occasions at three-year intervals for twins aged 50 years and older. These newer studies incorporate model-fitting approaches that allow the testing of various models concerning the transmission of genetic and environmental influences from time to time as well as the introduction of new, 'innovative' genetic or environmental variance at subsequent time points. In this fashion, more can be learned about continuity and change in cognitive development.

Infancy, childhood and adolescence

Reanalyses of the Louisville Twin Study data along with data from young adult twins and adoption study data (Plomin *et al.*, 1988) suggest that heritability in infancy and childhood increases from .10, .17, .18 and .26 at ages 1, 2, 3 and 4 years, respectively, to .50 in adulthood, with moderate influences of shared environments during childhood. These longitudinal results are consistent with cross-sectional analyses indicating that heritability increases early in development and shared environmental influences are of a consistent, moderate influence.

The nature of the transmission of genetic influences and the aetiology of continuity and change has been explored further in a series of analyses of CAP, MALTS and TIPS. Early analyses of CAP focused on continuity of genetic influences (Thompson *et al.*, 1985; DeFries *et al.*, 1987; Bergeman *et al.*, 1988). Because there were moderate to high longitudinal genetic correlations from infancy and childhood to adulthood, the findings indicate that there is substantial genetic continuity from 2, 3 and 4 years of age to adulthood.

With the collection of data from additional occasions in CAP as well as MALTS, subsequent analyses of these datasets, separately and pooled, have explored issues concerning age-to-age transmission of genetic and environmental influences, the role of these influences in continuity and change early in development, and potential structural changes. Longitudinal findings from CAP and MALTS suggest that the heritability of general cognitive abilities is somewhat greater than suggested by early reports and reanalyses of the Louisville Twin Study, rising from approximately .40 at age 1 to .57 at age 4 (Fulker *et al.*, 1993; Cherny *et al.*, 1994; Cherny *et al.*, 1996). There is considerable genetic continuity at these early ages. However some new genetic variance is introduced at each of the ages, stabilising by age 4. At age 7, when heritability increases to approximately .70, there is a considerable influx of new genetic variance which remains stable through ages 9 and 10. Fulker and colleagues suggest that the new genetic variance may arise 'in response to the novel intellectual demands imposed by schooling at this age' (Fulker *et al.*, 1993, p. 93).

Adulthood and ageing

Much of the research on individual differences in cognitive abilities during the second half of the life span has focused on whether declines in mean levels are accompanied by increasing total variance (Morse, 1993). Although cross-sectional findings suggest that individual differences in cognitive abilities increase across cohorts, little or no longitudinal evidence for increasing variance with age has been reported. Biometric analyses of cognitive abilities later in life provide important insights into the nature of potential cohort differences and relative longitudinal stability in individual differences with age.

Initial analyses from SATSA, based on cognitive data from two time points with a three-year interval, focused on the degree of phenotypic stability and the extent to which this reflected genetic and environmental influences (Plomin *et al.* 1994). As might be expected for this relatively short period of time, the phenotypic stability was quite high: r = .93, and there was little change in total variance. The heritabilities at both time points were similar and substantial (~.80). Further, genetic influences at Time 1 were more highly correlated with genetic influences at Time 2 than was the case for environmental influences. In other words, there was greater genetic than environmental stability across a three-year period. As heritabilities were substantial at both time points and the genetic correlation between occasions (i.e., genetic stability) was substantial (.83), phenotypic stability predominantly reflected genetic influences.

There are two limitations of these early analyses: first, only two time points were included and second, in order to be included in the analyses, both members of the pairs had to participate at both time points. With the inclusion of a third measurement occasion in SATSA, we could evaluate the consequences of these potential limitations. In a preliminary set of analyses, means and variances were plotted based on participation in SATSA. Figure 8.1 shows that there was a slight decline in mean levels across the three occasions for those pairs in which *both* members participated at *all three* times. There was an initial lower level followed

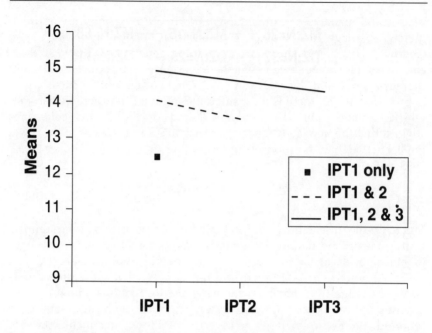

Figure 8.1 Mean levels in general cognitive abilities as a function of pairwise longitudinal participation in the Swedish Adoption/Twin Study of Aging. IPT = In Person Testing Session

by a slightly sharper decline in performance from Time 1 to Time 2 for pairs in which one or both ceased to participate after Time 2 and those pairs participating at Time 1 only performed the least well at that occasion. Most of the individuals who terminated participation were too sick to participate or died before the next testing occasion. This pattern of decline dependent on subsequent survival is known as 'terminal decline' (Berg, 1996), and suggests that there are substantial differences among those participating in one, two or three occasions. These mean differences, as well as accompanying differences in variances (not shown), further indicate that there are serious limitations in requiring that there are valid data available from both members of the pair at all occasions.

What is the consequence of these limitations for subsequent biometric analyses? Examination of intraclass correlations for MZ and DZ pairs, dependent on pairwise participation, indicates that similarity for pairs in which both participated on all three occasions is considerably more stable than similarity in other constellations of pairs (Figure 8.2). As the distance between the MZ and DZ correlations is similar across the three occasions, one would interpret findings for continuing participants to suggest that heritability is stable across six years. However, the relative

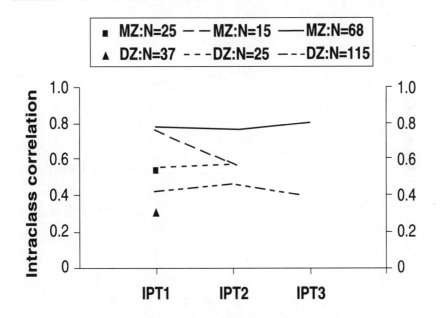

Figure 8.2 Intraclass correlations for general cognitive abilities as a function of participation in the Swedish Adoption/Twin Study of Aging. IPT = In Person Testing Session

distance between MZ and DZ correlations is smaller or decreases across time for the other two groups, suggesting that environmental influences may be important for the terminal decline phenomenon evidenced for the means. Thus, by requiring that both members participate in all occasions of measurement, we are limiting the likelihood of finding change in the relative importance of genetic and environmental influences.

Recent developments in various structural equation model-fitting programs allow for missing values for some participants and some variables. The three occasion SATSA cognitive data have recently been analysed using such a technique, and, at the same time, issues concerning cohort versus longitudinal trends in means, variances and components of variance have been examined (Finkel *et al.*, 1996). Cohort-sequential analyses combining cross-sectional (cohort) and longitudinal information confirm a general decline in mean levels of cognitive performance, but no change in total variance for general cognitive abilities. Thus, earlier predictions that individual differences should increase with advancing age were once again not supported. More interesting were the analyses of the genetic and environmental components of variance. When cross-sectional and longitudinal estimates of genetic and environmental variance are considered together, there appear to be no changes

Cross-sequential analysis of principal components

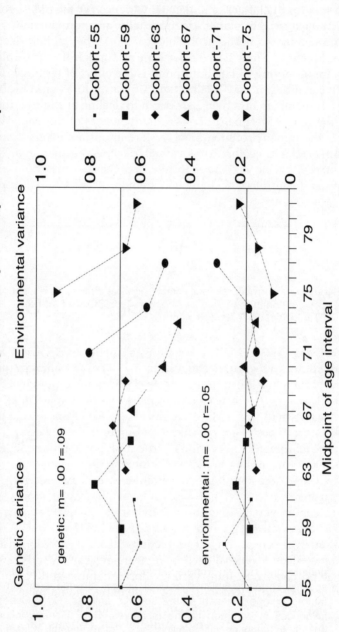

Figure 8.3 Cohort sequential analysis of genetic and environmental components of variance for general cognitive abilities

with age (regression lines in Figure 8.3). However, closer inspection of the longitudinal trends for the separate cohorts clearly demonstrates that there is a longitudinal *decrease* in genetic variance for the oldest cohorts. Heritability is relatively stable longitudinally at approximately 70 per cent in the younger cohorts. In the older cohorts, heritability decreases from 80 per cent at Time 1 to 60 per cent at Time 3. It is possible that what we are observing in late adulthood is the effect of terminal decline in cognitive abilities. It may be that twin similarity for cognitive abilities decreases as members of a twin pair begin to decline at slightly different times or the rate of decline differs for the members of the pair. Thus, it appears as though environmental factors are important for the timing of entry into or the trajectory of terminal decline. Further analyses of growth curves will be necessary to test hypotheses concerning genetic influences on the terminal decline phenomenon.

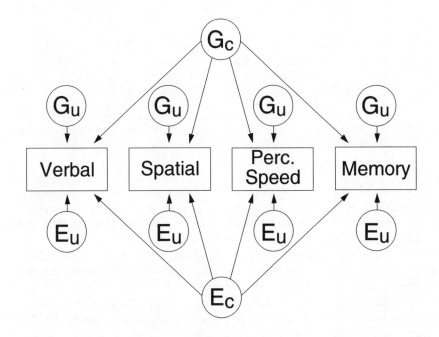

Figure 8.4 Example of Independent Pathway model in which there is one genetic and one environmental factor common to measures of specific cognitive abilities as well as genetic and environmental factors unique to each of the specific abilities. G_c = Genetic influences in common to the measures. G_u = Genetic influences unique to each specific ability. E_c = Environmental influences in common to the measures. E_u = Environmental influences unique to each specific ability

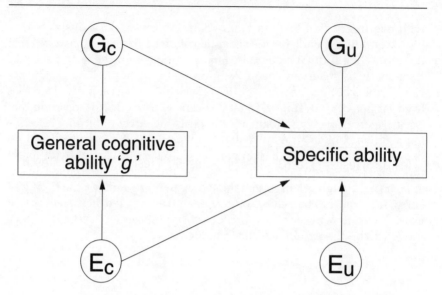

Figure 8.5 Design in which importance of genetic effects for individual measures of cognitive ability, independent of genetic effects for general cognitive abilities, g, can be evaluated. G_c = Genetic influences shared by general and specific cognitive abilities. G_u = Genetic influences unique to a specific ability. E_c = Environmental influences shared by general and specific cognitive abilities. E_u = Environmental influences unique to a specific ability

MULTIVARIATE ISSUES

Both general and specific cognitive abilities show genetic influence, although much less is known about the origins of individual differences in specific cognitive abilities. There is some evidence that verbal and spatial abilities may be more heritable than memory (Plomin, 1988). However, tests of specific abilities correlate substantially with g. This raises the question of the extent to which genetic influence on specific cognitive abilities can be accounted for by genetic influence on g (Jensen, 1992). Is there significant genetic influence on tests of specific cognitive abilities independent of genetic influence on general cognitive ability? Does the phenotypic structure of general and specific abilities reflect genetic or environmental covariation?

There are several multivariate biometric techniques that have been used to address these issues, most of which involve factor analytic procedures. One technique evaluates the importance of a single genetic (or environmental) factor in common to the tests (or subscales) as well as test (or scale) specific genetic (or environmental) factors (Figure 8.4). This design, also known as the independent pathway model (Neale and Cardon, 1992), tests directly whether there is genetic variance for the

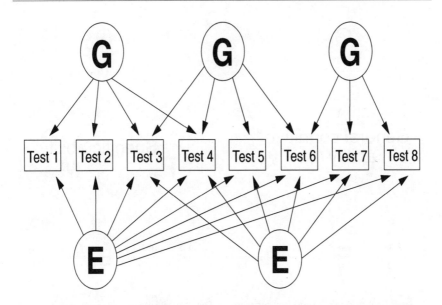

Figure 8.6 Example of multivariate biometric model in which there are different genetic and environmental structures

various abilities independent of a common genetic source. Bivariate analyses of tests of specific abilities and a general ability factor test whether the various tests are influenced by genetic effects independent of genetic effects for g (Figure 8.5). Expanding the independent pathway model to allow for multiple genetic and environmental factors (Figure 8.6) enables one to explore issues concerning whether the phenotypic factor structure more closely resembles the genetic or the environmental factor structure. Finally, hierarchical procedures enable one to address both the question of genetic variance independent of genetic variance for g as well as the questions concerning phenotypic, genotypic and environmental factor structure simultaneously. In Figure 8.7, the phenotypic factor structure is presented, with both first-order factors representing specific cognitive abilities and a second-order factor representing g. The biometric application of this model evaluates the importance of genetic and environmental influences on the individual test, the specific cognitive abilities (first-order factors) and g.

With regard to the first question, i.e., whether there is genetic variance for specific cognitive abilities independent of genetic variance for g, the empirical evidence from eleven twin and adoption studies indicates that the answer is *yes*. Although the studies utilise a variety of measures, populations and analytic designs that make detailed comparisons difficult, all the studies find genetic variance unique to both cognitive tests

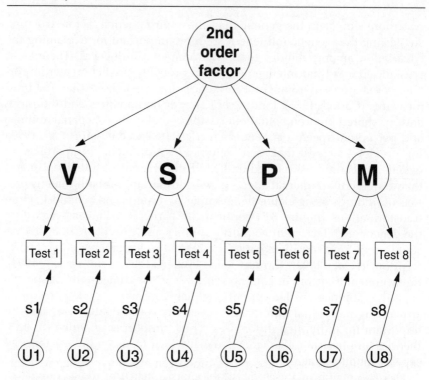

Figure 8.7 Hierarchical model of structure of specific cognitive abilities. Genetic and environmental influences are modelled for each of the latent traits (indicated by circles) as well as for the individual tests (indicated by squares)

and sub-scales not accountable by genetic variance for general cognitive abilities (Martin and Eaves, 1977; Martin *et al.*, 1984; Tambs *et al.*, 1986; Rice *et al.*, 1986; LaBuda *et al.*, 1987; Rice *et al.*, 1989; Cardon *et al.*, 1992; Pedersen *et al.*, 1994; Luo *et al.*, 1994; Loehlin *et al.*, 1994; Casto *et al.*, 1995). The consistency of this finding, across varying measures (e.g., WISC-R, WAIS, scholastic abilities, batteries of specific cognitive abilities) and in samples representing the entire life span (e.g., CAP, the National Merit Scholarship Qualifying Test sample of Twins, Norwegian twins and SATSA) provides resounding evidence that there is reliable genetic variance for specific cognitive abilities beyond *g*.

The results from these biometric studies also provide insight into the structure of cognitive abilities and, by extension, have implications for various theories concerning the psychometrics of intelligence. Many early studies found that multiple genetic and environmental factors best explained the covariation among the specific abilities (e.g., Martin *et al.*, 1984; LaBuda *et al.*, 1987). Furthermore, the phenotypic factor structure was more similar to the genetic than the environmental factor structure, suggesting that genetic influences are more important for explaining the covariation among abilities than environmental influences. Theories of crystallised and fluid intelligence would probably predict greater importance of shared environmental influences for crystallised than for fluid measures (Cattell, 1971). Findings of similar heritabilities and the influence of shared environmental effects for verbal abilities, spatial abilities and perceptual speed (e.g., Pedersen *et al.*, 1992; see Plomin *et al.*, 1990a for a review) suggest that there may not be a differential importance of genetic effects for crystallised and fluid dimensions of intelligence, and that shared environmental effects may be important for both dimensions. Recent findings using elaborate hierarchical designs and Schmid-Leiman transformations (Figure 8.7) confirm the earlier conclusions regarding the genetic architecture of cognitive abilities and provide further understanding of how specific abilities are related to general cognitive ability (Cardon *et al.*, 1992; Cardon and Fulker, 1994; Luo *et al.*, 1994). Environmental factors in common to the various dimensions of specific cognitive abilities are less important than a common genetic factor in structuring individual differences, yet ability-specific influences are also important for individual differences. Thus, support is provided for both theories emphasising *g* as well as those which focus on the existence of separate ability dimensions.

Developmental analyses of the biometric structure indicate that the genetic architecture of cognitive abilities is not constant throughout the life span. Cardon and Fulker (1994) demonstrated that different genetic and environmental influences were responsible for the structure of general and cognitive abilities at different occasions in childhood. Continuity of genetic effects in childhood is at the level of specific abilities rather than *g*. In other words, the genetic continuity is at the level of the components of intelligence, not at the level of genetic influences on *g* itself. Similarly, results from SATSA and MTSADA (Finkel *et al.*, 1995) provide insight into changes in cognitive performance late in life. In the oldest Swedish twins there was a dedifferentiation in structure, reflecting to a greater extent perceptual speed, as well as a decrease in genetic variance for the general cognitive factor in the older-old.

Influence of home environment

Research on environmental influence on behaviour has shown that, whereas there is little evidence for significant effects of shared environments on personality, these effects are important for specific cognitive abilities especially during childhood (Plomin and Daniels, 1987). Although studies of adolescents (Scarr and Weinberg, 1978) and adults (Bouchard *et al.*, 1990) fail to find significant evidence for shared environmental influence for cognitive abilities, recent results from SATSA affirm their importance for cognition later in life; shared environmental influences account for between 11 and 27 per cent of the variation in seven of the thirteen measures of specific cognitive abilities (Pedersen *et al.*, 1992).

The SATSA findings are particularly interesting for two reasons. First, the adoption/twin design of SATSA allows separate estimates of the importance of shared *rearing* environments (Es) and other forms of correlated environments (Ec). The former type of environmental effect is assessed by comparing the similarity of twins reared together (TRT) with twins separated at an early age and reared apart (TRA). When TRT are more similar than TRA, shared rearing effects are indicated. In SATSA, 11–14 per cent of the variation in four of thirteen tests was attributable to Es. Shared environmental experiences that are not exclusively attributable to the rearing situation (e.g., adult contact with co-twin or shared pre- and perinatal environment) are called correlated environments (Ec) and account for up to 27 per cent of the variation in three of the tests. Secondly, the SATSA sample for which cognitive data are available is composed of twins 44–87 years of age. The finding of significant shared environmental influences in this sample suggests that early rearing environment can cast a long shadow – the effect is observed nearly a half century after these individuals have left the families in which they were reared.

Two approaches to studying the influence of the environment on cognitive abilities have typically been taken. Within quantitative genetic designs as applied to behavioural phenotypes, the distinction between shared and non-shared environments refers to anonymous, aggregated sources of variation resulting in similarity and differences among relatives, respectively. The other approach has been to examine mean differences as the result of measured indicators of the environment. For example, several researchers have investigated the effects of general indices of the environment, such as socio-economic status, on cognitive abilities (Wolf, 1964; Marjoribanks, 1977) without regard to whether these effects are shared (resulting in similarities) or non-shared (resulting in differences among relatives). An implicit assumption in most developmental studies has been that if environmental influences are shown to be important during childhood, they contribute to sibling similarity, and thus are shared (McCall, 1983).

Environmentally oriented researchers dissatisfied with the lack of evidence for shared family effects frequently assert that behavioural genetics studies seldom use appropriate measures of the environment (Hoffman, 1991; Bronfenbrenner, 1986; Wachs, 1983; Wachs, 1992). As Rowe and Waldman (1993) point out, much of the critique rests on the emphasis by behavioural geneticists on the anonymous variance components rather than specific measures of environment. Lately, a growing number of behavioural genetic studies of cognitive abilities seek to identify specified environmental influences of importance for behaviour within the conceptualisation of components of variance. For example, using data from CAP, Rice and colleagues (Rice *et al.*, 1988) demonstrated that there is a direct relationship between an index of the home environment (Home Observation for Measurement of the Environment) and infant IQ. A current major effort is directed toward identifying *non-shared* environmental influences that cause *differences* among siblings (Hetherington *et al.*, 1993). Relatively little research has concentrated on specifying experiences that lead to sibling *similarity* and thus may be considered aspects of *shared* environmental effects for cognitive abilities (Coon *et al.*, 1990; Garfinkle, 1982; Spuhler and Vandenberg, 1978; Rowe and Waldman, 1993).

Recent analyses of SATSA data have explored the nature of shared environmental influences for cognitive abilities using measured indicators of the environment in a quantitative genetic design (Pedersen *et al.*, 1996). The results provide a heuristic example that illustrates the distinction between anonymous sources of environmental variation such as shared rearing environment or non-shared environment and measurable experiences in childhood such as familial Attitudes Toward Education (ATE) and the Intellectual-Cultural Orientation (Culture) sub-scale of the Moos Family Environment Scales (Moos and Moos, 1981). The analyses demonstrated that not only are ATE and Culture significantly associated with most of the measures of cognitive ability, but that they may be considered to be nearly comprehensive indicators of the otherwise anonymous variance component attributed to shared environmental effects for two cognitive measures (Thurstone's Picture Memory and Koh's Block Design) and partial indicators of shared environments for a third (Information). Although the effects of the measured environments in the present case were relatively small, the results demonstrate the general applicability of quantitative genetic methods to the study of the environment. It is possible to evaluate the relevance of measures of the environment as identifiable sources of variance within the rubric of shared environmental influence.

How can these results help us understand how the environment influences cognitive abilities? Perhaps not surprisingly, multiple regressions of ATE and Culture on the cognitive measures indicate that there is a rise in scores on these cognitive tests with increased scores on scales of parental attitudes toward education and familial orientation toward cultural and intellectual activities. Estimation of variance components, on the other hand, describes the extent to which and the manner in which environmental effects contribute to individual differences (variation around the mean) independent of genetic effects. These are anonymous variance components descriptive of individual differences in a population and are not descriptive of processes for individuals nor group differences. Shared and non-shared environmental effects together account for approximately 40 to 60 per cent of the variation in specific cognitive abilities in middle-aged and older adults. The inclusion of measures of the environment in the quantitative genetic model demonstrates that perceptions of familial attributes such as attitudes toward education and interest in culture contribute to environmental sources of sibling similarity for some cognitive abilities. What is also striking about these findings is that they suggest that early-rearing environmental effects are observed nearly a half century after these individuals have left the families in which they were reared.

As expected, these two childhood environmental measures clearly are not indicators of non-shared environments (that is, they do not contribute to differences among siblings) for cognitive abilities. However, one should keep in mind that non-shared environmental effects are *more* important than shared rearing effects for cognitive abilities. Furthermore, *both* shared and non-shared environmental effects can be important throughout the life span, operating in childhood as well as adulthood. As Goldsmith (1993, p. 331) points out, 'all experience that is shared by a pair of relatives (say, co-twins) does not occur in the family context, and experiences within the family often affect family members differently'. These considerations underscore significance of realising that idiosyncratic experiences during childhood can be of considerable importance and that consistency in home environment (such as attempting to treat all children the same) does not necessarily result in familial similarity for cognitive abilities later in life.

SUMMARY

Both genetic and environmental influences are important for individual differences in general and specific cognitive abilities. Both cross-sectional and longitudinal findings converge on the conclusion that heritability for general cognitive ability differs as a function of age, generally increasing from infancy through childhood and adolescence to a plateau in adulthood and with a decrease late in life (Figure 8.8). Multivariate analyses indicate that there is genetic variance for specific cognitive abilities independent of genetic influences for general cognitive ability, g, and that the genetic and environmental architecture of cognitive abilities changes with age. Finally, both shared and non-shared environmental effects are important sources of individual differences in cognitive abilities. Shared environmental effects exert a relatively stable influence throughout development whereas non-shared influences tend to be occasion and measure specific.

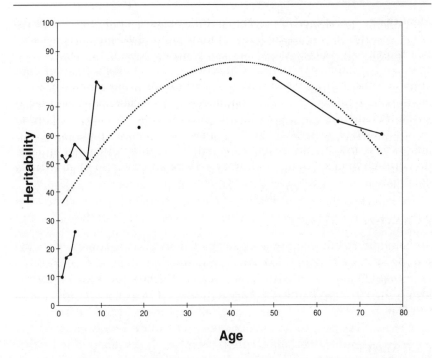

Figure 8.8 Summary of heritability estimates for general cognitive abilities across the life span. Longitudinal data for ages 1–4 (indicated by circles) are from the Louisville Twin Study (Wilson, 1985) and for ages 1–10 (indicated by squares) from CAP, MALTS and TIP (Cherny *et al.*, 1996; Fulker *et al.*, 1993). The single point at age 20 is based on twin data from Tambs *et al.*, 1989 and at 40 on data from Tambs *et al.*, 1986 and Bouchard *et al.*, 1990. Longitudinal data from 50 and above are from SATSA (Finkel *et al.*, 1996.) The dotted line is the polynomial regression line fitted to all the points

IN CONCLUSION

Genetic effects for cognitive abilities are polygenic and most likely pleiotropic, that is, a multitude of genes affect cognitive abilities and the effect of each gene is manifold. Although genetic effects account for the greatest proportion of variation for cognitive abilities, the study of the environment is still highly relevant. Environmental influences are also likely to be 'poly-environmental' and pleiotropic, that is, a multitude of environmental factors may be important for a behaviour, and there may be interactions among these environmental factors. Thus, the effect of any single environmental measure (or gene) is likely to be small. Analyses of measured environments may be considered as the environmental analogue to molecular genetic techniques which search for quantitative trait loci (McClearn *et al.*, 1991). In both cases, the focus is on identifying specific effects (genetic loci or measured environments) which may account for a moderate amount of the total phenotypic variation previously encompassed within broader rubrics of genetic and shared environmental variance. Concepts of anonymous sources of variation and the importance of measured indicators of the genome and the environment can be fruitfully combined by application of quantitative genetic/biometric models to the study of human behaviour. Further development of models integrating these two conceptualisations, i.e., anonymous and identified sources of individual differences, and application of such models to the wealth of data already collected in genetically informative populations should be encouraged.

ACKNOWLEDGEMENT

Preparation of this chapter was supported in part by grants from the John D. and Catherine T. MacArthur Foundation, the National Institute on Aging (AG 04563, AG 10175, AG 08724), the Swedish Council for the Co-ordination and Planning of Research and the Swedish Social Research Council.

REFERENCES

Baltes, P.B., Reese, H.W. and Lipsett, L.P. (1980) 'Life span developmental psychology', *Annual Review of Psychology* 31: 65–110.

Berg, S. (1996) 'Aging, behavior, and terminal decline', in J.E. Birren and K.W. Schaie (eds) *Handbook of the Psychology of Aging*, San Diego: Academic Press.

Bergeman, C.S., Plomin, R., DeFries, J.C. and Fulker, D.W. (1988) 'Path analysis of general and specific cognitive abilities in the Colorado Adoption Project: early childhood', *Personality and Individual Differences* 9: 391–395.

Boomsma, D.I. (1993) 'Current status and future prospects in twin studies of the development of cognitive abilities: infancy to old age', in T.J. Bouchard Jr. and P. Propping (eds) *Twins as a Tool of Behavioral Genetics*, New York: John Wiley.

Bouchard, T.J., Jr. and McGue, M. (1981) 'Familial studies of intelligence: a review', *Science* 212: 1,055–1,058.

Bouchard, T.J., Jr., Lykken, D.T., McGue, M., Segal, N.L. and Tellegen, A. (1990) 'Sources of human psychological differences: the Minnesota Study of Twins Reared Apart', *Science* 250: 223–228.

Bronfenbrenner, U. (1986) 'Ecology of the family as a context for human development', *Developmental Psychology* 22: 723–742.

Cardon, L.R. and Fulker, D.W. (1994) 'A model of developmental change in hierarchical phenotypes with application to specific cognitive abilities', *Behavioral Genetics* 24: 1–16.

Cardon, L.R., Fulker, D.W., DeFries, J.C. and Plomin, R. (1992) 'Multivariate genetic analysis of specific cognitive abilities in the Colorado Adoption Project at age 7', *Intelligence* 16: 383–400.

Casto, S.D., DeFries, J.C. and Fulker, D.W. (1995) 'Multivariate genetic analysis of Wechsler Intelligence Scale for Children-Revised (WISC-R) factors', *Behavior Genetics* 25: 25–32.

Cattell, R.B. (1971) *Abilities: Their Structure, Growth, and Action*, Boston: Houghton Mifflin.

Cherny, S.S., Fulker, D.W. and Hewitt, J.K. (1996) 'Cognitive development from infancy to middle childhood.', in R.J. Sternberg and E. Grigoranko (eds) *Intelligence: Heredity and Environment*, Cambridge: Cambridge University Press.

Cherny, S.S., Fulker, D.W., Emde, R.N., Robinson, J., Corley, R.P., Reznick, J.S., Plomin, R. and DeFries, J.C. (1994) 'A developmental-genetic analysis of continuity and change in the Bayley Mental Development Index from 14 to 24 months: The MacArthur Longitudinal Twin Study', *Psychological Science* 5: 354–360.

Chipuer, H.M., Rovine, M.J. and Plomin, R. (1990) 'LISREL modeling: genetic and environmental influences on IQ revisited', *Intelligence* 14: 11–29.

Coon, H., Fulker, D.W., DeFries, J.C. and Plomin, R. (1990) 'Home environment and cognitive ability of 7-year-old children in the Colorado Adoption Project: genetic and environmental etiologies', *Developmental Psychology* 26: 459–468.

DeFries, J.C., Plomin, R. and LaBuda, M.C. (1987) 'Genetic stability of cognitive development from childhood to adulthood', *Developmental Psychology* 23: 4–12.

DiLalla, L.F., Thompson, L.A., Plomin, R., Phillips, K., Fagan III, J.F., Haith, M.M., Cyphers, L.H. and Fulker, D.W. (1990) 'Infant predictors of preschool and adult IQ: a study of infant twins and their parents', *Developmental Psychology* 26: 759–769.

Eaves, L.J., Long, J. and Heath, A.C. (1986) 'A theory of developmental change in quantitative phenotypes applied to cognitive development', *Behavior Genetics* 16: 143–162.

Finkel, D., Pedersen, N.L., McGue, M. and McClearn, G.E. (1995) 'Heritability of cognitive abilities in adult twins: comparison of Minnesota and Swedish data', *Behavior Genetics* 25: 421–431.

Finkel, D., Pedersen, N.L., Plomin, R., McClearn, G.E. and Berg, S. (1996) 'Cross-sequential analysis of genetic influences on cognitive ability in the Swedish Adoption Twin Study of Aging', *Aging, Neuropsychology and Cognition* 3: 84–99.

Fulker, D.W., Cherny, S.S. and Cardon, L.R. (1993) 'Continuity and change in cognitive development', in R. Plomin and G.E. McClearn (eds) *Nature, Nurture, and Psychology*, Washington, DC: American Psychological Association.

Fulker, D.W., DeFries, J.C. and Plomin, R. (1988) 'Genetic influence on general mental ability increases between infancy and middle childhood', *Nature* 336: 767–769.

Garfinkle, A.S. (1982) 'Genetic and environmental influences on the development of Piagetian Logico-Mathematical Concepts and other specific cognitive abilities: a twin study', *Acta Geneticae Medicae et Gemellologiae* 31: 10–61.

Goldsmith, H.H. (1993) 'Nature–nurture issues in the behavior genetics context: overcoming barriers to communication', in R. Plomin and G.E. McClearn (eds) *Nature, Nurture and Psychology*, Washington, DC: American Psychological Association.

Hetherington, E.M., Reiss, D. and Plomin, R. (eds) (1993) *Separate Social Worlds of Siblings: Impact of Nonshared Environment on Development*, Hillsdale, NJ: Lawrence Erlbaum Associates.

Hoffman, L. (1991) 'The influence of the family environment on personality', *Psychological Bulletin* 110: 187–203.

Jarvik, L.F. and Bank, L. (1983) 'Aging twins: longitudinal psychometric data', in

K.W. Schaie (ed.) *Longitudinal Studies of Adult Psychological Development*, New York: Guilford Press.

Jensen, A.R. (1992) 'Vehicles of g', *Psychological Science* 3: 275–277.

Kallmann, F.J. and Sander, G. (1948) 'Twin studies on aging and longevity', *Journal of Heredity* 39: 349–357.

LaBuda, M.C., DeFries, J.C. and Fulker, D.W. (1987) 'Genetic and environmental covariance structures among WISC-R subtests: a twin study', *Intelligence* 11: 233–244.

Loehlin, J.C. (1989) 'Partitioning environmental and genetic contributions to behavioral development', *American Psychologist* 44: 1,285–1,292.

Loehlin, J.C., Horn, J.M. and Willerman, L. (1994) 'Differential inheritance of mental abilities in the Texas Adoption Project', *Intelligence* 19: 325–336.

Luo, D., Petrill, S.A. and Thompson, L.A. (1994) 'An exploration of genetic g: hierarchical factor analysis of cognitive data from the Western Reserve twin project', *Intelligence* 18: 335–347.

McCall, R.B. (1983) 'Environmental effects on intelligence: the forgotten realm of discontinuous nonshared within-family factors', *Child Development* 54: 408–415.

McCartney, K., Harris, M.J. and Bernieri, F. (1990) 'Growing up and growing apart: a developmental meta-analysis of twin studies', *Psychological Bulletin* 226–237.

McClearn, G.E., Plomin, R., Gora-Maslak, G. and Crabbe, J.C. (1991) 'The gene chase in behavioral science', *Psychological Science* 2: 222–229.

McGue, M., Bouchard, T.J., Jr., Iacono, W.G. and Lykken, D.T. (1993) 'Behavioral genetics of cognitive ability: a life-span perspective', in R. Plomin and G.E. McClearn (eds) *Nature, Nurture, and Psychology*, Washington, DC: American Psychological Association.

Marjoribanks, K. (1977) 'Socioeconomic status and its relation to cognitive performance as mediated through the family environment', in A. Oliverio (ed.) *Genetics, Environment and Intelligence*, Amsterdam: Elsevier/North-Holland Biomedical Press.

Martin, N.G. and Eaves, L.J. (1977) 'The genetical analysis of covariance structure', *Heredity* 38: 79–95.

Martin, N.G., Jardine, R. and Eaves, L.J. (1984) 'Is there only one set of genes for different abilities? A re-analysis of the National Merit Scholarship Qualifying Test (NMSQT) data', *Behavior Genetics* 14: 355–370.

Moos, R.H. and Moos, B.S. (1981) *Family Environment Scale Manual*, Palo Alto, CA: Consulting Psychologists Press.

Morse, C.K. (1993) 'Does variability increase with age? An archival study of cognitive measures', *Psychology and Aging* 8: 156–164.

Neale, M.C. and Cardon, L.R. (1992) *Methodology for Genetic Studies of Twins and Families*, Dordrecht: Kluwer Academic Publisher.

Paigen, K. (1980) 'Temporal genes and other developmental regulators in mammals', in T. Leighten and W.F. Loomis (eds) *The Molecular Genetics of Development*, New York: Academic Press.

Pedersen, N.L. (1991) 'Behavioral genetic concepts in longitudinal analyses', in D. Magnusson, L. Bergman, G. Rudinger and B. Törestad (eds) *Problems and Methods in Longitudinal Research: Stability and Change*, Cambridge: Cambridge University Press.

Pedersen, N.L., McClearn, G.E., Plomin, R., Nesselroade, J.R., Berg, S. and de Faire, U. (1991) 'The Swedish Adoption Twin Study of Aging: an update', *Acta Geneticae Medicae et Gemellologiae* 40: 7–20.

Pedersen, N.L., Plomin, R., Nesselroade, J.R. and McClearn, G.E. (1992) 'A quantitative genetic analysis of cognitive abilities during the second half of the life span', *Psychological Science* 3: 346–353.

Pedersen, N.L., Plomin, R. and McClearn, G.E. (1994) 'Is there G beyond g? (Is there genetic influence on specific cognitive abilities independent of genetic influence on general cognitive ability?)' *Intelligence* 18: 133–143.

Pedersen, N.L., Lichtenstein, P., Plomin, R. and McClearn, G.E. (1996) 'Identification of specific factors responsible for shared environmental effects for cognitive abilities', *Institute of Environmental Medicine Report*.

Plomin, R. (1985) 'Behavioral genetics', in D.K. Detterman (ed.) *Current Topics in Human Intelligence*, Norwood, NJ: Ablex.

—— (1986) *Development, Genetics and Psychology*, Hillsdale, NJ: Lawrence Erlbaum.

—— (1988) 'The nature and nurture of cognitive abilities', in R. Sternberg (ed.) *Advances in the Psychology of Human Intelligence (vol. 4)*, Hillsdale, NJ: Erlbaum.

Plomin, R. and Daniels, D. (1987) 'Why are children in the same family so different from one another?' *Behavioral and Brain Sciences* 10: 1–16.

Plomin, R. and DeFries, J.C. (1985) *Origins of Individual Differences in Infancy: The Colorado Adoption Project*, Orlando, FL: Academic Press.

Plomin, R., DeFries, J.C. and Fulker, D.W. (1988) *Nature and Nurture during Infancy and Early Childhood*, New York: Cambridge University Press.

Plomin, R., DeFries, J.C. and McClearn, G.E. (1990a) *Behavioral Genetics: A primer (2nd edn)*, New York: Freeman.

Plomin, R., Campos, J., Corley, R., Emde, R.N., Fulker, D.W., Kagan, J., Reznick, J.S., Robinson, J., Zahn-Waxler, C. and DeFries, J.C. (1990b) 'Individual differences during the second year of life: The MacArthur Longitudinal Twin Study', in J. Columbo and J. Fagan (eds) *Individual Differences in Infancy: Reliability, Stability and Predictability*, Hillsdale, NJ: Lawrence Erlbaum Associates.

Plomin, R., Pedersen, N.L., Lichtenstein, P. and McClearn, G.E. (1994) 'Variability and stability in cognitive abilities are largely genetic later in life', *Behavior Genetics* 24: 207–215.

Rice, T., Fulker, D.W. and DeFries, J.C. (1986) 'Multivariate path analysis of specific cognitive abilities in the Colorado Adoption Project', *Behavior Genetics* 16: 107–125.

—— (1988) 'Path analysis of IQ during infancy and early childhood and an index of the home environment in the Colorado Adoption Project', *Intelligence* 12: 27–45.

Rice, T., Carey, G., Fulker, D.W. and DeFries, J.C. (1989) 'Multivariate path analysis of specific cognitive abilities in the Colorado Adoption Project: conditional path model of assortative mating', *Behavior Genetics* 19: 195–207.

Rowe, D.C. and Waldman, I.D. (1993) 'The question "how" reconsidered', in R. Plomin and G.E. McClearn (eds), *Nature-Nurture and Psychology*, Washington, DC: American Psychological Association.

Scarr, S. and Weinberg, R.A. (1978) 'The influence of "family background" on intellectual attainment', *American Sociological Review* 43: 674–692.

Skodak, M. and Skeels, H.M. (1949) 'A final follow-up of one hundred adopted children', *Journal of Genetic Psychology* 75: 85–125.

Snyderman, M. and Rothman, S. (1987) 'Survey of expert opinion on intelligence and aptitude testing', *American Psychologist* 42: 137–144.

Spuhler, K.P. and Vandenberg, S.G. (1978) 'Relationship between family environment and children's and parent's cognitive performance (abstract)' *Behavior Genetics* 8: 114–115.

Tambs, K., Sundet, J.M. and Magnus, P. (1984) 'Heritability analysis of the WAIS subtests: a study of twins', *Intelligence* 8: 283–293.

—— (1986) 'Genetic and environmental contributions to the covariation between the Wechsler Adult Intelligence Scale (WAIS) subtests: a study of twins', *Behavior Genetics* 16: 475–491.

Tambs, K., Sundet, J.M., Magnus, P. and Berg, K. (1989) 'Genetic and environmental contributions to the covariance between occupational status, educational attainment, and IQ: a study of twins', *Behavior Genetics* 19: 209–222.

Thompson, L.A., Plomin, R. and DeFries, J.C. (1985) 'Parent–infant resemblance for general and specific cognitive abilities in the Colorado Adoption Project', *Intelligence* 9: 1–13.

Wachs, T.D. (1992) *The Nature of Nurture*, Newbury Park, CA: Sage Publications.

—— (1983) 'The use and abuse of environment in behavior genetic research', *Child Development* 54: 396–407.

Wilson, R.S. (1972) 'Similarity in developmental profiles among related pairs of human infants', *Science* 178: 1,005–1,007.

—— (1983) 'The Louisville Twin Study: developmental synchronies in behavior', *Child Development* 54: 298–316.

—— (1985) 'Continuity and change in cognitive ability profile', *Behavior Genetics* 16: 45–60.

Wolf, R.H. (1964) 'The identification and measurement of environmental process variables that are related to intelligence', unpublished doctoral dissertation, University of Chicago.

Chapter 9

Cognitive processes, mental abilities and general intelligence

Gerry Mulhern

> ... the search for the true single information-processing function underlying
> intelligence is likely to be as successful as the search for the Holy Grail.
> (Hunt, 1980, p. 457)

As a cognitive psychologist with an interest in individual differences, I
have had occasion to muse on the reasons why, in spite of a burgeoning
of experimental psychology throughout this century, an implicitly
'cognitive' construct like intelligence had received scant attention from
cognitive theorists and experimentalists until the 1970s. The circumstances that led to the development of the psychometry of intelligence
are well known and accounts may be found elsewhere (e.g., Carroll,
1993). In particular, the exigencies of mass selection and assessment in
both education and employment resulted in justifiable emphasis on test
validation, item analysis and associated factor analytic approaches.
These methodologies, while not necessarily incompatible with a cognitive approach, were simply not geared toward asking and answering
cognitive questions. Indeed, for some researchers the factor analytic
approach became something of a capricious end in itself, resulting in
immensely detailed descriptions of the structure of abilities that had
little or nothing to say about their underlying cognitive processes. Such
analyses ignored even basic issues such as why, precisely, some test
items are more difficult than others. A second issue that may be considered to have diverted researchers from asking some of the more
interesting cognitive questions about intelligence was a preoccupation
with the vitally important, but largely unproductive, nature–nurture
polemic.

Today, of course, the picture is rather different. The literature is replete
with research eschewing exclusively psychometric approaches and
claiming to 'model' psychometric intelligence in terms of cognitive and
biological processes. But how much has really changed since Cronbach's
(1957) plea for the unification of the psychometric and experimental
traditions? This chapter will argue that, in spite of clear statements of
philosophy and intent, the contribution of cognitive psychology in

explaining individual differences in mental ability remains far from convincing. Considerable effort has been put into uncovering the cognitive processes underlying mental abilities. However it may be argued that many of the 'processes' identified by researchers represent little more than an empirical confirmation of researchers' intuitions about what constitutes intelligent behaviour in a specified cognitive domain. Most particularly, a doubt must remain as to whether some of the processes that have been identified are necessary or even sufficient conditions for intelligent behaviour. Anderson (1992) identified several conundra which address this point.

> If intelligence is a reflection of knowledge structures, as the cognitivists would have us believe, why is it that tasks that require merely a simple perceptual discrimination can predict how many words a child will know? . . . This is easily answered if we consider intelligence to be a general property of our biology, as the neural-efficiency school would have us believe. However, if intelligence is a general property of our biology, why is it that some individuals of very low psychometric intelligence can perform remarkable cognitive feats such as, when given any date, calculating which day of the week it falls on (O'Connor and Hermelin 1984) or recognizing that a number is a prime number (Hermelin and O'Connor 1990)? . . .
>
> A closer look at knowledge highlights another conundrum. Some kinds of computationally simple problems like mental arithmetic are usually too difficult for mentally retarded children, but they can perform other, almost wondrous, computational feats, such as extracting three-dimensional representations from a retinal input or an important syntactic distinction from speech. Our most powerful computers do not come close to matching even the mentally retarded on these kinds of computations; but on simple mental arithmetic the same children could not compete with your digital wrist watch. There again, why is it that intelligence test performance predicts reading ability for the majority of children, but some very intelligent children are very bad at reading or spelling?
>
> (pp. 3–4)

While there have been notable attempts at rapprochement between the psychometric and cognitive traditions, some theorists offer little comfort to cognitivists. For example, Jensen (1987a, 1994 and this volume) has argued persuasively that consideration of the nature of 'intelligence' is misguided, and, that unlike the primary or first-order factors of intelligence, g cannot be described in terms of domain-specific knowledge or skills. He extends the argument to suggest that g cannot even be described in terms of theoretical cognitive processes and concludes that it is neither a psychological nor a behavioural variable, but an essentially biological one.

Given its definition (and derivation), this is an entirely reasonable view of *g*. However, the suggestion that a construct like general intelligence may be outside their jurisdiction is surely an uncomfortable one for cognitive psychologists. Admittedly, the fact that *g* represents a nebulous aggregation of a vast number of underlying cognitive abilities makes matters difficult for anyone attempting to model it and, to date, cognitive psychology has made no more than a modest contribution to the unravelling of *g* (or, for that matter, the lower-order factors of ability). Part of the problem lies in the differing views of what may constitute a cognitive description of intelligence. There is a vast array of phenomena that may legitimately be described as cognitive, ranging from metacognitions, frames, scripts, schemata, through domain-specific knowledge, logical constructs and reasoning strategies, through memory processes and basic information-processing mechanisms, through attentional and perceptual processes and down to cognitive neuropsychological phenomena. Just as cognitive psychologists may argue amongst themselves as to what constitute cognitive phenomena, similar issues arise when attempting to decide whether a particular approach to the study of intelligence is truly cognitive in nature or not. It may be argued that an emphasis on domain-specific abilities in cognitive research on intelligence has contributed to an even more circumscribed view of what may be considered 'cognitive'.

COGNITION AND MENTAL ABILITY

Cognitive correlates and cognitive components

Consideration of some early attempts to identify basic processes underlying intelligence lends further weight to Jensen's (1987a) contention. The cognitive correlates approach, first introduced by Hunt and his colleagues, was based on two basic principles: first, that individual differences in cognitive ability can be described in terms of a small number of 'basic' information-processing components, and second that such differences are due to variation in the speed of execution of these basic processes. In a series of papers, Hunt and his co-workers (Hunt, Frost and Lunneborg, 1973; Hunt *et al.*, 1975; Hunt, 1978, 1980) attempted to uncover the cognitive processes underlying verbal ability. They adapted a variety of experimental paradigms which had been developed by cognitive psychologists to investigate verbal memory, such as the letter matching task (Posner and Mitchell, 1967; Posner *et al.*, 1969; Posner, 1978), the short-term memory scanning task (S. Sternberg, 1966, 1975) and the sentence verification task (Clark and Chase, 1972; Chase and Clark, 1972). The basic approach was to see whether the speed with which subjects executed these tasks was correlated with psychometric verbal ability. Overall, the research proved inconclusive, with modest correlations and inconsistent patterns of results. While some findings were difficult to replicate (e.g., S. Sternberg, 1975; Hogaboam and Pellegrino, 1978), researchers were forced to conclude that the problem with cognitive correlates was one of emphasis. They realised that individual differences in psychometric intelligence were explained less by speed of processing *per se*, than by individuals' effectiveness in selecting, organising, executing, monitoring and adapting appropriate cognitive components to solve a particular problem (see, for example, Pellegrino and Glaser, 1979; Hunt, 1980).

The cognitive components approach was largely a response to the limitations of the cognitive correlates. The catalyst was R.J. Sternberg's (1977) seminal work in which he referred to a 'componential theory' of intelligence which was later referred to as 'cognitive components' by Pellegrino and Glaser (1979) and detailed fully by R.J. Sternberg (1983). This approach was elaborated further by R.J. Sternberg (1984, 1985), resulting in his triarchic theory of intelligence. Besides identifying components, the triarchic theory sought to take account of the cultural context of intelligence (contextual sub-theory) and to specify those tasks that required intelligent thought and those that did not (two-facet sub-theory).

The theory of cognitive components was based on two basic ideas: first, theoretical task analysis (the breaking down any cognitive task into information-processing sub-components) and secondly, the isolation of critical components (i.e., identification of those sub-components that were related to individual differences in performance). The cognitive tasks in question were the actual test items that were commonly found in psychometric tests of intelligence, and the cognitive components were the elementary processes thought to be used to solve these tasks.

According to the cognitive components approach there were three types of information-processing component. *Performance components* were those used in the solution of a particular cognitive task and were derived from task analysis. *Metacomponents* were used to marshal particular performance components in an appropriate sequence to permit successful solution of a cognitive task. *Knowledge-acquisition components* involved the selection and integration of new and existing information relevant to the solution of a particular cognitive task. R.J. Sternberg (1983) argued that these three types of information-processing component were highly interactive and integrative, although he also claimed that they had sufficient functional autonomy to permit an examination of the relationship of each to individual differences in psychometric intelligence.

Limitations of cognitive correlates and cognitive components

In spite of the considerable effort put into identifying correlates and components of intelligence, to what extent have these endeavours contributed to a real understanding of the cognitive basis of human abilities and, more particularly, how much closer are we to a cognitive model of general intelligence? Undoubtedly, both the cognitive correlates and cognitive components approaches provided an important focus for considering questions like 'what does it mean to score highly in some test of ability?' or 'what precisely does an intelligence test measure?'. It is questionable, however, whether either theory moved any closer to answering the question 'what is intelligence?'. There were problems associated with both approaches.

As we have already seen, the cognitive correlates approach involved taking a specific primary cognitive ability (e.g., verbal ability), identifying standard cognitive tasks or paradigms that looked as though they could sensibly be nested under the ability in question, and looking to see how quickly individuals could perform these tasks. The finding that individuals who performed quickly on these tasks also scored highly on the primary ability measure may be regarded as uncomfortably definitional, indeed bordering on circularity. It would surely not be surprising, for example, to discover that subjects with high verbal ability responded more quickly and accurately than those with low verbal ability to a task requiring them to decide whether or not a series of sentences were consistent with corresponding picture representations (MacLeod *et al.*, 1978), or that they could make judgements about homophones more readily than their low verbal counterparts (Goldberg *et al.*, 1977).

Similar problems are apparent in the cognitive components theory which appears prone to both methodological and theoretical problems (Pellegrino and Lyon, 1979). For example, various researchers (e.g., Anderson, 1992) have argued that Sternberg's componential theory seemed to be largely a redescription of the data, and that it represented more a framework for task description than a theory of mental operations underlying intelligence. It is significant that Neisser (1983), who is largely credited with coining the term 'cognitive psychology', should have made the following observation regarding R.J. Sternberg's (1983) description of metacomponents involved in analogical reasoning: '[they] are not separate elements in any genuine mental process; they are more like chapter headings in books on how to think' (p. 196).

Given the palpable difficulties in providing a cognitive description of various mental abilities, what then of *g*? Should cognitive psychologists still aspire to provide a coherent and, more importantly, useful description of the information-processing components underlying general intelligence? Clearly, such a model should not simply consist of some multi-stratum taxonomy of component processes with an appropriately aggregated 'higher order processing factor', in effect, the cognitive equivalent of psychometric g.

For a cognitive account of intelligence to prove useful, it must attempt to describe the information-processing basis of individual differences in g at the highest level of generality across cognitive task domains (R.J. Sternberg, 1983). Deary and Stough (1996) outline four 'desiderata' which they claim must be met before any information-processing measure may be considered to have contributed to a causal explanation for individual differences in psychometric intelligence. First, the measure must have a coherent theoretical rationale. Second, it must reliably produce correlations greater than 0.4 with psychometric intelligence among representative samples of the general population (although, like Hunt, 1980, they do not specify a sample size for this correlation). Third, it should be sufficiently 'basic' to suggest that it is a cause, rather than a symptom, of general intelligence. Finally, it should permit theoretical understanding of its relationship with psychometric intelligence.

Jensen (this volume) argues that psychometric g is so firmly established that even further psychometric research is unlikely to contribute to our understanding of it, and that its level of generality is such that it is a largely biological variable, reflecting properties of the human brain and not amenable to description in terms of cognitive processes. In this chapter, while acknowledging that the detailed study of brain structure and function in relation to g is of crucial importance, I argue that research should not be limited to a purely biological approach.

The remainder of this chapter considers several information-processing measures that have been found to correlate with psychometric intelligence and which have served as a focus for the debate about 'processing speed' versus 'knowledge-based' theories of g. These are reaction time (RT), inspection time (IT) and single-task measures of automaticity. Following a brief review of relevant research, the utility of each measure as a cognitive explanation of general intelligence is considered. This chapter does not present research linking evoked potentials to g since, although it has been argued that EEG components are influenced by cognitive strategies (e.g., Mackintosh, 1986), these measures may be regarded as more obviously physiological than other indices of processing speed, such as RT, IT and automaticity.

REACTION TIME AND GENERAL INTELLIGENCE

The rationale for investigating correlations between reaction time and psychometric g is that reaction time assesses individual differences in the speed or efficiency of neural processing. Such individual differences in neural functioning may appear in the cognitive domain as g. Research into speed of performance has a long-established provenance dating back to the work of Galton (1883), continued by (amongst others) Thorndike *et al.*, (1926), Eysenck (1967, 1986) and Jensen (1980, 1982, 1987b). Early research on RT and intelligence tended to focus on simple reaction time, while later work involved the study of more complex reaction time tasks. Jensen's (1980, 1982, 1987a) work is particularly noteworthy in terms of its contribution to the overall understanding of the relationship between RT and intelligence. His choice RT procedure involved various numbers of stimuli in the form of lights and their adjacent response buttons.

The basic paradigm allowed two components of overall response time to be measured, namely reaction time and movement time for each condition, and Jensen and a host of other researchers collected detailed information on the relationship between general intelligence and RT. In contrast to other cognitive models of intelligence, such as the cognitive correlates and cognitive components theories outlined above, Jensen proposed that psychometric measures of intelligence were predicted by a single, low-level measure of processing speed which was a neurophysiological phenomenon, rather than a property of higher-level cognitive processing.

Overall, studies relating RT to general intelligence have had limited success. In addition to modest correlations, the basic processes underlying RT paradigms have proved difficult to unpick, thereby reducing their explanatory power (e.g., Brody, 1992; Widaman and Carlson, 1989). In addition, some researchers have questioned Jensen's (1980, 1982, 1987b) view that RT performance is purely physiological and unaffected by differences in subjects' level of knowledge or strategies of knowledge use.

Their argument was based on the claim that individual differences in RT may be due, not only to neural processing efficiency (although this was undoubtedly important), but also to numerous other factors including attention, motivation, persistence, visual search strategies, encoding and task specific strategies such as guessing or anticipation. Longstreth (1984, 1986) pointed to possible confounding variables in Jensen's studies and suggested that the slower RTs among low-IQ individuals may have been due to poorer visual scanning strategies or less benefit from practice among these subjects, rather than to slower processing speed *per se*. Rabbitt (1985) argued that RT tasks required the complex control of high-level cognitive processes involving monitoring and control of response speed and error probability in order to optimise speed/error trade-off. He suggested that such task requirements could well explain RT performance, and in particular the higher degree of variability in RT found in low-IQ individuals (Jensen, 1980, 1982, 1992). Inconsistencies have also been reported in research involving task complexity, RT and IQ (e.g., Jenkinson, 1983; Nettelbeck and Kirby, 1983; Vernon, 1983, 1987), casting further doubt on the claim that the relationship between RT and general intelligence is due to shared processing speed. While not ruling out the processing speed hypothesis, the evidence from these studies would suggest that such an association can equally well be explained by shared use of high-level cognitive processing strategies in both RT tasks and in intelligence tests.

INSPECTION TIME AND GENERAL INTELLIGENCE

Inspection time (IT) has been defined as the minimum time required by an individual to make a single inspection of sensory input for which a discrimination of relative magnitude is required (Vickers et al., 1972; Vickers and Smith, 1986). Although most of the early work on IT had its origin in the field of psychophysics, unlike RT, research on IT has tended to remain largely within the domain of individual differences and has not attracted appreciable interest from experimental psychologists (Chaiken and Young, 1993).

While both RT and IT are assumed to be measures of processing speed, they differ in one important respect. While RT measures require subjects to make responses to stimuli as quickly as possible, IT makes no such requirement. Instead, subjects are required to make discriminative judgements about stimuli as accurately as possible, and speed of processing is estimated by incrementally reducing the exposure duration of stimuli until the speed of presentation is so impossibly fast that subjects' discriminations are no more than pure guesswork. Generally, an individual's inspection time is calculated as the stimulus exposure duration required to allow him or her to achieve a specified level of accuracy (for example, 80 per cent for a two-choice response procedure).

The first empirical attempt to relate IT to individual differences in psychometric intelligence was by Nettelbeck and Lally (1976), who reported correlations of -.92 (p<.01) and -.41 (p>.05) respectively between IT and the Performance and Verbal IQ scales of the WAIS. Following their study, researchers have reported variable findings, with correlations ranging from .2 to .9, although, a majority of studies have reported a negative and usually significant relationship between IT and some measure of IQ. In a review of twenty-nine IT studies, Nettelbeck (1987) concluded that approximately 25 per cent of variance in psychometric intelligence could be explained by IT. A meta-analysis by Kranzler and Jensen (1989) confirmed Nettelbeck's (1987) estimate, and more recent studies have consistently reported moderate correlations between IT and IQ measures (e.g., Bates and Eysenck, 1993; Chaiken and Young, 1993; Deary, 1993; Egan, 1994; Evans and Nettelbeck, 1993). More recently, Deary and Stough (1996) have claimed that IT correlates more consistently, more substantially and, arguably, more meaningfully with g than any RT measures, and that it represents a significant improvement on all previous measures of processing speed that have been correlated with general intelligence.

Notwithstanding this consistent, if moderate, association with psychometric intelligence, is IT a better contender than RT in the search for a basic process underlying *g*? The answer would appear to be a resounding 'maybe'. Certainly, IT appears to have fewer 'moving parts' than RT, with no need to consider movement time or speed/error trade-off. IT could also be considered to possess the necessary degree of generality (which seemed to elude RT) to allow it to explain individual differences in *g*. Moreover, given its psychophysical provenance, IT might be considered to have a solid theoretical peg upon which to hang. However, as with RT, all may not be well.

We saw in the case of RT that two equally plausible explanations emerged which could explain its correlation with psychometric intelligence, namely, either that individual differences in RT are basic to (and possibly cause) intelligence, or that individual differences in RT are a consequence of *g*. In spite of its initial promise, similar competing explanations of individual differences in IT have also emerged. As for RT, the argument that IT performance may be a consequence rather than a 'cause' of intelligence stems from a claim that the IT task itself is more complex than it at first appeared (e.g., Anderson, 1992; Deary and Stough, 1996). Recently, in a series of dual-task studies, Hecker and Mapperson (1996) reported that the presence of high-level secondary cognitive tasks could interfere with IT performance. They concluded that these findings were compatible with the notion that IT involves higher-level cognitive processing and that the IT–IQ correlation was unlikely to be due solely to some elemental factor, such as pure processing speed, underlying both tasks. However, in considering the implications of such findings for the 'high-level' and 'low-level' explanations of *g*, Anderson (1992) cautions against throwing the baby out with the bathwater:

> Although these progressively simpler tasks [RT and IT] are not as simple as they at first appear, the ways in which they become complicated simply put more emphasis on variation in low level parameters of processing . . . The only sense of 'complicated' that is critical for the essence of the high-level argument is if knowledge regarding the nature of 'simple' tasks can be used to find *other ways* (different strategies) of doing them . . . If, on the other hand, a simple mechanism has more parameters than we first thought, and, crucially, those parameters are not within the strategic control of the subject, then this does not invalidate the proposition that low-level mechanisms vary in speed or efficiency with level of intelligence.
>
> (pp. 48–49)

Thus it would seem that there may still be considerable mileage in attempting to explain general intelligence in terms of basic processing speed. The question remains, however, as to whether low-level correlates of intelligence such as RT and IT can offer the prospect of more than an essentially biological explanation of g?

AUTOMATICITY AND COGNITIVE ABILITY

If individual differences in psychometric intelligence were explicable only in terms of neural efficiency, this would be a blow to cognitive psychologists – and, of course to others (such as teachers and parents) who try to maximise children's intellectual potential through broadly cognitive interventions. So are individual differences in g simply not amenable to cognitive investigation and, consequently, to cognitive intervention?

We have already seen that at least some of the variance in individuals' RT and IT may be accounted for by factors other than processing speed *per se*. In addition to task-specific strategies identified above, Carroll (1993) also identified 'motivation, persistence, and tendency to guess, to omit items, or to abandon attempts at solution' (p. 507) as non-specific influences on speeded task performance. To this list could be added a host of other personal characteristics, including ponderosity, impulsivity, obsessionality and test anxiety. Might an answer lie in attempting to identify an information-processing mechanism which, while constrained by basic processing speed, is not limited to speed *per se*?

One possible approach may be to consider whether automaticity for basic knowledge-based functions can predict individual differences in higher-level cognitive ability in various knowledge domains. While this apparent fractionation of g may at first sight appear to be a somewhat retrograde step in 'the search for the true single information-processing function underlying intelligence' (Hunt, 1980, p. 457), it may be argued that the identification of a common processing mechanism in different domains may provide converging evidence for just such a function.

The role of automaticity in problem solving, reading and writing, mathematics and procedural and motor skill acquisition is well known, but it has received relatively little attention from researchers interested in individual differences in intelligence. Research on automaticity is based on the idea that, since the capacity of working memory is limited, the more automatic basic cognitive operations become, the less attentional resource is required for their execution. More working memory may therefore be made available for more complex cognitive processes. In attempting to explain individual differences in general intelligence, it could be argued that it is not processing speed *per se* that underlies intellectual ability, but the degree of cognitive facilitation which individuals can bring to tasks requiring intelligent thought.

A possible reason for the comparative lack of interest in automaticity as a basis for explaining performance on tests of mental ability may be found in the methods used to measure it. Overwhelmingly, researchers have tended to use dual-task paradigms to infer the amount of working memory resource available to subjects when performing cognitive tasks. The use of dual-task procedures gives rise to problems, including secondary tasks that either do not permit quantitative assessment of automaticity or that make such estimates difficult. Typically, these paradigms can do little more than establish the presence or absence of automaticity in a specified knowledge or skill domain by assessing the degree of interference occurring in a primary task following the introduction of a secondary task. For example, in Nicholson and Fawcett's (1989) study of reading automaticity among children diagnosed as dyslexic, they investigated the effect of two tasks – reading and beam balancing. They reported a substantial deterioration in dyslexic children's beam balancing when the reading task was introduced compared with their beam balance performance in single-task mode. While Nicholson and Fawcett (1989) interpreted these results to indicate a lack of automaticity for reading among dyslexic children, their dual-task procedure did not allow them to quantify children's levels of automaticity. Clearly, the degree of disruption to the beam balance task may have given some indication of the extent of automaticity, but it would not have allowed automaticity to be measured. In addition to the problem of quantification, dual-task procedures are prone to similar criticisms of strategic and other non-specific influences levelled at RT and IT paradigms.

Gray and Mulhern (1995) attempted to address some of the problems associated with dual-task measures of automaticity. They introduced a single-task measure of automaticity for simple mental addition based on Groen and Parkman's (1972) chronometric paradigm. Essentially, the approach was based on the frequently reported observation that so-called 'tie' combinations (1+1, 2+2, etc.) were much more highly automatised than 'non-tie' combinations (e.g., 1+2, 5+3, etc.). Subjects were presented with addition combinations in the form 'x + y = ?' and were required to produce the correct answer as quickly as possible. Automaticity was estimated by considering the discrepancy in addition times between tie and non-tie combinations. In a study of ten-year-old children, Gray and Mulhern (1995) reported a significant correlation between this chronometric estimate of automaticity for simple addition facts and children's performance on a widely used test of mathematical ability. More recently, Mulhern, Wylie and Sawey (forthcoming) developed a similar chronometric procedure for estimating automaticity for spelling and, in a study of some 60 adult subjects, obtained a highly significant correlation between this measure and performance on the Nelson-Denny Reading Comprehension Test (Brown *et al.*, 1973).

The single-task procedure appears promising for several reasons. First, subjects' levels of automaticity can be readily quantified by considering the discrepancy between response times to two types of stimuli contained in the same stimulus set. In the case of the addition task, these were tie and non-tie combinations, while for the spelling task, they were words paired with either common mis-spellings or jumbled letter sequences. Secondly, each individual acts as his or her own baseline, thus controlling for many of the possible extraneous effects identified in RT and IT procedures, including non-specific influences on speeded task performance. Thirdly, by focusing on automaticity rather than processing speed *per se*, it may be possible to offer a unitary account of individual differences in mental abilities, and ultimately in *g*, involving processing speed *and* domain specific explanations.

Research using single-task measures of automaticity is at an early stage and results so far may raise more questions than they answer. Are differences in automaticity a 'cause' or a 'symptom' of intelligence? To what extent does automaticity predict sub-components of primary abilities? Could intervention studies involving automaticity training (e.g., rote learning) result in increases in psychometric measures of ability? What would be the implications of this for our understanding of psychometric *g*? Hunt's (1980) Holy Grail may continue to prove as elusive as ever. It remains to be seen whether automaticity offers a fresh perspective, or merely proves to be another piece of glass in Jensen's (1987a) 'perpetual kaleidoscope of concepts, notions, and philosophies concerning the definition of "intelligence"' (p. 194).

REFERENCES

Anderson, M. (1992) *Intelligence and Development*, Oxford: Blackwell.
Bates, T.C. and Eysenck, H.J. (1993) 'Intelligence, inspection time, and decision time', *Intelligence* 17: 523–531.
Brody, N. (1992) *Intelligence* (2nd edn), San Diego, CA: Academic Press.
Brown, J.I., Nelson, M.J. and Denny, E.C. (1973) *The Nelson-Denny Reading Test*, Boston: Houghton Mifflin.
Carroll, J.B. (1993) *Human Cognitive Abilities: A Survey of Factor-Analytic Studies*, Cambridge: Cambridge University Press.
Chaiken, S.R. and Young, R.K. (1993) 'Inspection time and intelligence: attempts to eliminate the apparent movement strategy', *American Journal of Psychology* 106: 191–210.
Chase, W.G. and Clark, H.H. (1972) 'Mental operations in the comparison of sentences and pictures', in L. Gregg (ed.) *Cognition in Learning and Memory*, New York: Wiley.

Clark, H.H. and Chase, W.G. (1972) 'On the process of comparing sentences against pictures', *Cognitive Psychology* 3: 472–517.

Cronbach, L.J. (1957) 'The two disciplines of scientific psychology', *American Psychologist* 12: 671–684.

Deary, I.J. (1993) 'Inspection time and WAIS-R IQ subtypes: a confirmatory factor analysis study', *Intelligence* 17: 223–236.

Deary, I.J. and Stough, C. (1996) 'Intelligence and inspection time: achievements, prospects and problems', *American Psychologist* 51: 599–608.

Egan, V. (1994) 'Intelligence, inspection time and cognitive strategies', *British Journal of Psychology* 85: 305–316.

Evans, G. and Nettelbeck, T. (1993) 'Inspection time: a flash mask to reduce apparent movement effects', *Personality and Individual Differences* 15: 91–94.

Eysenck, H.J. (1967) 'Intelligence assessment: a theoretical and experimental approach', *British Journal of Educational Psychology* 37: 81–98.

—— (1986) 'The theory of intelligence and the psychophysiology of cognition', in R.J. Sternberg (ed.) *Advances in the Psychology of Human Intelligence*, Hillsdale, NJ: Erlbaum.

Galton, F. (1883) *Inquiries into Human Faculty and its Development*, London: Macmillan.

Goldberg R.A., Schwartz, S. and Stewart, M. (1977) 'Individual differences in cognitive processes', *Journal of Educational Psychology* 69: 9–14.

Gray, C. and Mulhern, G. (1995) 'Does children's memory for addition facts predict general mathematical ability?', *Perceptual and Motor Skills* 81: 163–167.

Groen, G.J. and Parkman, J.M. (1972) 'A chronometric analysis of simple addition', *Psychological Review* 97: 329–343.

Hecker, R. and Mapperson, B. (1996) 'Sources of individual differences in IT', *Personality and Individual Differences* 21: 697–709.

Hermelin, B. and O'Connor, N. (1990) 'Factors and primes: a specific numerical ability', *Psychological Medicine* 20: 163–169.

Hogaboam, T.W. and Pellegrino, J.W. (1978) 'Hunting for individual differences in cognitive processes: verbal ability and semantic processing of pictures and words', *Memory and Cognition* 6: 189–193.

Hunt, E. (1978) 'Mechanics of verbal ability', *Psychological Review* 85: 109–130.

—— (1980) 'Intelligence as an information processing concept', *British Journal of Psychology* 71: 449–474.

Hunt, E.B., Frost, N. and Lunneborg, C. (1973) 'Individual differences in cognition: a new approach to intelligence', in G. Bower (ed.) *Advances in Learning and Motivation Volume 7*, New York: Academic Press.

Hunt, E.B., Lunneborg, C. and Lewis, J. (1975) 'What does it mean to be high verbal?', *Cognitive Psychology* 7: 194–227.

Jenkinson, J.C. (1983) 'Is speed of information processing related to fluid or crystallized intelligence?', *Intelligence* 7: 91–106.

Jensen, A.R. (1980) 'Chronometric analysis of mental ability', *Journal of Social and Biological Structures* 3: 181–224.

—— (1982) 'Reaction time and psychometric *g*', in H.J. Eysenck (ed.) *A Model for Intelligence*, Berlin: Springer-Verlag.

—— (1987a) 'Psychometric *g* as a focus of concerted research effort', *Intelligence* 11: 193–198.

—— (1987b) 'Process differences and individual differences in some cognitive tasks', *Intelligence* 11: 107–136.

—— (1992) 'The importance of intraindividual variation in reaction time', *Personality and Individual Differences* 13: 869–881.

—— (1994) 'Phlogiston, animal magnetism, and intelligence', in D.K. Detterman (ed.) *Current Topics in Human Intelligence Volume 4: Theories of Intelligence*, Norwood, NJ: Ablex.

Kranzler, J.H. and Jensen, A.R. (1989) 'Inspection time and intelligence: a meta-analysis', *Intelligence* 13: 329–347.

Longstreth, L.E. (1984) 'Jensen's reaction time investigations: a critique', *Intelligence* 8: 139–160.

—— (1986) 'The real and the unreal: a reply to Jensen and Vernon', *Intelligence* 10: 181–191.

Mackintosh, N.J. (1986) 'The biology of intelligence?', *British Journal of Psychology* 77: 1–18.

MacLeod, C.M., Hunt, E.B. and Mathews, N.N. (1978) 'Individual differences in the verification of sentence-picture relationships', *Journal of Verbal Learning and Verbal Behavior* 17: 493–508.

Mulhern, G., Wylie, J. and Sawey, M. (forthcoming) 'Predicting reading ability from a chronometric measure of spelling', *Proceedings of the British Psychological Society.*

Neisser, U. (1983) 'Components of intelligence or steps in routine procedures?' *Cognition* 15: 189–197.

Nettelbeck, T. (1987) 'Inspection time and intelligence', in P.A. Vernon (ed.) *Speed of Information Processing and Intelligence*, Norwood, NJ: Ablex.

Nettelbeck, T. and Kirby, N.H. (1983) 'Measures of timed performance and intelligence', *Intelligence* 7: 39–52.

Nettelbeck, T. and Lally, M. (1976) 'Inspection time and measured intelligence', *British Journal of Psychology* 67: 17–22.

Nicholson, R.I. and Fawcett, A.J. (1989) 'Automaticity: a new framework for dyslexia research?', *Cognition* 35: 159–182.

O'Connor, N. and Hermelin, B. (1984) 'Idiot savant calendrical calculators: maths or memory?', *Psychological Medicine* 14: 801–806.

Pellegrino, J.W. and Glaser, R. (1979) 'Cognitive correlates and components in the analysis of individual differences', in R.J. Sternberg and D.K. Detterman (eds) *Human Intelligence*, Norwood, NJ: Ablex

Pellegrino, J.W. and Lyon, D.R. (1979) 'The components of a componential analysis', *Intelligence* 3: 169–186.

Posner, M.I. (1978) *Chronometric Explorations of Mind*, Hillsdale, NJ: Erlbaum.

Posner, M.I. and Mitchell, R.F. (1967) 'Chronometric analysis of classification', *Psychological Review* 74: 392–409.

Posner, M.I., Boies, S.J., Eichelman, W.H. and Taylor, R.L. (1969) 'Retention of visual and name codes of single letters', *Journal of Experimental Psychology* 79: 1–16.

Rabbitt, P.M.A. (1985) 'Oh *g* Dr. Jensen! or, *g*-ing up cognitive psychology?', *Behavioral and Brain Sciences* 8: 238–239.

Sternberg, R.J. (1977) *Intelligence, Information Processing and Analogical Reasoning*, Hillsdale, NJ: Erlbaum.

—— (1983) 'Components of human intelligence', *Cognition* 15: 1–48.

—— (1984) 'Toward a triarchic theory of human intelligence', *Behavioral and Brain Sciences* 7: 269–315.

—— (1985) *Beyond IQ: A Triarchic Theory of Human Intelligence*, Cambridge: Cambridge University Press.

Sternberg, S. (1966) 'High speed scanning in human memory', *Science* 153: 652–654.

—— (1969) 'The discovery of processing stages: extensions of Donders' method', *Acta Psychologica* 30: 276–315.

—— (1975) 'Memory scanning: new findings and current controversies', *Quarterly Journal of Experimental Psychology* 27: 1–32.

Thorndike, E.L., Bregman, E.O., Cobb, M.V., Woodyard, E. and the Staff of the Division of Psychology of the Institute of Educational Research of Teachers College, Columbia University (1926) *The Measurement of Intelligence*, New York: Bureau of Publications, Teachers College, Columbia University.

Vernon, P.A. (1983) 'Speed of information processing and intelligence', *Intelligence* 7: 53–70.

—— (ed.) (1987) '*Speed of Information Processing and Intelligence*', Norwood, NJ: Ablex.

Vickers, D. and Smith, P. (1986) 'The rationale for the inspection time index', *Personality and Individual Differences* 7: 609–624.

Vickers, D., Nettelbeck, T. and Willson, R.J. (1972) 'Perceptual indices of performance: the measurement of "inspection time" and "noise" in the visual system', *Perception* 1: 263–295.

Widaman, K.F., and Carlson, J.S. (1989) 'Procedural effects on performance on the Hick paradigm: bias in reaction time and movement time parameters', *Intelligence* 13: 63–86.

Chapter 10

Epilogue

Paul Kline

I was asked by the editors of this volume to write the epilogue to attempt to bring some kind of order to the huge amounts of research into psychometrics which have been discussed. This is a tall order but the comments which I shall make shall, I hope, achieve this end.

The title seems to me to be highly significant: *Processes in Individual Differences*. When I started out in psychometrics such a title could have commanded almost no empirical work. The fact that in the fields of ability and personality, and to a far lesser extent in mood and motivation, there are considerable bodies of systematic data and the beginnings of good theories indicates how far progress has been made. This introduces the first point.

As has been stated in most of the chapters in this volume, there is a necessity to go beyond the identification of factors in tests and questionnaires simply from their loadings on items. Yet in much of psychometrics, as all reviewers must know, there is still insufficient attention paid to this essential point. This is, of course, because the factor analysis of items is the easy part; the psychological identification of factors is difficult.

There are various ways in which this can be done: the characteristics of high and low scorers on the scales can be investigated; the factors can be located in factor space, which is especially useful if there are clear marker factors such as g or anxiety; the factors can be related to underlying physiology and neurology; heritability indices can be computed, and finally they can be tied in to well-established psychological theories. These procedures are complementary and with some factors, such as ability factors, much progress has been made. I am in complete agreement with the point made by Hans Eysenck in this volume that, as Cronbach argued, correlational and experimental psychology must be integrated. As the chapters make clear, many of these approaches have been adopted.

I shall amplify briefly some of these important issues with reference to some of the chapters in this volume. Paul Barrett's chapter sketches in the exciting prospects which lie ahead in research into the physiological and neural substrates underpinning g. The search for biological g has become realistic. If, or more optimistically, *when* this proves successful we shall have a real understanding of the nature of intelligence. Ideally it would be useful to use these same methods to extend our understanding of personality and other ability factors, although the work in these fields is less well developed and more complex.

In many ways research into the genetics of individual differences is the most exciting field of psychology. With the modern understanding of DNA and the unfolding of the human genome, which is proceeding even more rapidly than at first appeared likely, the fundamental questions about the inheritance of all characteristics, not simply psychometric variables, are likely to be answered – or at least to become answerable. Both the chapters in this volume on this topic illustrate clearly how biometric analyses can illuminate the nature of psychometric factors.

One of the most interesting and perhaps surprising findings of biometric analyses of both personality and ability factors was the relative unimportance of the common, shared, environment. This, of course, runs counter to most sociological accounts of human behaviour, and is none the worse for that. However, it is counter-intuitive. Pedersen and Lichtenstein's chapter, where they discuss the SATSA study, indicates that these early claims were perhaps too simplistic. In some instances the shared environment assumes some influence, although small. Also important in this work (and clearly a subject for much further investigation) is the inclusion of measures of the environment, thus answering criticisms concerning the anonymity of the environmental variance. Stevenson's careful study of twins indicated that anti-social behaviour in childhood was determined by common environmental influence; he suggested marital discord and parent criminality. This is particularly interesting for several reasons, namely that it indicates that genetic and environmental effects differ with age – for delinquency in adults and adolescents has a clear genetic component – and that, for once, the shared environment is important.

Michael Eysenck's chapter reports studies that make an important point, namely that it is simplistic to regard questionnaire scores, even of a variable as well established as anxiety, as entirely valid measures of the latent trait. Eysenck demonstrates how high scores can be contaminated by social desirability with consequently misleading results. This exemplifies a more general point about the factor analysis of personality questionnaires and rating scales which I believe is generally ignored but which renders findings dubious for theoretical purposes. This relates to the differences between ability and personality test items.

In an ability test, the items are exemplars of the ability under investigation, provided that it is a good test. Each item in an ability test presents a problem which requires intelligence for its solution. This is not the case with personality questionnaires. Putting the keyed response 'Yes' to the item 'I like to keep my desk tidy' is not an example of conscientious behaviour. Part of my PhD involved the development of the Ai3Q to measure obsessional personality. When answering the item 'Can you take firm decisions?' not a few subjects had clearly altered their response several times before endorsing 'Yes'. My psychometric response was to abandon the test item but the wider implications of the item were conveniently repressed.

Clearly, this difference in the nature of items must be reflected in the nature of the factors emerging. Ability factors really do reflect abilities, and this is demonstrated by their widespread effectiveness in selection and prediction. But what do personality factors reflect? In many cases, unless there is key evidence to attest to their validity, these factors seem to me to be semantic – to reflect nothing other than that the items are essentially of similar meaning. Such semantic factors have been called tautologous or bloated specifics. They are not of considerable psychological interest, whatever their name. The importance of this problem has increased considerably in recent years on account of the plethora of studies on the Big Five, through questionnaires and rating scales. That is why it is unfortunate that the Big Five factors, other than extraversion and anxiety, have little theoretical basis.

I must mention the beautifully clear exposition of the social psychology of personality by Sarah Hampson because I believe this constructivist model of personality to be largely mistaken. It has included in the definition of personality two aspects which are not traditionally dealt with – the observer component and the self-observer component. However it is difficult to see how these really form part of personality. This is not to say that they are not worthy of study, but they are really just aspects of social psychology. Thus suppose person X is highly anxious, worrying about everything. It makes no sense to say that this could be affected by the fact that there were or were not observers. Everybody has felt anxious on their own and in a crowd. Suppose that one observer was a poor judge of personality and considered that X was stolid and stable. So what? The status of X on the anxiety variable would not be changed. This example demonstrates that the social psychology of personality is not about personality but about the *perception* of personality. Actually, of course, there could be no perception of personality unless there was something to perceive, but that is another question.

I also want to make a few more general points before concluding this epilogue. One of the disappointing features of recent psychology is the apparent demise of the London School originating with Spearman and continued so brilliantly by Burt, Cattell and Hans Eysenck. Yet the work reported in this book demonstrates that the spirit lives on. In the fields of both personality and motivation, research is concentrating on the meaning of the factors which have emerged. All these studies of processes are a long way removed from the literally infinite possible factorings of items and tests. Many of these findings will be able to be used as building blocks for the necessary integration of experimental psychology, physiology and psychometrics. Biometric analyses are also moving forward, revealing the subtle interplay of environmental and genetic factors developmentally – vital information for a real understanding of personality and ability.

I have taken part in the study of individual differences over more than thirty years. On many occasions it seemed unclear to me where it was going, or worse, that it was going astray, away from psychology and psychological theory and into statistical methodology and actuarial prediction. However it is clear from this book that there is a fruitful future for the psychometric study of individual differences and already that there are many rich areas for research.

Author index

Abramson, L.Y. 6, 8, 9, 18, 21
Adamson, M. 23, 35
Allport, G.W. 7, 18
Almagor, M. 99, 105
Alper, J.S. 54, 55
Anderson, B. 121, 122
Anderson, M. 150, 153, 157, 160

Baltes, P.B. 128, 144
Bandura, A. 6, 8, 18
Barrett, P.T. 1, 12, 13, 18, 22, 37, 76, 90,
    118, 120, 123, 164
Bassili, J.A. 80, 86
Bates, T.C. 13, 21, 156, 160
Battistich, V. 53, 55
Baumeister, R.F. 73, 86
Beck, A.T. 64, 71
Benet, V. 26, 35
Benjamin, J. 54, 56
Ben-Porath, Y. 26, 35
Berg, S. 130, 132, 144, 145, 146, 148
Berger, P. 75, 86
Block, J. 26, 35
Boomsma, D.I. 124, 128, 144
Borkenau, P. 79, 86
Bouchard, T.J., Jr 127, 128, 139, 144, 146
Bower, G.H. 91, 105
Boyle, G.J. 17, 18
Brand, C. 26, 35
Brewer, M.B. 79, 80, 81, 86, 88
Brody, G.H. 53, 56
Brody, N. 155, 160
Bronfenbrenner, U. 140, 144
Brown, J.I. 160
Bullock, W.A. 11, 18
Buss, A.R. 47, 52, 56

Calil, H.M. 104, 105

Cardon, L.R. 42, 57, 136, 138, 139, 144,
    145, 146
Carroll, J.B. 6, 7, 18, 115, 123, 149,
    158, 160
Casselden, P.A. 84, 86
Casto, S.D. 138, 144
Cattell, R.B. 4, 5, 7, 8, 17, 18, 19, 26, 35,
    36, 91, 92, 93, 94, 95, 105, 139,
    145, 166
Chaiken, S.R. 156, 160
Chase, W.G. 151, 160, 161
Cherny, S.S. 131, 145
Chipuer, H.M. 127, 145
Church, I. 26, 35
Claeys, W. 82, 83, 86
Clark, H.H. 151, 160, 161
Clark, L.A. 59, 65, 98, 105
Cloninger, C.R. 12, 18, 26, 35, 54, 56
Cohen, D.J. 47, 56, 58
Cohen, R.L. 3, 19
Cohn, S.J. 119, 123
Conley, J.J. 63, 71
Cooley, C.H. 73, 87
Coolidge, F. 26, 35
Coon, H. 141, 145
Cooper, C. 89, 92, 93, 94, 95, 100, 101,
    105, 106
Costa, P.T., Jr 8, 20, 35, 59, 72, 74, 76, 87,
    88, 90
Craske, M.G. 65, 71
Crick, F. 115, 123
Cronbach, L.J. 8, 26, 30, 35, 149,
    161, 164
Csikszentmihalyi, M. 101, 106

Davis, P.J. 70, 71
Deary, I.J. 12, 19, 36, 120, 123, 154, 156,
    157, 161

Subject index

ability: general 1–5, 7, 9, 12, 13, 15, 16,
    89–97, 101–105, 108–122, 127–142,
    150–160, 164–167; crystallised 13,
    139; fluid 121, 139; verbal 1, 151–153
act categorisation 77–79, 81, 85
action decrement 29, 30
activation 11, 62, 70
actor 9, 73–77, 81–86
adolescence 39, 46, 47, 48, 49, 52, 53, 91,
    128, 130, 139, 142, 165
adoption 39, 42, 118, 126, 129, 130, 132,
    133, 137, 140
AEP *see* evoked potential
affect intensity 90, 101
age 29, 46, 47, 48, 74, 78, 83, 116, 118,
    120, 121, 127–142, 144, 165
aggression 46
altruism 46, 52, 53, 79
antisocial behaviour 39, 46, 47, 48, 50,
    52, 53
anxiety 3, 10–12, 16, 58–70, 89, 91–94,
    96, 158, 164–166
arithmetic 150
arousal 11, 13, 28, 29, 31, 32, 92
Ascending Reticular Activating
    System 11
attention 10, 67, 68, 69, 70, 78, 113,
    151, 155
attentional bias 68, 70
attitudes 33, 141
attribution, of personality 6, 8, 53,
    77–82, 84, 85
automaticity 154, 158–160

behaviour 1–7, 9, 10–16, 18, 25, 28, 29,
    32, 33, 39, 40, 44, 46–55, 60–66,
    70–86, 91, 96, 101–103, 108–115, 117,
    121, 122, 126, 127, 139, 143, 150, 151,
    165, 166
Big Five model of personality 7, 26,
    76, 166
biometric analyses 15, 126, 129, 131,
    132, 165, 167
brain size 108, 112, 119

cancer 33
change 18, 47, 63, 64, 70, 94, 95, 97, 99,
    102–104, 127–142, 149, 166
character 4, 11, 83; *see also* personality
Cholesky decomposition 44, 45, 50
clinical psychology 74, 86
cognition 2, 3, 6, 7, 8, 9, 16, 46, 74, 79,
    103, 111, 113, 121, 140, 151
cognitive ability 2, 3, 7, 39, 127, 128,
    136, 139, 141, 142, 151, 153, 158
cognitive components approach
    152, 153
Colorado Adoption Project 39, 130
common environment *see* shared
    environment
comparator 62, 63
conditioning 29, 118
consciousness 66, 78, 91, 109, 111, 114
consistency of behaviour 26, 63, 76,
    82–84, 85, 142
construction of personality 6, 10,
    74–77, 85, 86
constructionist models 6, 10, 75, 76, 85
constructivist models 6, 9, 73–77,
    85, 166
correlated vectors, method of 115, 116,
    118–121
cortex 11, 108, 113, 120, 121
criminality 32, 47, 52, 112, 165
crystallised ability *see* ability